Rand McNally

Road Atlas & Travel Guide

United States • Canada • Mexico

MW01717147

Contents

Jack A. Wolf

ALONG THE ROAD

Roads and streets in the United States total nearly 4 million miles, of which over 3 million are outside towns and cities. The first roads in this country were the waterways, then came the post roads, so named as they were used by the "mail carriers," who rode horseback. The first engineered and planned road was the privately constructed toll turnpike from Philadelphia to Lancaster, Pennsylvania, built in 1793-94. The next was the Cumberland Road (National Pike) opened in 1818 between Cumberland, Maryland, and Wheeling, West Virginia. Improved roads came as a result of the bicycle, but the greatest improvement came with the invention of the automobile. Today the network of roads and streets provides complete mobility and freedom so that the motorist can travel to a variety of vacation destinations. Towns and cities along the roads are shown on the following pages, and are described in the points of interest; the letter-number key following each town or city name indicates its location on the map page.

ALABAMA / Map page 4

Anniston, C-4. Anniston Museum of Natural History has unusual bird and Egyptian collections.

Birmingham, C-3 (see map p. 65). Visit the Museum of Art and the Botanical Gardens. Ride the elevator to the top of the iron statue of Vulcan on Red Mountain.

Cheaha State Park, C-4. Hike trails on Cheaha Mountain for a view of the Talladega National Forest.

Clanton, D-3. Tour the power plants at both Lay and Mitchell dams on the Coosa River. Boating and fishing.

Florence, A-2. Tour W. C. Handy's Home & Museum, Pope's Tavern, and Indian Mound and Museum. Helen Keller's birthplace is at nearby Tuscumbia.

Fort Payne, B-4. DeSoto State Park has a 110-foot waterfall and one of the deepest gorges east of the Rockies. Manitou and Sequoyah caves are nearby.

Huntsville, A-3. You can experience the sights and sounds of space first-hand at the Alabama Space & Rocket Center. NASA tours available through Marshall Space Flight Center.

Mobile, H-1. A charming city with lovely antebellum homes, live oak trees draped with Spanish moss, and an Azalea Trail late February through early April. There are several important museums and forts, and Mobile has its own Mardi Gras. The battleship *Alabama* and submarine *Drum* are open to visitors. Twenty miles south are Bellingrath Gardens and Home, especially beautiful from May through October.

Montgomery, E-4. The First White House of the Confederacy, where Jefferson Davis lived when Montgomery was the Confederacy capital, now houses Davis family memorabilia; open to the public.

Russell Cave National Monument, A-4. Indians lived in the cave as long ago as 7000 B.C. Dioramas and explanations in the Visitor Center.

Talladega, C-4. Alabama International Motor Speedway is the home of NASCAR'S Winston and Talladega annual 500 auto racing events.

Tuskegee, E-4. Tuskegee Institute National Historic Site includes the Historic Campus District, "The Oaks," home of Booker T. Washington, the George Washington Carver Museum, with Dr. Carver's laboratory and artwork, and an antebellum museum.

ALASKA / Map page 5

Anchorage, C-3. Alaska's largest city offers both modern urban and wildlife areas. East is Chugach State Park with rugged peaks, glaciers, open alpine valleys. Wildlife abounds. Forty miles southeast is Mount Alyeska, large year-round ski resort.

Denali National Park, C-3. The continent's highest peak soars over the wildlife park. Observe grizzly bear, caribou, moose, and mountain sheep.

Fairbanks, B-3. A major tourist center, this is the starting point for many side trips—inquire at the Visitor Information Center. Riverboat excursions on stern-wheelers available May-September. University Museum has Indian and Eskimo exhibits.

Glacier Bay National Park, D-4. Boats operate May-September to take visitors on a long cruise; see wildlife, massive icebergs, and glaciers.

Juneau, D-5. Alaska's capital city. Mendenhall Glacier is 13 miles west; see salmon spawn at nearby Steep Creek, mid-July-November. Alaska State Museum has Indian and Eskimo artifacts.

Katmai National Park, D-2. Visitors must fly to the area, then travel by bus to see the awesome "Valley of 10,000 Smokes" from the 1912 volcanic upheaval. Sport fishing in the park is excellent.

Kodiak, D-3. Erskine House was built by the Russians circa 1793 as a store. Now the Baranof Museum.

Nome, B-2. Accessible by plane or by steamer June-September. Museum is open daily, and Eskimo artisans here are famous for their walrus and mastodon ivory carvings. Numerous tours available.

Petersburg, D-5. City's Visitor Center is in Clausen Memorial Museum; collection includes historical fishing gear. Little Norway Festival is in Mid-May.

Sitka, D-5. First capital of Alaska. The past is present in Pioneer Home, Sheldon Jackson Museum, an 1842 Russian Mission, and reconstructed St. Michael Russian Orthodox Cathedral, with its priceless ikons.

Sitka National Historical Park, D-5. Site of the 1804 fort and battle which marked the last major Tlingit Indian resistance to Russian colonization. Spectacular totem poles mark the site.

Skagway, C-5. Klondike Gold Rush National Historical Park preserves historic buildings, Skagway's main street, and portions of Chilkoot and White Pass Trails over which prospectors struggled to the Klondike Gold Fields. Inside Passage ends here.

Valdez, C-3. The southern terminal of the Alaskan pipeline. Nearby are scenic Keystone Canyon and Worthington Glacier. Gold fields gateway.

Wrangell, D-5. A favorite starting point for hunters and fishermen. Bear Tribal House, tribal house of the Bear Clan, has totem collection.

ARIZONA / Map page 6

Bisbee, G-5. Tours of old Queen Mine and Lavender Open Pit Mine; Mining and Historical Museum.

Canyon de Chelly National Monument, B-6. Cliff dwellings built by the Pueblo Indians beginning circa A.D. 350. Navajos live and farm here.

Casa Grande Ruins National Monument, E-4. Well-preserved ruins of a massive four-story building constructed by Indians who farmed here 600 years ago. A museum here has archaeological exhibits.

Flagstaff, C-4. Museum of Northern Arizona has exhibits of Hopi and Navajo crafts. Guided tour of Lowell Observatory and Planetary Research Center, weekdays at 1:30 p.m. At nearby San Francisco peaks, Arizona Snow Bowl's chair lift operates for sightseers during summers; popular ski center.

Grand Canyon National Park, A-3. This giant canyon carved by the Colorado River is overwhelming in magnitude and beauty. The view from South Rim attracts international visitors; scenic auto routes to the rim. The Visitor Center here provides tour information.

Lake Havasu City, D-1. London Bridge originally constructed across the Thames River in 1824-31 was reconstructed here in 1972. Browse in the London Bridge English Village nearby, and enjoy water recreation on Lake Havasu and the Colorado River.

Lake Powell, A-4. Man-made impoundment lies between towering red sandstone cliffs and canyon walls in Arizona and Utah. Fishing, boating, lake tours.

Petrified Forest National Park, C-5. Petrified logs up to 100 feet long lie in Rainbow Forest.

Phoenix, E-3 (see map p. 77). State Capitol has interesting murals and a museum featuring prehistoric Indian cultures and modern Indian crafts. Heard Museum has anthropological and primitive art exhibits from Africa, Asia, and the Pacific islands as well as American Indian Kachina dolls. Arizona Museum features pioneer exhibits. See also the Phoenix Art Museum and the Arizona Mineral Museum. In Papago Park are the famous Desert Botanical Gardens and the zoo.

Tempe, E-4. Man-made waves of the Big Surf make it possible to use surfboards in the middle of the desert.

Tombstone, G-5. The site of Wyatt Earp's Battle of OK Corral, historic newspaper Tombstone *Epitaph* still printing. Tour Bird Cage Theatre, Tombstone Courthouse, and Wells Fargo Museum.

Tucson, F-4. A set built here for the movie *Arizona* is now the outskirts village Old Tucson, a replica of historic Tucson in Old West days. Nearby is Arizona-Sonora Desert Museum, perhaps the world's most interesting living museum of desert plants and animals. The beauty of Mission San Xavier del Bac is timeless. The great 80-inch solar telescope is at Kitt Peak National Observatory, about 45 miles southwest.

Window Rock, B-6. A unique eight-sided chamber is the headquarters of the Navajo Tribal Government. A short distance to the east is the headquarters of the Navajo Arts and Crafts Guild. Navajo Tribal Museum depicts Navajo history and culture.

Winslow, C-5. Meteor Crater, with a diameter of 4,150 feet and a rim 560 feet above the center, is by far the nation's largest. Open daily.

Yuma, F-1. Of interest are the Yuma Territorial Prison and the Imperial National Wildlife Refuge, along the Colorado River.

ARKANSAS / Map page 7.

Arkansas Post National Memorial, E-5. Nearby Arkansas Post County Museum has original buildings from an 1830s homesite; agricultural museum and a historical display.

Batesville, B-5. An old river port with antique appeal in its architecture. 1867 waterpower mill nearby.

Blanchard Springs Caverns, A-4. Said to be the most important cave discovery of the 20th century. In Ozark National Forest, it has been completely prepared for visitors, including those in wheelchairs. Visitor Center offers educational movie and two types of tours.

Buffalo National River, B-3. Drift in a canoe or johnboat down this river, which courses past multicolored bluffs and numerous caves and springs.

Crater of Diamonds State Park, E-2. Gems are on the surface for the picking, if you're lucky. One find was appraised at over $100,000.

Crossett, F-4. Tours of a paper mill are hosted here by Georgia Pacific Corp., which also will tell you about its scientific tree farming in the area.

Dogpatch USA, A-3. A theme park, about 10 miles south of Harrison, that presents live portrayals of Al Capp's famous comic-strip characters.

Eureka Springs, A-2. Hundreds of streets that never cross each other, a church you enter through the bell tower, and many other oddities are in this town built against the side of a steep cliff. Attend the *Great Passion Play* and the Ozark Folk Festival. Visit Christ of the Ozarks statue, tour Victorian mansions, historical museums, and arts and craft shops.

Fort Smith, B-1. Where Hanging Judge Isaac Parker sent about 79 frontier badmen to the gallows. His courtroom and the gallows have been restored.

Hot Springs National Park, D-3. A city of 15 certified bathhouses, this spa has been popular for almost a century. Many amusements for young and old. Animal Wonderland has a dolphin show. *Country Music Story* is presented in the summer; Magic Springs Family Attraction and Mid-America Center Museum are worthwhile.

Little Rock, D-4. Handsome Metrocenter Mall for shoppers features a Henry Moore statue in a parklike setting. Visit the Arkansas Territorial Restoration, Old State House, and State Capitol.

Morrilton, C-3. The Museum of Automobiles, founded by the late Gov. Winthrop Rockefeller, features an attractive display of antique and classic cars.

Mountain Home, A-4. Resort town in the center of water activities. Bull Shoals Lake to the west, Norfolk Lake to the east are major impoundments featuring water sports. Good trout fishing in the White and North Fork rivers.

Old Washington Historic State Park, E-2. Restoration of the 1830s Greek Revival town where Gen. Sam Houston announced his plans for the liberation of Texas, the Bowie knife was forged by a local knifesmith, and the Confederate government met while Little Rock was occupied by Union forces.

Ozark Folk Center, B-4. At Mountain View, watch genuine mountain craftsmen at work, and listen to them play their centuries-old tunes at evening performances in one of the Midwest's newest and finest auditoriums, in 10-channel stereo. An authentic preservation of Anglo-Saxon arts and crafts. This state park also offers fine lodging and local cuisine at its hilltop restaurant. Magnificent scenery.

Stuttgart, D-5. Ducks and geese winging down the Mississippi flyway stop in rice fields here. Visitors are welcome at the Fish Farming Experimental Station, operated by the U.S. Department of Interior.

Tallmena Scenic Drive, D-1. This unusual highway (State 88 in Arkansas; State 1 in Oklahoma) across the summits of the Ouachita ("Wash ee-taw") Mountains in the Ouachita National Forest has many lookout points along its 55-mile route from Mena, Arkansas, to Talihina, Oklahoma. Queen Wilhelmina Inn and State Park are on the Arkansas portion of the route.

CALIFORNIA / Map page 8–9

Anaheim, J-4 (see map p. 72). America's most famous theme park, Disneyland, is here. A loop train trip will familiarize you with the park; a museum near the entrance tells the story of Walt Disney's dreams and career. In the park you'll see Town Square, Main Street USA of the 1890s, and six themed areas—Tomorrowland, Frontierland, Fantasyland, Adventureland, Bear Country, and New Orleans New Square.

Arcadia, J-4 (see map p. 72). Los Angeles State and County Arboretum, a large horticultural research center, is here. Santa Anita Park is one of the nation's best-known thoroughbred racing tracks.

Barstow, I-5. Calico Ghost Town, about 11 miles east, is a reconstruction of a silver mining boom town. Also in the area is the Calico Early Man Site.

Berkeley, E-1 (see map p. 78). Beautiful University of California campus has a 307-foot campanile modeled like one in Venice. Red-tiled buildings give the campus a Mediterranean quality.

Beverly Hills, J-4 (see map p. 72). The home of a number of film and television personalities. See via bus tour.

Borrego Springs, K-5. From mid-January to April wild flowers turn the desert into a sea of color at the half-million-acre Anza-Borrego State Park. Guided tours.

Buena Park, J-4 (see map p. 72). Knott's Berry Farm now includes Ghost Town, Fiesta Village, and Roaring 20's. Pan for gold, ride a cable car, travel on a steam train, board a stagecoach, and more theme areas. Nearby Movieland has 240 lifelike figures of the stars.

Coloma, E-3. At Marshall Gold Discovery State Historic Park you can see where James Marshall struck it rich on Sutter's Creek and started the '49 Gold Rush.

Death Valley National Monument, G-5. The castle here is just about the way Death Valley Scotty left it. Lowest point in the Western Hemisphere, summer temperatures frequently reach 135 degrees Fahrenheit, yet October to May are comfortable.

Lassen Volcanic National Park, C-3. Considered the most active volcanic section of the conterminous U.S. Stay on proper trails at all times in hot water or steaming areas. The park is a unique experience with strange odors, gurgling and roaring sounds, and blasts of hot water and steam from ominous cracks.

Long Beach, J-4 (see map p. 72). One of the world's great passenger ships, *Queen Mary,* is permanently docked here and can be toured. An 8-mile-long beach attracts thousands during most months of the year.

Los Angeles, J-4 (see map p. 72). See show tapings at ABC, CBS, NBC; tour Burbank, Warner Bros., and Universal Studios and museums at Exposition and Griffith parks. See El Pueblo de Los Angeles State Historic Park, Farmers Market, the Music Center, Hollywood Bowl, Southwest Museum, Los Angeles Zoo, and Chinatown. See downtown Los Angeles in a ride on the Minibus.

Monterey, G-1. Cannery Row, detailed in John Steinbeck's novel, is an excellent place to shop. Visit Fisherman's Wharf. Handsome seascapes surround the peninsula, which is popular with artists.

Mission Trail, E-2-L-5. Along hundreds of seacoast miles from San Diego to north of San Francisco and clustered close to I-5, State 1, and U.S. 101 are a score of missions ranging in age from 200 to more than 300 years. Among them are Mission San Miguel Arcangel, Mission Santa Barbara, and San Juan Capistrano.

Oakland, E-1 (see map p. 78). Visit the old haunts of the author of frontier stories by walking the neighborhood of Jack London Square. Jack London Village nearby.

Oceanside, K-4. Visit nearby Mt. Palomar, home of the 200-inch reflecting telescope, the Western Hemisphere's largest; visit marine base Camp Pendleton.

Palo Alto, F-1. Leland Stanford Jr. Museum at Stanford University displays the Golden Spike that was driven in 1869 where the Central Pacific and Union Pacific met completing the first transcontinental railroad.

Pasadena, J-4 (see map p. 72). Home of the Rose Bowl and the annual Tournament of Roses Parade. In nearby San Marino visitors can see the famous Gainsborough painting *The Blue Boy* and a priceless Gutenberg Bible at the Huntington Library, Art Gallery, and Botanical Gardens; library outstanding.

Redwood National Park, A-2. This 109,226-acre park on the northern coast between Crescent City and Orick is the place to see giant redwoods towering in their virgin groves. The tallest at 368 feet is at Orick.

Sacramento, E-2. Sutter's Fort, where the city began, depicts John Sutter's life; also here is the State Indian Museum. The Old Sacramento Historic District has been restored to re-create the 1850–80 period, recalling the days of the pony express, the arrival of the Central Pacific Railroad, and the gold rush. The State Capitol and the Governor's Mansion may also be toured.

San Diego, L-4 (see map p. 77). Home of the great San Diego Zoo, in Balboa Park (the zoo's Wild Animal Park is north of the city). At Old Town San Diego State Historic Park visitors can inspect the site of the original mission and settlement of 1769. Sea World is a marine showplace in a Polynesian setting; located in Mission Bay Park. Junipero Serra Museum tells the story of the Spanish missions. Cabrillo National Monument memorializes Cabrillo's discovery of the west coast in 1542. See naval vessels in San Diego Bay.

San Francisco, E-1 (see map p. 78). One of America's great cities has Chinatown, Fisherman's Wharf for fine seafood, and the world-famous cable cars for nostalgic transportation. Five restored ships are docked at the Hyde Street Pier. Other places to see are Golden Gate Park, site of several fine museums; Union Square; Japan Town; Nob Hill; Golden Gate Bridge; the Presidio; and the view from Twin Peaks. Follow the 49 Mile Scenic Drive sign for a tour to the many points of interest in this city of many hills.

San Jose, F-2. Visit Happy Hollow, a children's playground in Kelly Park; Overfelt Botanical Gardens; 160-room Winchester Mystery House, built by an eccentric heiress to warn off evil spirits (she kept adding rooms until she died).

Santa Clara, F-2. Marriott's Great America theme park has rides, entertainment, restaurants, and craft shops in five areas.

Sequoia and Kings Canyon National Parks, G-4. Groves of giant Sequoias, world's largest living things; Mount Whitney is the highest peak in the conterminous U.S.; enormous canyons of the Kings River.

Desert Flowers, Anza Borrego State Park, California

San Diego Convention & Visitors Bureau

Backpacking in San Juan Mountains, Ouray, Colorado

Yosemite National Park, F-4. Granite peaks and domes rise above broad meadows in the heart of the Sierra Nevada. One of the most beautiful national parks. Famous sites are El Capitan and Half Dome.

COLORADO / Map page 12

Antonito, F-4. Ride the narrow-gauge Cumbres & Toltec Scenic Railroad between Antonito and Chama, New Mexico, early June to mid-October.

Aspen, D-3. This onetime silver town is famous for its winter sports; year-round resort center. The Aspen Music Festival presents summer concerts. World-famous names are on the agenda of the Aspen Music School.

Bent's Old Fort National Historic Site, E-6. Once center of vast fur-trading empire in the West.

Black Canyon of the Gunnison National Monument, D-2. Over 13,000 acres containing the deepest and most scenic portion of the Gunnison River gorge.

Boulder, C-4. The city has a chain of parks, including the Flatirons; drive up Flagstaff Scenic Highway for a beautiful view. Visit National Center for Atmospheric Research and National Bureau of Standards.

Canon City, D-4. Drive across Royal Gorge on the suspension bridge or ride the incline railroad to the bottom and take the aerial tram across.

Central City, C-4. The Opera House and ornate Teller House recall the past. Both have shows.

Colorado Springs, D-5. Visit the U.S. Air Force Academy and Garden of the Gods. Drive up to Pikes Peak or ride the world's highest cog railway.

Cripple Creek, D-4. Ride the Cripple Creek and Victor Railroad during the summer, or take a tour of the Mollie Kathleen Gold Mine. Melodramas presented at the Imperial Hotel during the tourist season.

Denver, C-5 (see map p. 68). The State Capitol's gold dome is as beautiful as the view from the dome itself. Explore the art museum and the Colorado Heritage Center; see Molly Brown House and "Millionaire's Row" and take your pick of summer theatre at Elitch's Gardens or a performance at Boettcher Concert Hall, in the Arvata Center for the Arts & Humanities.

Durango, F-2. Ride the Silverton narrow-gauge passenger train through the mountains from Durango to Silverton. Runs mid-May–late October; make advance reservations. National civic engineering landmark.

Estes Park, B-4. An aerial tramway carries passengers to the top of Prospect Mountain; also scenic drives in the area.

Georgetown, C-4. William Hamill House has goldplated door knobs, and the Hotel de Paris still has a faded elegance; both are museums.

Golden, C-4. Visit the mining and geology museums at the Colorado School of Mines and the Colorado Railroad Museum. Buffalo Bill is buried atop Lookout Mountain. Adolph Coors brewery has tours.

Great Sand Dunes National Monument, E-4. Climb the highest inland sand dunes in America.

Idaho Springs, C-4. Drive the highest road in North America to the top of 14,260-foot Mount Evans.

Mesa Verde National Park, F-1. Walk the twisting streets of Indian ghost towns featuring multistoried apartment buildings constructed more than two centuries before Columbus discovered America.

Rocky Mountain National Park, B-4. In the park is some of the country's grandest scenery; drive Trail Ridge Road across Continental Divide.

CONNECTICUT / Map pages 10–11

Bridgeport, G-2. Memorabilia of the circus provides many a chuckle at P. T. Barnum Museum. State's largest zoo is Beardsley Zoological Gardens.

Brooklyn, E-5. This historic northeastern village has a fine Unitarian Church, Episcopal church Old Trinity, and a number of 18th-century houses.

East Granby, east of Granby, D-3. Old Newgate Prison was once a copper mine and later a colonial and state prison; now a unique museum of early penology.

East Haddam, F-4. Home of the Goodspeed Opera House, a Victorian gem devoted to musical comedies. Gillette Castle, home of actor William Gillette (Sherlock Holmes), is southeast on State 148. Take the Ferry from Hadlyme to Chester for a beautiful ride across the river.

Essex, F-4. In summer, steam cars of the Valley Railroad chug from here up to Chester.

Hartford, E-3. Of interest are the Victorian State Capitol, the Old State House, and the State Library Museum, which has priceless displays. Visit also the homes of Mark Twain and Harriet Beecher Stowe.

Litchfield, E-2. Set in the foothills of the Berkshire Chain (Litchfield Hills) the town is virtually unchanged from the days of George Washington, a frequent visitor at the time. Historical museum and America's first law school, Tapping Reeve, of interest.

Mystic, F-5. The last of the wooden whalers, the *Charles W. Morgan,* is docked at Mystic Seaport, a museum of old maritime days. Nearby is Mystic Marinelife Aquarium.

New Haven, G-3. Yale University, the Yale University Art Gallery, the Yale Center for British Art, and Peabody Museum of Natural History are all open to visitors.

New London, F-5. Check in advance for times of base tours and cadet reviews, then tour the U.S. Coast Guard Academy and view the submarine base.

Rocky Hill, E-4. Dinosaur State Park has dinosaur tracks from Triassic Period (200 million years ago).

Stratford, G-2. Enjoy Shakespeare, opera, ballet, music, and Broadway plays at the American Shakespeare Theatre, replica of the Old Globe Theatre.

DELAWARE / Map page 13

Dover, B-7. Capital of the first state to ratify the Constitution. Delaware's State House, built in 1793, has been restored; State Museum is a complex including three historic buildings.

Lewes, C-8. Zwaanendael Museum has a fine collection of maritime exhibits. Ride the Cape May–Lewes Ferry, connecting Delaware with New Jersey.

New Castle, A-7. There are many historic homes centered on The Green. Settled in 1651.

Rehoboth Beach, C-8. Fun-in-the-sun of the beaches and boardwalks.

Wilmington, A-8. Visit the restored Grand Opera House on the Market Street Pedestrian mall. Close by see the Port of Wilmington. The Wilmington & Western Railroad ride to Hockessin is a short distance from the Hagley Museum, founded by the Du Pont Family. Northwest of the city is Henry Francis du Pont's Winterthur, with over 100 rooms of American antiques and palatial estate grounds open to the public.

DISTRICT OF COLUMBIA / Maps page 80

Washington. In the nation's capital city, two buildings—the U.S. Capitol and the White House—generally receive the greatest number of visitors. Take a conducted tour of the Capitol. Your congressman or an office assistant can arrange a VIP tour of the White House. The National Park Service operates a Tourmobile along the East and West Malls. The Library of Congress, Supreme Court Building, and the U.S. Botanic Garden Conservatory are within walking distance from the Capitol. On the Mall are the Washington Monument and the Smithsonian Institution and several of its 14 museums—Museum of Natural History, Museum of History and Technology, National Air and Space Museum, National Gallery of Art, Hirschorn Museum and Sculpture Garden. Near the White House are the U.S. Treasury and Ford's Theatre. Also rewarding to visit are the Lincoln and Jefferson memorials.

FLORIDA / Map page 14

Apalachicola, H-3. Learn local history at John Gorrie State Museum. Northwest is Apalachicola National Forest.

Bartow, D-3. Phosphate Valley Exposition has dioramas telling the story of fossils from the phosphate mines, which are nearby.

Cape Canaveral, D-5. The John F. Kennedy Space Center offers a tour of launch sites, many used for putting weather and communications satellites into orbit today as a part of the NASA program.

Cocoa Beach, D-5. This city offers the best view for missile and space-vehicle watching.

Cypress Gardens, near Winter Haven, D-3. These famous, lovely gardens where water ski shows originated over 30 years ago have four ski shows daily, boat cruises, and 14 acres of new attractions.

Everglades National Park, G-4. Nation's largest subtropical wilderness, it is famed for exotic birds, unusual tropical vegetation, and numerous species of fish. Visitors can cruise the swamps, salt prairies, pine islands, sawgrass marshes, and mangrove forests.

Key Drive, G-5-H-4. From the mainland to Key West, a 158-mile tour over the Overseas Highway, one of the world's longest island-hopping bridge drives. You'll see marshlands, the ocean, and many islands on the way to Key Largo, Islamorada, Marathon, Big Pine Key, and Key West. Area water sports year-round.

Miami, G-5 (see map p. 71). Places of interest include Hialeah Park for horse racing. Miami Seaquarium, Miami Serpentarium, Planet Ocean, Monkey Jungle, Parrot Jungle, and Vizcaya, former estate of James Deering and now the Dade County Art Museum.

Miami Beach, G-5 (see map p. 71). Inspect nine miles of sandy beach, explore and enjoy luxury hotels.

St. Augustine, B-4. On the upper East Coast, this is the oldest European settlement in the U.S. Spanish-colonial architecture is revived in San Agustin Antiguo. Castillo de San Marcos National Monument is the site of the oldest masonry fort in the U.S.

Sarasota, E-3. The onetime winter home of the circus is now the Ringling Museum of Art, Ringling residence, Asolo Theater, and Ringling Museum of the Circus.

Silver Springs, near Ocala, C-3. Thousands of feeding fish can be observed in the crystal waters through glass-bottom boats. Jungle Cruise and Deer Park.

Tallahassee, A-1. Visit the interesting State Capitol, Junior Museum, and St. Marks National Wildlife Refuge.

Tampa, D-3. Busch Gardens "The Dark Continent" is a theme park with an excellent exhibition of wild animals and performing birds.

Walt Disney World, D-3. Just off I-4 southwest of Orlando, this is one of the world's great entertainment complexes. The Magic Kingdom is segmented into Fantasyland, Tomorrowland, Main St. USA, Adventureland, Frontierland, and Liberty Square. Outside the Magic Kingdom are areas such as Fort Wilderness and the new EPCOT Center-Experimental Prototype Community of Tomorrow.

GEORGIA / Map page 15

Atlanta, C-2 (see map p. 63). This southern state capital has long been famous for its beautiful buildings and its beautiful flowers and trees. Visit the Atlanta Historical Society, Woodruff Arts Center, gold-domed State Capitol, Peachtree Center, Omni Complex, and Fernbank Science Center. Martin Luther King, Jr. Memorial grave site, church, and birthplace are here and visited by many.

Brunswick, F-6. Gateway to the "golden isles"—Sea Island, St. Simons Island, and Jekyll Island. Sea Island has the famous Cloisters resort and gorgeous modern homes; Jekyll Island has beautiful beaches and remains of an 1886 Millionaire's Village.

Dahlonega, B-2. Site of America's first gold rush (1828). Visit Dahlonega Courthouse Gold Museum. Pan for gold at Crisson Mines.

Helen, north of Cleveland, A-3. This lovely alpine village was created from remains of an old lumber mill village. Surrounded by the scenic beauty of Chattahoochee National Forest.

Lumpkin, E-1. Travelers back in time will find an 1850's village in nearby Westville; authentic structures.

Macon, D-3. A lovely old southern town whose antebellum mansions are often open to the public. Hay House and Old Cannonball House and Museum open regularly. Grand Opera House is an example of 1886 opulence. Ocmulgee National Monument nearby.

Pine Mountain, D-1. Callaway Gardens, on U.S. 27, includes 2,500 acres of scenic woodland and beautiful flowering formal gardens; picnicking, swimming, and fishing facilities. Circus and water ski shows.

Plains, E-2. This is Jimmy Carter's hometown. Visitors can browse in the shops, visit the railway station, tour landmarks.

Savannah, E-6. This gracious old city is noted for its cobblestone streets, beautiful gardens, and stately mansions. Start with a walking tour of the restored nine-block Savannah Waterfront, filled with restaurants, galleries, museums, and craft shops. Harbor tours on cruise boats scheduled regularly.

Six Flags Over Georgia, C-2. Ten miles west of Atlanta, this popular theme park has six sections representing periods in the state's history. Rides, stage shows.

Stone Mountain Park, B-3. A 3,200-acre park centered on massive Stone Mountain. Take a skylift to the summit for a view of the Confederate Memorial Carving.

Tifton, F-3. Stroll through Georgia Agrirama, a 19th-century Georgia farm community, with a print shop, farmstead, sawmill, turpentine still, and cotton gin.

Warm Springs, D-2. The "Little White House" of Franklin D. Roosevelt is located here.

Waycross, F-4. Southeast off U.S. 1/23 are Okefenokee National Wildlife Refuge and the Okefenokee Swamp Park, both open year-round.

HAWAII / Map page 5

Hawaii, G-5. The "big island" is marked by lava flows that have surged down the mountains of Mauna Kea and Kilauea since the dawn of time. Here are Pu'uhonua o Honaunau National Historic Park and Hawaii Volcanoes National Park.

Kauai, E-1. Four botanical gardens are open to the public. Old Russian Fort was built for the czar in 1817 in an attempt to seize the island. Paradise Pacifica is a 23-acre collection of gardens, lagoons, rain forest, Polynesian village, and more.

Lanai, F-3. Luahiwa Petroglyphs, best preserved in the state. Lanai City resembles a New England village.

Maui, F-4. Haleakala National Park preserves features of Haleakala Crater and Kipahulu Valley's ecosystems.

Molokai, F-3. Kapuiwa Grove has more than 1,000 coconut trees in a 10-acre plot. Palaau State Park here.

Oahu, G-3. The "aloha isle." Crossroads of the Pacific is the state capital, Honolulu, whose Capitol is of Polynesian design. Bishop Museum has fine Pacificana displays. Magnificent Iolani Palace has the only throne room under the American flag. National Memorial Cemetery of the Pacific, overlooking Pearl Harbor, Honolulu, and Waikiki, is the final resting place of thousands of World War II, Korean and Vietnam veterans. Waimea Falls Park is a narrow canyon.

IDAHO / Map page 16

Boise, F-1. Largest city and capital of the state. Visit the Boise Gallery of Art, Idaho State Historical Society Museum; Ann Morrison Memorial Park, and Julia Davis Park. Gateway to Boise National Forest.

Cataldo, B-2. Old Mission is the oldest surviving (restored) building in the state; now a state park.

Coeur d'Alene, B-1. Excursion boats leave the city for daily six-hour trips up the lake and into St. Joe River. Passengers lunch at Heyburn State Park.

Craters of the Moon National Monument, G-3. Nation's greatest variety of volcanic basalt. Volcanic cones, craters, lava flows, and caves make this astonishing landscape.

Dworshak Reservoir, near Orofino, C-2. Visit the national fish hatchery, rent a fishing boat, or take a pleasure boat trip on the reservoir.

Fort Hall, G-4. Shoshone and Bannock Indian crafts can be purchased in local tribal shops.

Hells Canyon, E-1. On the Oregon border, the Snake River has cut a 7,900-foot-gorge, the deepest canyon in America. Try a one-day boat trip.

Idaho City, F-2. Boot Hill has the graves of miners who died with their boots on. There's a historical museum here and buildings of the gold rush 1860s.

Idaho Falls, G-4. Intermountain Science Center, exhibits, nature trails. The historic nuclear reactor EBR-1 at the Idaho National Engineering Laboratory, west on U.S. 20 about 50 miles, may be seen June 15-September 15. Potato-growing area.

Kellogg, B-1. Tour the above-ground concentrator and mine operations at the Bunker Hill properties.

Lewiston, D-1. One of the world's largest lumber mills offers free tours. For a breathtaking view of the region, drive up the Lewis and Clark Highway (US 12), which parallels the Lewis and Clark Trail east to Montana.

Nez Perce National Historical Park, D-2. Visit 24 sites representative of history and culture of these Indians.

Salmon, E-3. Jet boats take visitors down the Salmon River through steep-walled gorges difficult to scale.

Sawtooth National Recreation Area, F-2. This magnificent area comprises several hundred lakes and trails and facilities for camping. Information available at the Stanley Ranger Station, south of Stanley, and the Visitors Center, on Red Fish Lake, both on State 75.

Snake River Birds of Prey Natural Area, southwest of Boise, F-1. Eagles, falcons, ospreys, owls, and various species of hawks will interest birdwatchers. Obtain directions from Division of Tourism, Capitol, Boise.

Sun Valley, F-3. One of the world's best known year-round sports centers because of its exceptional snow conditions and sheltered bowl in the mountains. Wide range of excursions, camping, and fishing trips in the encircling Sawtooth Mountains and National Forest.

Twin Falls, H-3. Shoshone Falls, at 212 feet, are higher than Niagara Falls. Impressive view from bridge.

ILLINOIS / Map page 17

Chicago, B-5 (see map p. 66). Take an elevator to the top of Sears Tower, world's tallest building, or a close rival, the John Hancock Center. There are lakefront facilities for swimming and boating; Lincoln Park and the Lincoln Park Zoo and suburban Brookfield Zoo are popular family attractions. The city offers a broad spectrum of entertainment, from Lyric Opera to Chicago Symphony to theater and night club big-name shows. Visit the Art Institute, Field Museum, Shedd Aquarium, and Adler Planetarium; young and old alike love the do-it-yourself exhibits of the Museum of Science and Industry. Enjoy the architecture and many sculptures, from the Picasso at the Richard J. Daley Center, to the Chagall Wall, to the Calder Flamingo, to the Miró. Summertime concerts in Grant Park, the city's many plazas, and at Ravinia, near Highland Park. In nearby Oak Park, tour the Frank Lloyd Wright Historic District (Visitors Center at 158 N. Forest St. in Oak Park).

Galena, A-2. Home tours in June and September attract thousands of visitors to admire the fine Victorian architecture and visit the area antique shops. The Ulysses S. Grant home is open daily.

Great America Theme Park, in Gurnee, west of Waukegan, A-4. Marriott's family recreation park features five different theme areas, stage shows, rides.

Harrisburg, G-4. Headquarters for the 258,000-acre Shawnee National Forest. Scenic drives beautiful in spring and fall; camping and fishing popular.

Lincoln, D-3. Postville Courthouse State Historic Site is a replica of the building where Lincoln attended court when he rode the law circuit. Lincoln College has a fine collection of Lincolniana in its library.

Lincoln's New Salem State Park, D-3. Much-visited restoration of the town of New Salem, where Lincoln lived and worked for six years. During summer an outdoor drama uses Lincoln's own words.

Nauvoo, C-1. This quaint old town on the Mississippi River was the headquarters of The Church of Jesus Christ of Latter-day Saints from 1839 to 1846. Later a socialist French sect left its mark on the little town. See the Nauvoo Restoration, Joseph Smith Historic Center, and Old Carthage Jail in nearby Carthage.

Springfield, D-3. Illinois' capital is on the Lincoln Heritage Trail—Lincoln practiced law here, was married here, and left here to become president. He is also buried here. See the Lincoln Home National Historic Site, Lincoln Law Offices, Lincoln Tomb State Historic Site. The Old State Capitol is beautifully restored; light and sound show nightly during summer. Also of interest are Parks Telephone Museum and nearby Clayville Rural Life Center and Museum.

Union, A-4. Illinois Rail Museum displays an 1851 railroad station and steam engines, streetcars, the works. Seven Acres Museum and Village nearby.

Woodstock, A-4. Circa-1900 town square features specialty shopping and a restored Opera House and Courthouse-Jail complex.

INDIANA / Map page 18

Auburn, A-5. Auburn-Cord-Duesenburg Museum is housed in the original showroom of the Auburn Automobile Co. Twenty makes of automobiles.

Bloomington, F-3. Lake Monroe, Indiana's largest, is 10 miles southeast of town, providing all types of recreation. On Indiana University's beautiful wooded campus are fine museums of art, archaeology, history, and rare books; many handsome buildings.

Columbus, F-4. The town has restored Victorian buildings and invited some of the world's greatest architects to create contemporary buildings, including churches, schools, and homes.

Fort Wayne, B-5. Historic Fort Wayne is a careful reconstruction of the last American frontier military post in Indiana. Children's zoo has miniature safaris, paddleboat, and pony rides. Living museum.

Indianapolis, E-3 (see map p. 73). Three fine museums —Indiana State Museum, Indianapolis Museum of Art, and the wonderful Children's Museum—are musts. See State Capitol building and Monument Circle. Indianapolis Motor Speedway Hall of Fame is located inside the famous Indianapolis 500 track. Famous auto race and trials held here each Memorial Day weekend.

Jeffersonville, G-4. Howard Steamboat Museum is the only one of its type. Take a sidetrip to see the falls of the Ohio fossil bed in nearby Clarksville.

Lafayette, C-2. Ft. Ouiatenon, built by the French in 1717 along the Wabash River, is now a county park with reconstructed blockhouse and museum. Purdue University welcomes visitors to its campus.

Lincoln Boyhood National Memorial, H-2. Lincoln grew from boyhood to manhood on his father's farm near the old Pigeon Creek settlement.

Metamora, E-5. An operating gristmill houses a museum overlooking the sluiceway of the Whitewater Canal. Ride the canal boat *Valley Belle*.

Michigan City, A-2. International Friendship Gardens have continuous garden shows early spring through late fall. Indiana Dunes State Park is 11 miles west on US 12 and State 49.

Nashville, F-3. Visitors to this long-time popular artists' colony can browse in numerous art, craft, and specialty shops, with live entertainment offered throughout the year. Nearby is scenic Brown County State Park; fall foliage magnificent.

New Harmony, H-1. In 1814 the town was settled by the Rappites, a religious sect which created a thriving and uniquely civilized town out of the wilderness. The Harmony Society moved east in 1825, selling its property to Welsh-born Robert Owen, who made the town the site of an ambitious utopian experiment. An ambitious restoration program has now restored several buildings and added new ones.

Noblesville, D-4. Indiana in the 1830s comes alive again at Conner Prairie Pioneer Settlement, with costumed guides at the Farmstead and the Village.

Rockville, E-2. Billie Creek Village has a re-created turn-of-the-century village and farmstead. Covered bridge buffs leave this county seat for a tour of 38 of these structures in Parke County.

Santa Claus, H-2. Santa Claus Land is popular not only at Christmas but throughout the year.

Vincennes, G-1. Tour Grouseland, home of William Henry Harrison, then walk to the nearby *Western Sun* Print Shop and the small building that served as the first territorial capitol. George Rogers Clark National Historical Park, near Lincoln Memorial Bridge, commemorates seizure of Fort Sackville from the British.

IOWA / Map page 19

Amana Colonies, C-6. The seven villages welcome visitors to their shops, furniture factory, and woolen mill. The Amana Inns serve German-style meals.

Burlington, E-7. Ripley's "Believe It Or Not" called Snake Alley the crookedest street in the world—it makes five turns in just one block.

Cedar Rapids, C-7. Near downtown is Czech Village. Czech celebrations held throughout the year.

Clermont, A-6. Montauk was built by one of Iowa's governors in 1874. Enjoy this beautifully restored home and outstanding scenery.

Council Bluffs, D-1. The Historic General Dodge House was built in 1869 by the retired Civil War general and railroad builder. Bluffs overlook river.

Davenport, D-8. At the Museum-Art Center are the Davenport Art Gallery and the Putnam Museum.

Decorah, A-6. Vesterheim, the Norwegian-American Museum, has a comprehensive collection. The three buildings include a stone mill and blacksmith shop.

Des Moines, D-4. Guests tour the State Capitol and the Art Center, designed by Eliel Saarinen, which is as outstanding as the works it contains. There is a delightful children's zoo and Living History Farms. Adventureland Park has turn-of-the-century theme.

Dubuque, B-8. Board a sternwheeler for a Mississippi River trip; ride a cable car to towering bluffs. See the Civil War shot tower; lock, dam, and bridges.

Keokuk, E-7. The *George M. Verity* is a sternwheel towboat which has been turned into a museum of river memorabilia. Keokuk Dam stretches one mile across the Mississippi River; built in 1913.

Mason City, A-5. The Kinney Pioneer Museum is 7 miles west of town. An annual band festival keeps alive the tradition of the movie *Music Man.* Also in town is the Charles H. MacNider Museum, an art center featuring changing and permanent exhibits with emphasis on American art. The Margaret M. MacNider Park offers swimming, fishing, hiking, picnicking, and camping.

McGregor, A-7. Spook Cave has an underground water tour. Explore the fascinating formations by boat; temperature constant 47 degrees Fahrenheit.

Pella, D-5. Wyatt Earp's boyhood home is part of the Pella Historical Village. In spring Dutch descendants scrub the streets to get ready for the tulip festival.

West Branch, C-7. The Herbert Hoover National Historical Site contains Hoover's birthplace, a replica of his father's blacksmith shop, a Quaker Meeting House, and impressive library. Open daily.

KANSAS / Map page 22

Abilene, C-6. The home where Dwight Eisenhower was raised and the Eisenhower Memorial Museum are close to each other. The late president and famous general and his wife, Mamie, are buried in the nearby chapel. Old Abilene Town recalls frontier days.

Chanute, D-7. Safari Museum houses photographs and artifacts of the South Seas, Borneo, and East Africa collected by the famous explorers Martin and Osa Johnson during the early 1900s.

Coffeyville, E-7. The Dalton Museum tells the story of the 1892 raid the Daltons made on Coffeyville's banks.

Dodge City, D-3. Front Street is a lively reconstruction of the days of Earp, Hickock, and Masterson. View relics of the past at Boot Hill Museum.

Hays, C-3. Some original buildings of old Fort Hays still stand in Frontier Historical Park; buffalo graze on the grounds. Visit Sternberg Memorial Museum and Ellis County Historical Society and Museum.

Kansas City, B-8 (see map p. 71). Indian children went to school at Old Shawnee Town. Wells Fargo Express office and the First Territorial Jail are nearby.

Larned, D-4. Kit Carson, Wild Bill Hickok, Buffalo Bill, and George Custer were all stationed at Fort Larned, now a national historic site. Santa Fe Trail Center is nearby.

Leavenworth, B-8. Custer's pay wagon is in the U.S. Army Museum at Fort Leavenworth, one of the country's oldest continuously active military posts.

Lindsborg, C-5. Swedish culture abounds in this small town, home of Bethany College, the Birger Sandzen Memorial Gallery, and world-famous Messiah Festival during Holy Week. Visit McPherson County Old Mill Museum & Park.

Salina, C-5. Tour flour mills to see how prairie wheat is processed. Indian artifacts and a prehistoric burial pit are 4 miles east; interesting archaeological findings.

Topeka, B-7. Tour the State House and Kansas State Historical Society Museum. The zoo has a tropical rain forest and more than 400 animals.

Wichita, D-5. The Mid-America All-Indian Center pays tribute to the Indians; Old Cowtown Museum takes visitors back to the Old West. Visit Omnisphere Earth-Space Center for a look into the future.

KENTUCKY / Map pages 20–21

Abraham Lincoln Birthplace National Historic Site, C-7. President Lincoln was born here in a cabin now preserved in an impressive marble memorial.

Bardstown, C-7. My Old Kentucky Home State Park is the site of Judge John Rowan's Federal Hill mansion, which inspired Stephen Foster. In summer a musical drama of the composer's story is presented.

Bowling Green, D-6. Beech Bend Park has luxury campgrounds in its 1,000 acres. Indoor roller skating, miniature golf, zoo, more.

Covington, A-8. The Cathedral Basilica of the Assumption is a fine example of French-Gothic architecture. The great transept window is thought to be the largest stained-glass window in the world. Heroic murals by Kentucky artist Frank Duveneck and sculpture by Clement Barnhorn.

Fort Boonesborough State Park, C-9. Daniel Boone was the builder of the original fort, now restored.

Fort Knox, C-7. See General Patton Museum of Cavalry and Armor. Sorry, no gold on display.

Frankfort, B-8. The interior of the beautiful State Capitol is patterned after the Palace of Versailles and the Paris Opera House. Kentucky Military History Museum displays Pontiac's tomahawk and Boone's rifle. The Boones' graves are in Frankfort Cemetery.

Harrodsburg, C-8. Old Fort Harrod State Park is a reproduction of the fort built by James Harrod and his settlers in 1774; first permanent English settlement west of the Allegheny Mountains.

Henderson, C-5. In John James Audubon State Park visit memorial museum, which features many paintings by Audubon and his sons plus 126 first-edition prints.

Land Between the Lakes, D-4. In the southwest corner of the state. Visit the Environmental Education Center.

Lexington, B-8. Several of the famed horse farms admit visitors. Visit Kentucky Horse Park, magnificent multimillion-dollar tribute to the horse. Man O'War's statue is at the park entrance.

Louisville, B-7 (see map p. 70). See Churchill Downs where the celebrated Kentucky Derby is run each spring. Take an Ohio River boat ride on the *Belle of Louisville*.

Mammoth Cave National Park, D-6. Guided cave tours throughout the day. Have lunch in Snowball Dining Room, 267 feet below the surface.

Paducah, D-3. The former home of Vice-President Alben W. Barkley has been refurbished. Market House is now a museum, art gallery, and theater.

Pleasant Hill, C-8. Southwest of Lexington, Shakertown, an experiment in religious communal living, has been handsomely restored with lodging facilities and dining rooms. Costumed workers show how Shakers farmed and made high quality, utilitarian furniture.

Wickliffe, D-3. Near the confluence of the Mississippi and Ohio rivers are mounds built by prehistoric Americans of 1,000 years ago. Their origin remains a mystery, but evidence of their high culture may be seen.

LOUISIANA / Map page 23

Baton Rouge, C-4. Start at the tourist information center in the Old State Capitol, a Gothic castle built in 1847. The "new" capitol of Huey Long fame is interesting, and LSU Rural Life Museum and Burden Research Center has an antebellum overseer's dwelling. Many magnificent plantations in the area.

Lafayette, E-3. Famous for its spring azalea trail and rice festival. Acadian Village has authentic buildings representative of an early Cajun bayou village.

Monroe, A-3. Louisiana Purchase Gardens have 100 acres of blooms along walks and waterways. Poverty Point State Commemorative Area has a complex of man-made earthen mounds dating from 1700–700 B.C.

New Iberia, E-4. Shadows-on-the-Teche is one of the most beautiful of plantation homes. Nearby Avery Island has exotic gardens, a large bird sanctuary, and the McIlhenny Tabasco Factory.

New Orleans, E-6 (see map p. 74). Enjoy the cuisine, shops, jazz, and architecture of the French Quarter and the French Market. Visit the St. Louis Cathedral and impressive Cabildo. Walking or driving tours of the Garden District give a glimpse of the city's Greek Revival and mid-Victorian architecture.

St. Francisville, D-4. Stop at West Feliciana Historical Society for a tour map of the many antebellum and post-bellum homes in the area.

St. Martinville, E-4. Ornate old St. Martin of Tours Catholic Church has gifts from Louis XVI and Marie Antoinette; on the church grounds are Evangeline's grave and Le Petit Paris Museum. Visit the huge Evangeline oak, then go north to the Longfellow-Evangeline State Commemorative Area.

Shreveport, A-1. The State Exhibit Museum, adjacent to Louisiana State Fairgrounds, offers a variety of art and historic relics. American Rose Society Gardens, headquarters for America's largest plant society, is outside of town. Roses bloom from the months of April through December.

MAINE / Map page 24

Acadia National Park, F-4. Watch awesome cliffs and listen to the surf pounding incessantly at them.

Allagash Wilderness Waterway, B-2. Enjoy whitewater canoeing. Explore miles of beautiful woods.

Andover, F-1. Inspect the interesting Comsat space vehicles at the reception center of the nearby satellite tracking station.

Bath, G-2. Maine Maritime Museum depicts the history of shipbuilding, a major industry here. *Virginia,* the first ship launched in America, was built here.

Baxter State Park, C-3. In this magnificent wilderness area is 5,268-foot-high Mt. Katahdin.

Boothbay Harbor, G-2. Two restored rail depots offer the opportunity to ride a narrow-guage steam train and visit the Railway Museum. Take an excursion boat on a harbor cruise; enjoy a clambake.

Brunswick, G-2. On the Bowdoin College campus is the Peary-MacMillan Arctic Museum.

Kennebunkport, H-1. Visitors swim at Cleaves Cove and Goose Rocks Beach and fish in the ocean. Seashore Trolley Museum is a favorite of adults and children.

Orono, E-3. Visit the campus of the University of Maine, home of "The Stein Song."

Poland, G-1. The unusual communal way of life once followed by the Shakers is depicted at Shaker Museum. Poland Spring water made this one of the best-known resorts in the East.

Rangeley Lake, E-1. A four-seasons resort that offers fishing, sailing, hiking, skiing, and more.

MARYLAND / Map page 13

Aberdeen, B-6. Visit the U.S. Army Ordnance Museum at the Proving Ground where army weapons are tested.

Annapolis, C-6. See the State House and parades and sports events at the U.S. Naval Academy.

Baltimore, B-6 (see map p. 65). Visitors are attracted to U.S. Frigate *Constellation,* the nation's oldest warship. See the city's fine museums, Fort McHenry, and the B & O Railroad Museum and roundhouse. The National Aquarium is at Pier 3, Pratt Street.

Deep Creek Lake, B-1. Maryland's largest freshwater lake with miles of shoreline. Cross-country skiing at Herrington Manor and New Germany state parks.

Frederick, B-4. Barbara Fritchie House, Roger Brooke Taney Home and Francis Scott Key Museum, and Historical Society of Frederick County Museum are of interest.

Ocean City, D-8. Vacationers flock to the waterfront amusement area and beaches. The Assateague Island National Seashore, nearby, has wild ponies and waterfowl.

St. Mary's City, D-6. See the Old State House at the site of Maryland's first capital. Here also are archeological digs and a re-created 17th-century vessel.

St. Michaels, west of Easton, C-6. In the town where James Michener wrote *Chesapeake,* see bay boats at the Chesapeake Bay Maritime Museum.

Acadia National Park, Maine

Leith Rohr

MASSACHUSETTS / Map pages 10–11

Boston, C-7 (see map p. 64). The capital of Massachusetts, this is one of the most historic cities in the U.S. Walk the Freedom Trail, which meanders past such landmarks as Faneuil Hall, the Boston Common, the Old State House, the Boston Massacre site, Benjamin Franklin's birthplace, Paul Revere's House, Old North Church and more. Other sites, some on the trail and some not, are Beacon Hill, the U.S.S. *Constitution* (Old Ironsides), Prudential and Government centers, Copley Square, Copp's Hill Burying Ground, and the markets. Harvard University, Radcliffe College, and the Massachusetts Institute of Technology are in Cambridge. Each has outstanding buildings.

Deerfield, B-4. Historic Deerfield, Inc. is a national landmark with 12 museum houses. Also in town is the Indian House Memorial.

Fall River, E-7. A fine concentration of World War II naval vessels can be visited at Battleship Cove.

Hancock, B-2. Hancock Shaker Village, a restored historic landmark, contains 18 handsome buildings of a 1790 Shaker settlement. Open summer and fall.

Minute Man National Historical Park, B-7 (see map p. 64). Site of the fighting which started the American Revolution. Here are North Bridge, Minute Man statue, Battle Road, and Nathaniel Hawthorne's home.

New Bedford, E-8. New Bedford Whaling Museum, Seamen's Bethel, New Bedford Glass Museum, and the County Street historic district recall the days when this was acclaimed the "whaling capital of the world."

Plymouth, D-8. Here are Plymouth Rock, *Mayflower II,* living museum Plimouth Plantation, and Cole's Hill, where early colonists were buried.

Provincetown, D-10. Quaint streets and shops attract visitors to this onetime whaling town.

Quincy, C-8 (see map p. 64). The homes of John Adams and John Quincy Adams are on the same street.

Salem, B-8. Visit Nathaniel Hawthorne's "House of the Seven Gables," Hathaway House, Retire Becket House, and Hawthorne's birthplace.

Springfield, D-4. Basketball Hall of Fame is at Springfield College, where the game of basketball was invented is open to visitors.

Sturbridge, D-5. Craftsmen in costume work at early-day crafts at Old Sturbridge Village, re-creating a New England community dating from 1790 to 1840.

MICHIGAN / Map page 25

Ann Arbor, G-4. Peaceful uses for atomic energy are researched at Phoenix Memorial Laboratory on the campus of the University of Michigan. Also open to visitors are several fine museums and the stadium, which seats some 101,000 spectators.

Battle Creek, G-3. Of interest are the Postum Club art exhibit and nearby Kellogg Bird Sanctuary.

Beaver Island, C-2. In Lake Michigan 32 miles out from the harbor at Charlevoix. Water and snow sports, miles of scenic beauty, and century-old historic sites. In the 1840s this was a Mormon colony ruled by James Jesse Strang, the only king ever to reign in the U.S.

Dearborn, G-5 (see map p. 69). Greenfield Village contains fascinating structures collected from around the nation by Henry Ford. Among the buildings are Luther Burbank's garden office; an original 1913 carousel in the village's Suwanee Park. Henry Ford Museum, with its 8-acre Hall of Technology, is adjacent to the museum.

Detroit, G-5 (see map p. 69). The Motor City is proud of its new Renaissance Center, a modern city within a city; a Science Center; Detroit Institute of Arts; the Cranbrook museums; Children's Museum; Detroit Historical Museum; Philip A. Hart Memorial Plaza; the zoo; auto plant tours, and much more.

Fayette, C-2. A picturesque and well-preserved historic townsite (iron smelting) of the last century. Visitors can fish in Snail Shell Harbor with proper license and camp beneath the towering trees of Fayette State Park.

Flint, F-4. A living museum, Historical Crossroads Village contains nearly 40 structures. Alfred P. Sloan, Jr. Museum is outstanding. Tours of several General Motors' plants are available. Suggest you call in advance.

Frankenmuth, F-4. A town of Bavarian charm with quaint shops; Bronner's, which has one of America's largest displays of Christmas decorations; and the Bavarian Inn and Zehnder's, famous for family-style chicken dinners.

Grand Rapids, G-2. Gerald R. Ford spent his boyhood here; the city has many fine museums and parks.

Holland, G-2. Visitors can view vast tulip fields and see wooden shoes being carved. Visit the Dutch Village. See an authentic Dutch mill, the over-200-year-old Windmill De Zwaan, only authentic mill in the U.S.

Interlochen, D-2. Home of the National Music Camp, where concerts, plays, and ballets are performed during the summer. Interlochen Arts Academy is the camp's winter counterpart. Summer concerts.

Jackson, G-4. The illuminated Cascades at the Sparks Foundation are a 500-foot-long stream that courses over 16 separate waterfalls in an array of light, color, and music. The Michigan Space Center depicts the state and nation's space role achievements.

Lansing, G-3. Capital city of Michigan; daily tours of the Capitol. Places to visit are Impression Five Science Museum, Abrams Planetarium, Michigan State University at East Lansing, and Potter Park and Zoo.

Mackinac Island State Park, C-3. Autos and trucks are banned on the island, but you can take a horsedrawn carriage ride. Grand Hotel has one of the longest porches in the world. Visit historic Old Fort Mackinac.

Monroe, H-5. Monroe County Historical Museum has Indian memorabilia from the River Raisin Massacre of 1813 (War of 1812) and personal items of George Armstrong Custer, who lived here when young.

Bayou near Pascagoula, Mississippi

© Southern Living. Photo by Beth Maynor

Munsing, B-2. Longfellow's "Hiawatha" made the Pictured Rocks famous. They can be visited via cruise boats from Municipal Pier. National lakeshore area.

Sault Ste. Marie, B-4. Connected by bridges with its twin city in Ontario. A Soo Tour Train takes visitors for a ride around town. Chief attraction is Soo Locks (St. Mary's Falls Ship Canal).

MINNESOTA / Map page 26

Apple Valley, southwest of Minneapolis, G-4. Visit the new Minnesota Zoological Garden; over 375 species of animals and 2,000 varieties of plants.

Bemidji, D-2. Statues of Paul Bunyan and Babe the Blue Ox stand on the shore of Lake Bemidji.

Brainerd, E-3. Lumbertown, U.S.A. includes 1870s vintage buildings; ride a train and riverboat. Paul Bunyan Amusement Center nearby. Open daily in summer.

Chisholm, C-4. Learn about iron and the area at the Iron Range Interpretative Center in the southwest part of the city. Less than a mile away is the Minnesota Museum of Mining, which acquaints you with the mining process, miners' tools; numerous exhibits.

Duluth, D-5. I-35 gives you a panoramic view of the international harbor. Also visit Marine Museum and the St. Louis County Heritage and Arts Center.

Eveleth, D-4. The U.S. Hockey Hall of Fame is located just off U.S. 53, north of town.

Faribault, G-4. The state's peony capital every June; mapped tours of historic buildings.

Grand Portage National Monument, A-5. Follow scenic North Shore Drive from Duluth to this historic fur trading post where traders and trappers rendezvoused. The Grand Portage post of the Northwest Company has been reconstructed.

International Falls, B-4. Gateway to the forested lake country of Voyageurs National Park, popular for camping, fishing, and boating.

Little Falls, E-3. Walk across a footbridge built by 12-year-old Charles A. Lindbergh at his boyhood home, now a state park and interpretive center.

Minneapolis, G-4 (see map p. 74). City of lovely parks, fine buildings and museums, including the Minneapolis Institute of Arts, the Walker Art Center, and the world-famous Tyrone Guthrie Theater. Stroll Nicollet Mall; see the Crystal Court of the IDS Building. See native plants and birds at the Eloise Butler Wildflower Bird Sanctuary. On the University of Minnesota campus are the Bell Museum of Natural History and University Art Gallery. Visit nearby Minnehaha Park and the Minnehaha Falls.

Mountain Iron, west of Virginia, C-4. Climb the observation tower for a look into the first pit in the Mesabi Range; discovered in 1890, now a historic landmark.

Park Rapids, D-2. Rapid River Logging Camp is self-guided; nearby 28,000-acre Itasca State Park, where the Mississippi River begins, has heavy forests and Lake Itasca, source of the mighty river.

Pipestone National Monument, H-1. Learn the history of the Indian pipes at the visitor center; in summer watch Indians quarrying the stone. Hike the trail to the quarries and shop in the Upper Midwest Indian Cultural Center. Pipes of peace carved by Indians are popular souvenirs.

Rochester, H-4. Tour Mayo Clinic, visit Olmsted County Museum, Mayo Medical Museum, and Dr. Charles Mayo's estate.

St. Paul, G-4 (see map p. 74). The beautiful State Capitol has tours. The Omnitheater at the Science Museum simulates underwater and space travel. Cathedral of St. Paul is one of the country's largest. Historic Fort Snelling overlooks the Minnesota and Mississippi rivers; fort built in the 1820s.

Shakopee, G-3. Valleyfair is a theme park with rides and shows. Stagecoach Museum nearby.

Two Harbors, D-5. See the Lake County Historical & Railroad Museum and watch ore boats being loaded. Mallet locomotive is on display.

Virginia, C-4. Watch operating open-pit mine from observation tower at Rouchleau Mine.

Winona, H-5. The Wilkie Steamboat Center has Fulton steamboat documents and the Wilkie riverboating collection of artifacts and documents.

MISSISSIPPI / Map page 27

Biloxi, H-4. On the Gulf of Mexico the city has a rich heritage from having been under six flags—France, Spain, Great Britain, Republic of West Florida, Confederacy, and United States. An important shrimp port, the city celebrates a ceremonious blessing of its fleet annually in the early part of June. Beauvoir, last home of Jefferson Davis, and a number of old Spanish houses, and Biloxi Lighthouse are worth visiting.

Greenville, C-2. Winterville Mounds Historic Site, 5 miles north, is a restored meeting place of prehistoric Lower Mississippi Valley Indians.

Gulfport, H-4. An important Gulf Coast resort with miles of sand beaches. Take a boat trip to Ship Island in Gulf Islands National Seashore.

Jackson, E-3. See the State Capitol, Governor's Mansion, Municipal Art Gallery, The Old Capitol, and Jackson Zoo, one of the largest in the South.

Natchez, F-1. An important river port from the early 1800s, this was the locale for lavish plantations and many great mansions. During a prominent pilgrimage held here during March and early April, 35 antebellum homes are open to the public.

Picayune, H-3. The NASA National Space Technology Laboratories, 13 miles south of the city, has interesting tours, by appointment only. Write NASA, N.S.T.L. Public Affairs Office, Bay St. Louis, MS 39529.

Vicksburg, E-2. The city's almost impregnable fortifications and commanding location on the Mississippi River made the "Gibraltar of the Confederacy" vital to the survival of the South in the War between the States. Vicksburg National Military Park is dedicated to maintaining the history of the great siege in the battle between the states.

MISSOURI / Map page 28

Big Spring, near Van Buren, E-5. Part of Ozark National Scenic Riverways, the first of the national riverways, this is one of the largest single-outlet springs (276 million gallons daily) in the United States.

Branson, F-3. Hub of the White River Lakes area. Shepherd of the Hills Farm, the setting of Harold Bell Wright's famous novel, is 7 miles west of town. Old Mill Theatre dramatizes the story on summer evenings.

Fulton, C-4. Churchill's "Iron Curtain" speech was given at Westminster College, location of a three-century-old Christopher Wren church reconstructed from materials brought from London.

George Washington Carver National Monument, E-2. Nature trails and experimental gardens grace the forest glen where one of the world's greatest scientists, the noted botanist and educator, spent his boyhood.

Hannibal, B-5. At the foot of Cardiff Hill, the "Holiday Hill" of the Mark Twain stories, tourists can see life-size statues of Tom Sawyer and Huck Finn. Tour the historic area surrounding Twain's boyhood home (Tom Sawyer's in the book) and see the Becky Thatcher home, Clemens law office, and the famous fence, which is the subject of a national whitewashing contest every 4th of July.

Independence, C-2. Visit Harry S. Truman Library and Museum, where the president's papers and historic mementoes are housed. The Mormon Visitors' Center displays artifacts and films on the life of Christ and Mormon history. Saints Auditorium, headquarters of the Reorganized Church of Jesus Christ of Latter-day Saints, has a 6,000-pipe organ.

Jefferson City, C-4. The handsome State Capitol building, set on a bluff overlooking the Missouri River, contains the excellent State Museum and world-famous murals by Thomas Hart Benton.

Kansas City, B-2 (see map p. 71). Among the places to see are the Plaza (shopping center), Nelson-Atkins Museum of Art, Museum of History and Science, Liberty

Continued on p. ix, following p. 80.

Rand McNally

Interstate Road Atlas

CONTENTS

MAP LEGEND

Complete | Under Construction | Proposed

TOLL / FREE — Multilane Controlled Access

Other Multilane

(Proposed highway alignments are generalized. Many locations are undetermined)

Toll Barrier — Interchanges

paved | unpaved

Principal Through Highways

Other Through Roads

Other Roads

64 National Interstate Highways (Markers partially erected)

20 ALT 20 BYP 20 U.S. Highways (Alternate, Bypass)

2 20 200 State and Provincial Highways

515 Secondary State, County, and Provincial Highways

Trans-Canada Highway

85 Mexican Highways

COMPARATIVE DISTANCE SCALE

km. 0 5 10 20 30 40 50 60 70 80 90 100 — 1 mile = 1.609 kilometers

mi. 0 5 10 20 30 40 50 60 — 1 kilometer = .621 miles

All persons (aliens and American citizens) must stop and report for customs inspection before entering the United States. There is a penalty for failure to report. It is advisable that persons departing from the United States check with customs officials regarding re-entry.

State Maps

Accumulated mileage between red pointers

City Areas

State and National Recreation Areas, Parks and Monuments

Points of Interest Areas, Military and Indian Reservations

U.S. National Forests

State and Provincial Parks (with camping facilities)

State and Provincial Parks (no camping facilities)

State Memorials, Monuments, Historic Sites

U.S. and Canadian Nat'l. Parks

U.S. National Cemeteries, Historic Sites

U.S. National Monuments

Recreational Areas and Campsites

State Capitals

Points of Interest

City Maps

Red accumulated mileages between red dots
Other mileages between towns, junctions & interchanges

Airports: Scheduled Service — Military — Other

Points of Interest

Winter Sports Areas

Campsites

A B State Parks and Recreation Areas
A: Camping B: No Camping

National Cemeteries

National Forests

National Parks

State Parks

Military Reservations, Points of Interest

Indian Reservations

Other Parks

Rand McNally & Company
P.O. Box 7600, Chicago, Illinois 60680
10 East 53rd St., New York, New York 10022
595 Market St., San Francisco, California 94105

Library of Congress Catalog Number 82-061807

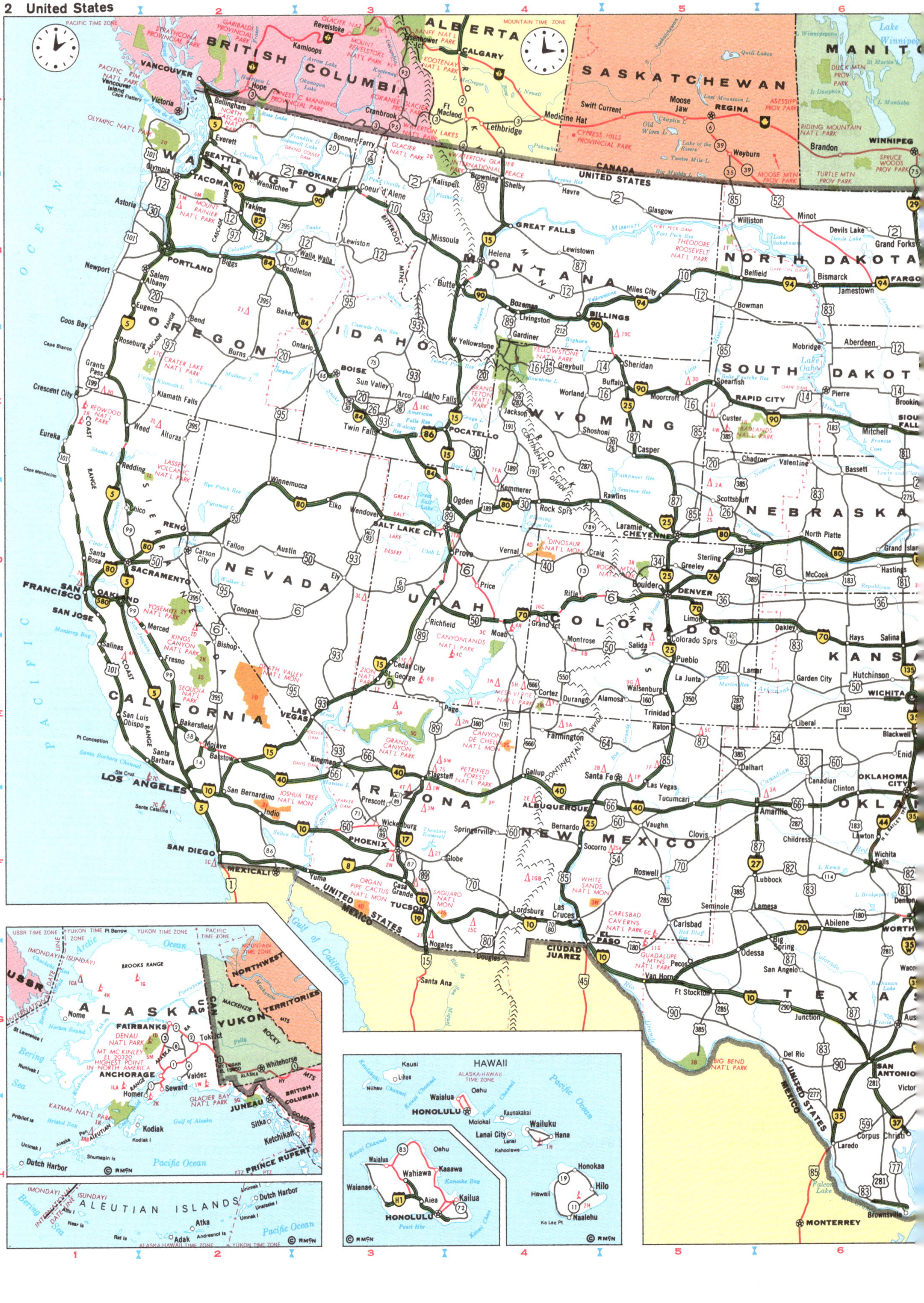

PACIFIC TIME ZONE
MOUNTAIN TIME ZONE
BRITISH COLUMBIA
ALBERTA
SASKATCHEWAN
MANITOBA
CANADA
UNITED STATES
PACIFIC OCEAN
WASHINGTON
OREGON
CALIFORNIA
NEVADA
IDAHO
MONTANA
WYOMING
UTAH
COLORADO
ARIZONA
NEW MEXICO
TEXAS
NORTH DAKOTA
SOUTH DAKOTA
NEBRASKA
KANSAS
OKLAHOMA
MEXICO
Vancouver
Victoria
Kamloops
Revelstoke
Calgary
Lethbridge
Medicine Hat
Regina
Moose Jaw
Swift Current
Weyburn
Brandon
Winnipeg
Seattle
Tacoma
Olympia
Everett
Bellingham
Spokane
Yakima
Wenatchee
Astoria
Portland
Salem
Albany
Eugene
Bend
Coos Bay
Roseburg
Medford
Klamath Falls
Pendleton
Walla Walla
Lewiston
Coeur d'Alene
Boise
Twin Falls
Pocatello
Idaho Falls
Sun Valley
Missoula
Kalispell
Great Falls
Helena
Butte
Bozeman
Livingston
Billings
Lewistown
Miles City
Glasgow
Havre
Shelby
Williston
Minot
Bismarck
Devils Lake
Grand Forks
Fargo
Jamestown
Bowman
Mobridge
Aberdeen
Pierre
Rapid City
Custer
Spearfish
Sheridan
Buffalo
Gillette
Casper
Cody
Worland
Riverton
Rock Springs
Rawlins
Laramie
Cheyenne
Kemmerer
Jackson
Ogden
Salt Lake City
Provo
Price
Vernal
Richfield
Cedar City
St George
Moab
Eureka
Redding
Chico
Sacramento
Reno
Carson City
San Francisco
Oakland
San Jose
Fresno
Merced
Bakersfield
Santa Barbara
Los Angeles
San Bernardino
San Diego
Barstow
Mojave
Indio
Las Vegas
Ely
Elko
Winnemucca
Tonopah
Bishop
Austin
Fallon
Denver
Boulder
Greeley
Sterling
Colorado Springs
Pueblo
Grand Junction
Durango
Cortez
Alamosa
Trinidad
La Junta
Lamar
Limon
North Platte
McCook
Hastings
Scottsbluff
Chadron
Valentine
Hays
Salina
Hutchinson
Wichita
Garden City
Dodge City
Liberal
Flagstaff
Prescott
Kingman
Phoenix
Wickenburg
Globe
Tucson
Yuma
Casa Grande
Nogales
Douglas
Gallup
Albuquerque
Santa Fe
Las Vegas
Farmington
Socorro
Las Cruces
Roswell
Carlsbad
Clovis
Tucumcari
El Paso
Ciudad Juarez
Amarillo
Lubbock
Odessa
Big Spring
San Angelo
Abilene
Dalhart
Childress
Pecos
Van Horn
Del Rio
Laredo
San Antonio
Corpus Christi
Brownsville
Monterrey
Santa Ana
Mexicali
Gulf of California
ALASKA
Fairbanks
Anchorage
Nome
Valdez
Seward
Homer
Kodiak
Juneau
Sitka
Ketchikan
Whitehorse
Prince Rupert
Dutch Harbor
Bering Sea
Gulf of Alaska
YUKON
NORTHWEST TERRITORIES
USSR
BROOKS RANGE
MT MC KINLEY EL 20320 HIGHEST POINT IN NORTH AMERICA
DENALI NAT'L PARK
KATMAI NAT'L PARK
GLACIER BAY NAT'L PARK
ALEUTIAN ISLANDS
Atka
Adak
HAWAII
ALASKA-HAWAII TIME ZONE
Kauai
Oahu
Molokai
Lanai City
Wailuku
Hana
Honolulu
Hilo
Kailua
Wahiawa
Aiea
Waianae
Waialua
Kaneohe Bay
OLYMPIC NAT'L PARK
MOUNT RAINIER NAT'L PARK
CRATER LAKE NAT'L PARK
REDWOOD NAT'L PARK
LASSEN VOLCANIC NAT'L PARK
YOSEMITE NAT'L PARK
KINGS CANYON NAT'L PARK
SEQUOIA NAT'L PARK
DEATH VALLEY NAT'L MON
JOSHUA TREE NAT'L MON
GLACIER NAT'L PARK
YELLOWSTONE NAT'L PARK
GRAND TETON NAT'L PARK
ZION NAT'L PARK
CANYONLANDS NAT'L PARK
GRAND CANYON NAT'L PARK
PETRIFIED FOREST NAT'L PARK
MESA VERDE NAT'L PARK
ROCKY MTN NAT'L PARK
DINOSAUR NAT'L MON
CANYON DE CHELLY NAT'L MON
ORGAN PIPE CACTUS NAT'L MON
SAGUARO NAT'L MON
WHITE SANDS NAT'L MON
CARLSBAD CAVERNS NAT'L PARK
GUADALUPE MTNS NAT'L PARK
BIG BEND NAT'L PARK
BADLANDS NAT'L PARK
THEODORE ROOSEVELT NAT'L PARK
GREAT SALT LAKE
GREAT SALT LAKE DESERT
CONTINENTAL DIVIDE
ROCKY MTS
SIERRA NEVADA
CASCADE RANGE
COAST RANGE
© RMcN

NATIONAL MONUMENTS

2A	Agate Fossil Beds	D-5
3A	Alibates Flint Quarries	F-6
3AB	Aniakchak	H-1
5A	Aztec Ruins	E-4
2B	Bandelier	E-5
4B	Black Canyon of the Gunnison	E-4
5B	Booker T. Washington	E-10
1C	Cabrillo	F-2
2C	Canyon de Chelly	E-4
1CA	Cape Krusintern	G-1
5C	Capulin Mountain	E-5
8C	Casa Grande Ruins	F-3
9C	Castillo de San Marcos	G-10
10C	Castle Clinton	C-11
11C	Cedar Breaks	E-3
15C	Chiricahua	F-4
16C	Colorado	D-4
17C	Congaree Swamp	F-10
18C	Craters of the Moon	C-3
19C	Custer Battlefield	C-5
1D	Death Valley	E-2
2D	Devils Postpile	D-2
3D	Devils Tower	C-5
4D	Dinosaur	D-4
1E	Effigy Mounds	C-7
2E	El Morro	F-4
1F	Florissant Fossil Beds	E-5
1FA	Fort Frederica	F 10
2F	Fort Jefferson	H-10
3F	Fort McHenry	D-11
4F	Fort Mantazas	G-10
5F	Fort Pulaski	F-10
5FA	Fort Stanwix	C-11
6F	Fort Sumter	F-10
7F	Fort Union	E-5
7FA	Fossil Butte	D-4
1GA	George Washington Birthplace	D-11
1GAA	George Washington Carver	E-7
1GB	Gila Cliff Dwellings	F-4
6G	Grand Portage	B-8
9G	Great Sand Dunes	F-5
2H	Hohokam Pima	F-3
3H	Homestead	D-6
5H	Hovenweep	E-4
1J	Jewel Cave	C-5
2J	John Day Fossil Beds	B-2
3J	Joshua Tree	F-2
2L	Lava Beds	C-2
3L	Lehman Caves	D-3
3M	Montezuma Castle	F-3
4M	Mound City Group	D-9
5M	Mount St. Helens	B-2
7M	Muir Woods	D-1
1N	Natural Bridges	E-4
2N	Navajo	E-4
1O	Ocmulgee	F-9
3O	Oregon Caves	C-1
4O	Organ Pipe Cactus	F-3
1P	Pecos	E-5
4P	Pinnacles	E-1
5P	Pipe Spring	E-3
6P	Pipestone	C-7
1R	Rainbow Bridge	E-4
4R	Russell Cave	F-9
1S	Saguaro	F-3
1SA	Saint Croix Island	B-12
2SA	Salinas	F-5
2S	Scotts Bluff	D-5
5S	Statue of Liberty	D-11
7S	Sunset Crater	E-3
1TA	Timpanogos Cave	D-4
2T	Tonto	F-3
3T	Tumacacori	F-3
4T	Tuzigoot	F-3
1W	Walnut Canyon	E-3
3W	White Sands	F-4
5W	Wupatki	E-3
1Y	Yucca House	E-4

NATIONAL PARKS

1A	Acadia	B-12
4A	Arches	D-4
1B	Badlands	C-5
3B	Big Bend	G-5
3BA	Biscayne	H-11
6B	Bryce Canyon	E-3
3C	Canyonlands	E-4
4C	Capitol Reef	E-4
6C	Carlsbad Caverns	F-5
7C	Channel Islands	E, F-2
17C	Crater Lake	C-2
1D	Denali	G-2
3E	Everglades	H-10
1G	Gates of The Arctic	G-1 & 2
2G	Glacier	A-3
3G	Glacier Bay	H-2
5G	Grand Canyon	E-3
7G	Grand Teton	C-4
10G	Great Smoky Mountains	E-9
11G	Guadalupe Mts	F-5
1H	Haleakala	H-4
2H	Hawaii Volcanoes	H-4
4H	Hot Springs	F-7
1I	Isle Royale	B-8
1K	Katmai	H-1
2K	Kenai Fjords	H-2
3K	Kings Canyon	E-2
4K	Kobuk Valley	G-1
1LA	Lake Clark	G-1
1L	Lassen Volcanic	C-2
1M	Mammoth Cave	E-9
2M	Mesa Verde	E-4
6M	Mount Rainer	B-2
3N	North Cascades	A-2
2O	Olympic	A-2
3P	Petrified Forest	F-4
2R	Redwood	C-1
3R	Rocky Mountain	D-5
3S	Sequoia	E-2
4S	Shenandoah	D-10
1T	Theodore Roosevelt	B-5
1V	Voyageurs	B-7
4W	Wind Cave	C-5
1W	Wrangell-St. Elias	H-2
1Y	Yellowstone	C-4
2Y	Yosemite	D-2
1Z	Zion	E-3

ALABAMA

Population: 3,893,978
(1980 Census)
Land Area: 50,766 Sq. Mi.
Capital: Montgomery

Cities and Towns

Abbeville........F-5
Alabaster........D-3
Albertville........B-4
Alexander City........D-4
Aliceville........D-1
Andalusia........G-3
Anniston........C-4
Ashford........G-5
Ashland........C-4
Ashville........C-4
Athens........A-3
Atmore........G-2
Attalla........B-4
Auburn........E-5
Bay Minette........G-2
Bellamy........E-1
Bessemer........C-3
Birmingham........C-3
Boaz........B-4
Brewton........G-3
Bridgeport........A-4
Brundidge........F-4
Butler........E-1
Camden........F-2
Castleberry........G-3
Centre........B-4
Centreville........D-2
Chatom........F-1
Childersburg........C-3
Clanton........D-3
Clayton........F-5
Cleveland........B-3
Collinsville........B-4
Columbiana........D-3
Cottondale........D-2
Courtland........A-2
Cullman........B-3
Dadeville........D-4
Decatur........A-3
Demopolis........E-2
Dothan........G-5
Double Springs........B-2
E. Brewton........G-3
Elba........F-4
Enterprise........G-4
Eufaula........F-5
Eutaw........D-1
Evergreen........F-3
Fairfield........C-3
Fairhope........H-1
Fayette........C-2
Florala........G-4
Florence........A-2
Ft. Payne........B-4
Frisco City........F-2
Gadsden........B-4
Geneva........G-4
Georgiana........F-3
Goodwater........D-4
Grand Bay........H-1
Greensboro........D-2
Greenville........F-3
Grove Hill........F-2
Guntersville........B-3
Hackleburg........B-2
Haleyville........B-2
Hamilton........B-1
Hanceville........B-3
Hartford........G-4
Hartselle........B-3
Hayneville........E-3
Heflin........C-4
Homewood........C-3
Huntsville........A-3
Jackson........F-1
Jacksonville........C-4
Jasper........C-2
Lafayette........D-5
Lanett........D-5
Leeds........C-3
Linden........E-2
Livingston........E-1
Loxley........H-2
Luverne........F-4
Mc Kenzie........F-3
Maplesville........D-3
Marion........E-2
Mobile........H-1
Montevallo........D-3
Montgomery........E-4
Moulton........B-2
Mountain Brook........C-3
Mt. Vernon........G-1
Muscle Shoals........A-2
New Brockton........F-4
Normal........A-3
Northport........D-2
Oneonta........B-3
Opelika........D-5
Opp........G-4
Ozark........F-4
Phenix City........E-5
Piedmont........B-4
Prattville........E-3
Prichard........H-1
Rainbow City........C-4
Ramer........E-4
Red Bay........B-1
Roanoke........D-5
Robertsdale........H-2
Rogersville........A-2
Russellville........B-2
Samson........G-4
Saraland........G-1
Scottsboro........A-4
Selma........E-3
Sheffield........A-2
Siluria........D-3
Stapleton........H-2
Stevenson........A-4
Stockton........G-1
Sulligent........B-1
Sylacauga........D-4
Talladega........C-4
Tallassee........E-4
Tarrant City........C-3
Thomaston........E-2
Thomasville........F-2
Troy........F-4
Tuscaloosa........D-2
Tuscumbia........A-2
Tuskegee........E-4
Union Sprs........E-4
Uniontown........E-2
Vernon........C-1
Vincent........C-3
Wedowee........C-5
Wetumpka........E-4
Winfield........B-2
York........E-1

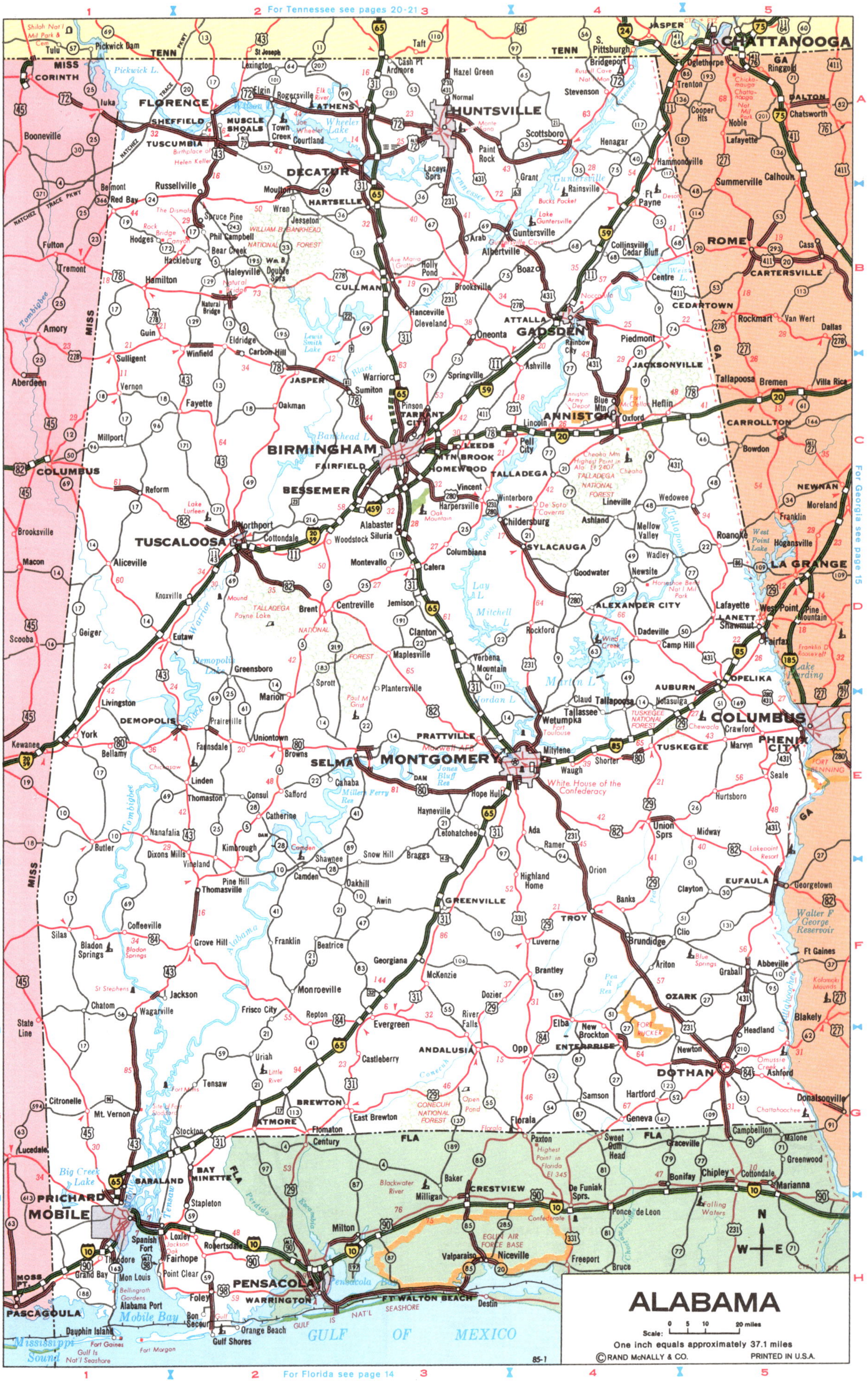

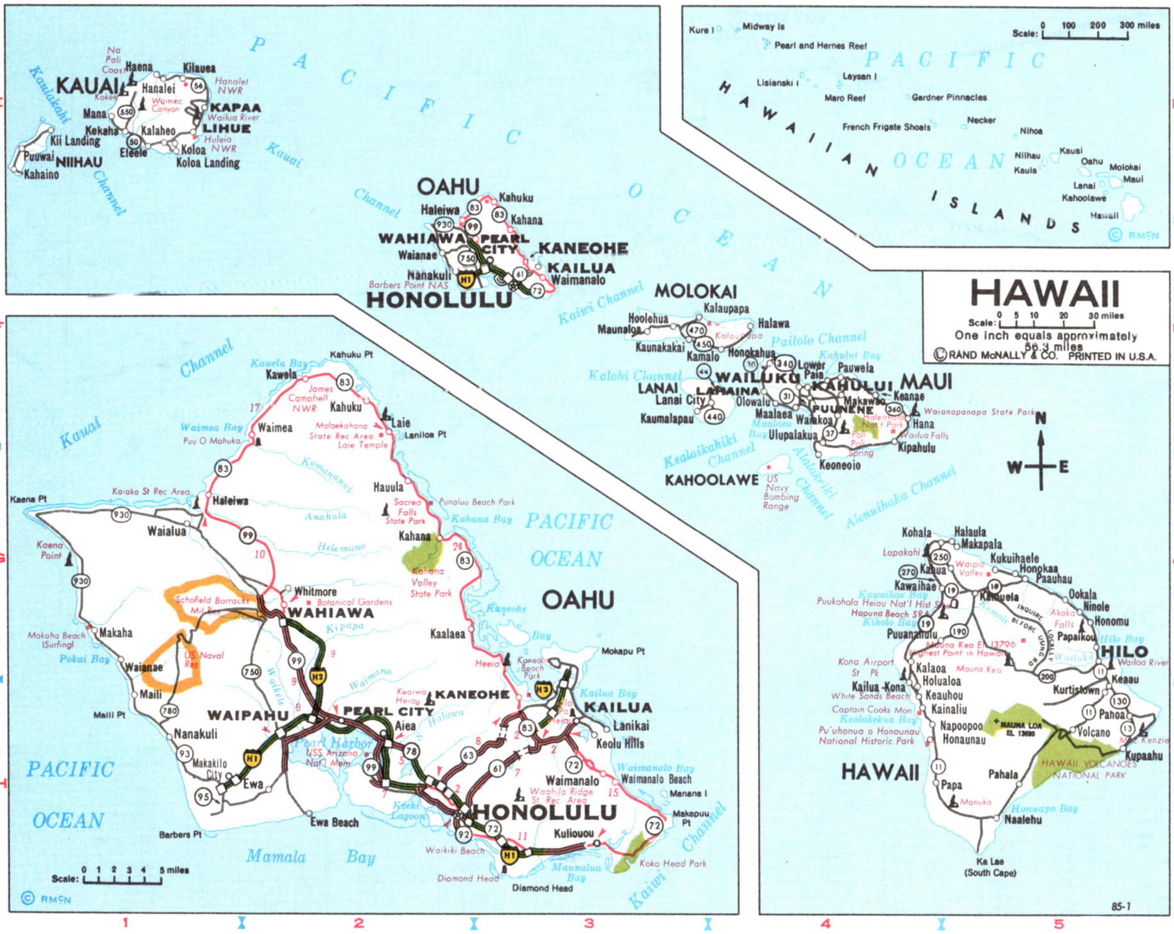

ALASKA

Population: 401,851
(1980 Census)
Land Area: 570,833 Sq. Mi.
Capital: Juneau

Cities and Towns

Alakanuk.........B-1
Allakaket.........B-3
Anchorage.........C-3
Anvik.........C-2
Barrow.........A-3
Bethel.........C-2
Big Delta.........B-3
Buckland.........B-2
Cantwell.........C-3
Chena Hot Sprs.........B-3
Chignik.........D-2
Chugiak.........C-3
Circle.........B-4
Circle Hot Sprs.........B-4
College.........B-3
Cordova.........C-3
Delta Junction.........B-3
Dillingham.........C-2
Douglas.........D-5
Eek.........C-2
Fairbanks.........B-3
Ft. Randall.........D-1
Fort Yukon.........B-3
Homer.........C-3
Hoonah.........D-5
Hooper Bay.........C-1
Inuvik.........A-4
Juneau.........D-5
Kaltag.........B-2
Karluk.........D-2
Kenai.........C-3
Ketchikan.........D-5
Kodiak.........D-3
Kotzebue.........B-2
Kwethluk.........C-2
Kwigillingok.........C-1
McGrath.........C-2
Mekoryuk.........C-1
Nenana.........B-3
Newhalem.........C-2
Noatak.........A-2
Nome.........B-2
Nondalton.........C-2
Palmer.........C-3
Perryville.........D-2
Petersburg.........D-5
Port Graham.........C-3
Pt. Hope.........A-2
Ruby.........B-2
Saint Michael.........B-2
Savoonga.........B-1
Scammon Bay.........C-1
Shungnak.........B-2
Sitka.........D-5
Skagway.........C-5
Soldotna.........C-3
Spenard.........C-3
Stony River.........C-2
Tanana.........B-3
Taylor.........B-2
Tok Junction.........B-4
Umiat.........A-3
Valdez.........C-3
Wainwright.........A-2
Willow.........C-3
Wiseman.........B-3
Wrangell.........D-5

HAWAII

Population: 964,691
(1980 Census)
Land Area: 6,427 Sq. Mi.
Capital: Honolulu

Cities and Towns

Alea.........H-2
Ewa.........H-2
Ewa Beach.........H-2
Halaula.........G-5
Haleiwa.........G-1
Hana.........F-4
Hauula.........G-2
Hilo.........G-5
Holualoa.........H-4
Honaunau.........H-5
Honokaa.........G-5
Honolulu.........H-3
Honomu.........G-5
Hoolehua.........F-3
Kahuku.........F-2
Kahului.........F-4
Kailua.........H-3
Kailua-Kona.........H-4
Kainaliu.........H-4
Kalaheo.........E-1
Kalaupapa.........F-3
Kamuela.........G-5
Kaneohe.........H-3
Kapaa.........E-1
Kaunakakai.........F-3
Kawaihae.........G-4
Keaau.........H-5
Kekaha.........E-1
Kilauea.........E-1
Kohala.........G-4
Koloa Landing.........E-1
Kukuihaele.........G-5
Kurtistown.........H-5
Lahaina.........F-4
Laie.........F-2
Lanai City.........F-3
Lihue.........E-1
Lower Paia.........F-4
Maalaea.........F-4
Maili.........H-1
Makakilo City.........H-1
Makaha.........G-1
Makapala.........G-5
Makawao.........F-4
Maunaloa.........F-3
Naalehu.........H-5
Nanakuli.........H-1
Ninole.........G-5
Ookala.........G-5
Pahala.........H-5
Pahoa.........H-5
Papaikou.........G-5
Pauwela.........F-4
Pearl City.........H-2
Puunene.........F-4
Volcano.........H-5
Wahiawa.........G-2
Waialua.........G-1
Waianae.........G-1
Wailuku.........F-4
Waimanalo.........H-3
Waimanalo Beach.........H-3
Waimea.........F-2
Waipahu.........H-2
Whitmore.........G-2

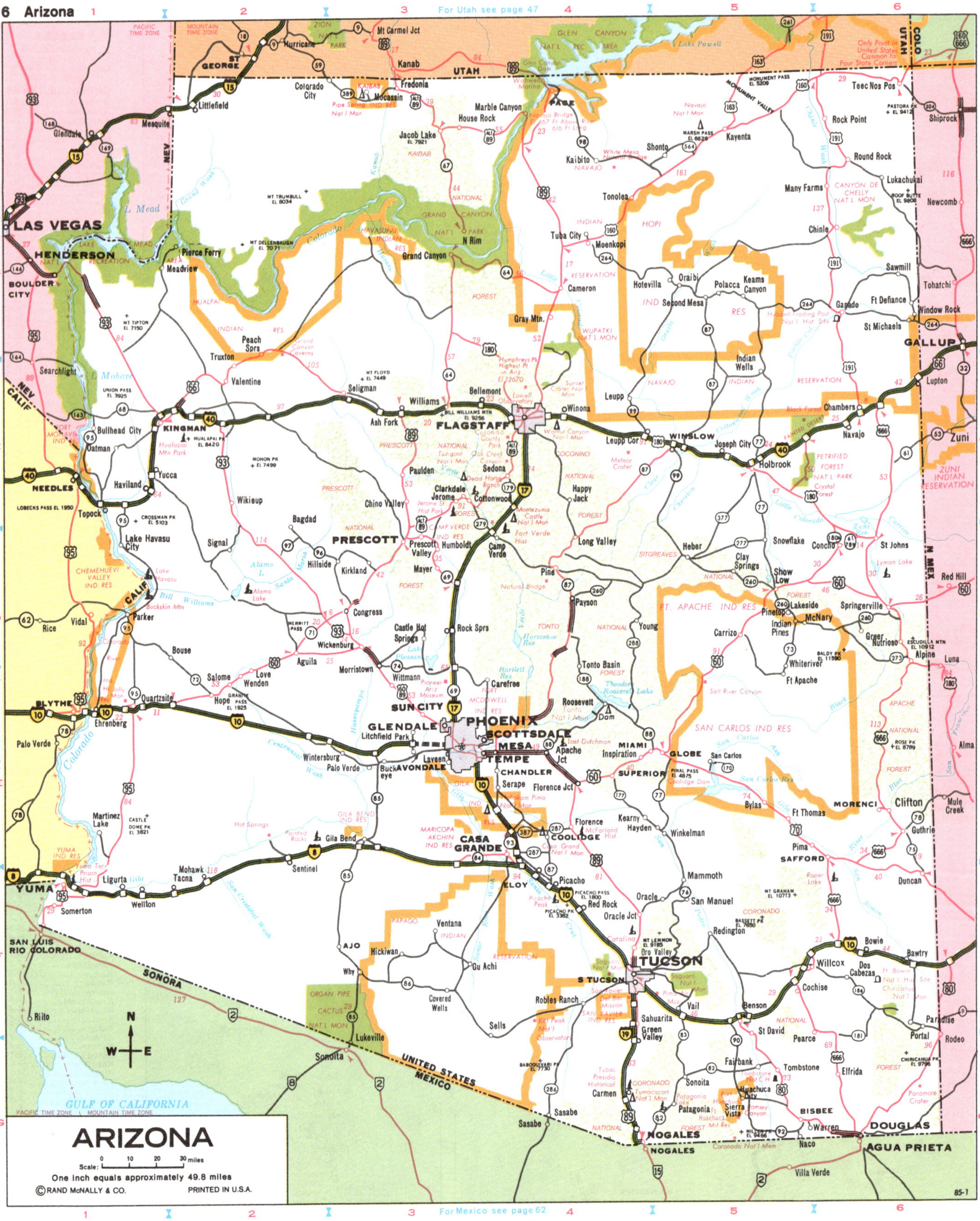

ARIZONA

Population: 2,718,425
(1980 Census)
Land Area: 113,510 Sq. Mi.
Capital: Phoenix

Cities and Towns

ARKANSAS

Population: 2,286,419
(1980 Census)
Land Area: 52,082 Sq. Mi.
Capital: Little Rock

Cities and Towns

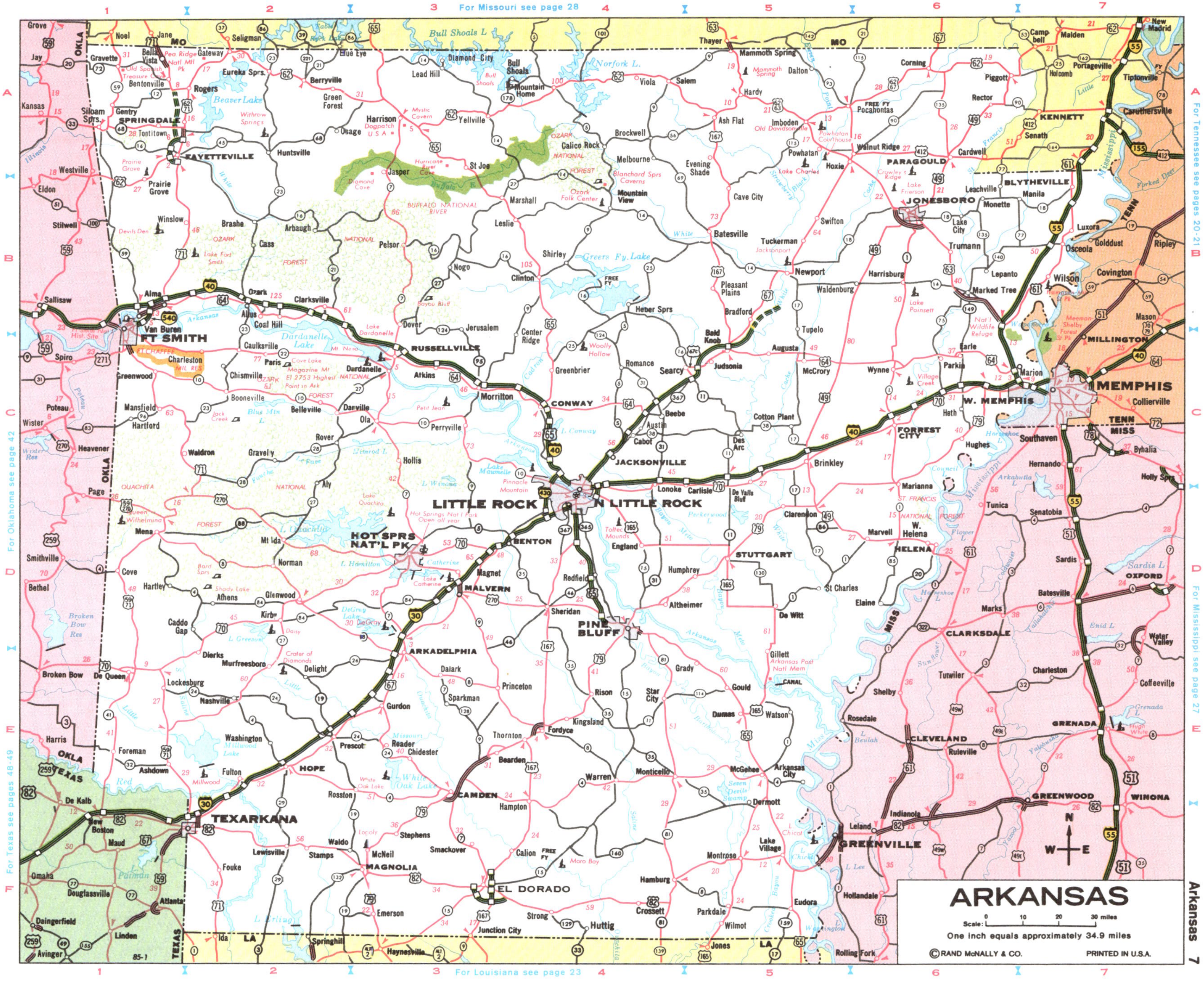

CALIFORNIA

Population: 23,667,837
(1980 Census)
Land Area: 156,297 Sq. Mi.
Capital: Sacramento

Cities & Towns

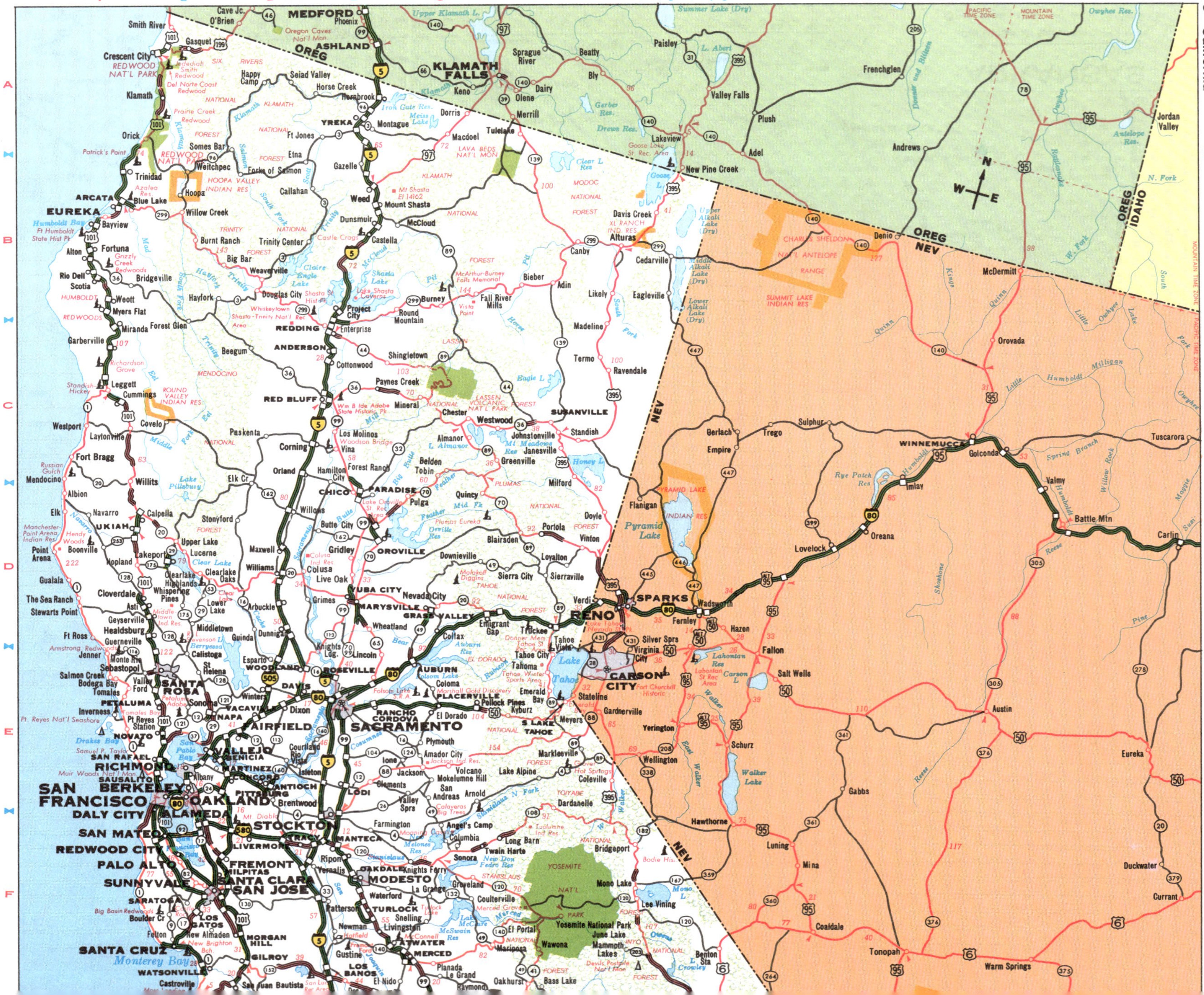

CALIFORNIA
Scale: 0 5 10 20 miles
One inch equals approximately 51.9 miles
©RAND McNALLY & CO.
PRINTED IN U.S.A.
85-1
P A C I F I C
O C E A N
SALINAS
MONTEREY
PACIFIC GROVE
FRESNO
CLOVIS
MADERA
VISALIA
HANFORD
TULARE
PORTERVILLE
BAKERSFIELD
OILDALE
SAN LUIS OBISPO
SANTA MARIA
LOMPOC
SANTA BARBARA
VENTURA
OXNARD
LANCASTER
PALMDALE
BARSTOW
VICTORVILLE
BURBANK
GLENDALE
PASADENA
BEVERLY HILLS
SANTA MONICA
LOS ANGELES
LONG BEACH
ANAHEIM
SANTA ANA
SAN BERNARDINO
RIVERSIDE
ONTARIO
POMONA
OCEANSIDE
SAN DIEGO
CHULA VISTA
TIJUANA
MEXICALI
YUMA
LAS VEGAS
NEV
ARIZ
MEXICO
NELLIS AIR FORCE RANGE
NEVADA TEST SITE
DEATH VALLEY NATIONAL MONUMENT
CHINA LAKE NAVAL WEAPONS CENTER
FORT IRWIN MILITARY RESERVATION
TWENTYNINE PALMS MARINE CORPS BASE
JOSHUA TREE NATIONAL MONUMENT
ANZA-BORREGO DESERT STATE PARK
Salton Sea
Gulf of Santa Catalina
Santa Barbara Channel
For Arizona see page
For Mexico see page 62

For Vermont see page 32

For New Hampshire see page 32

For New York see pages 34-35

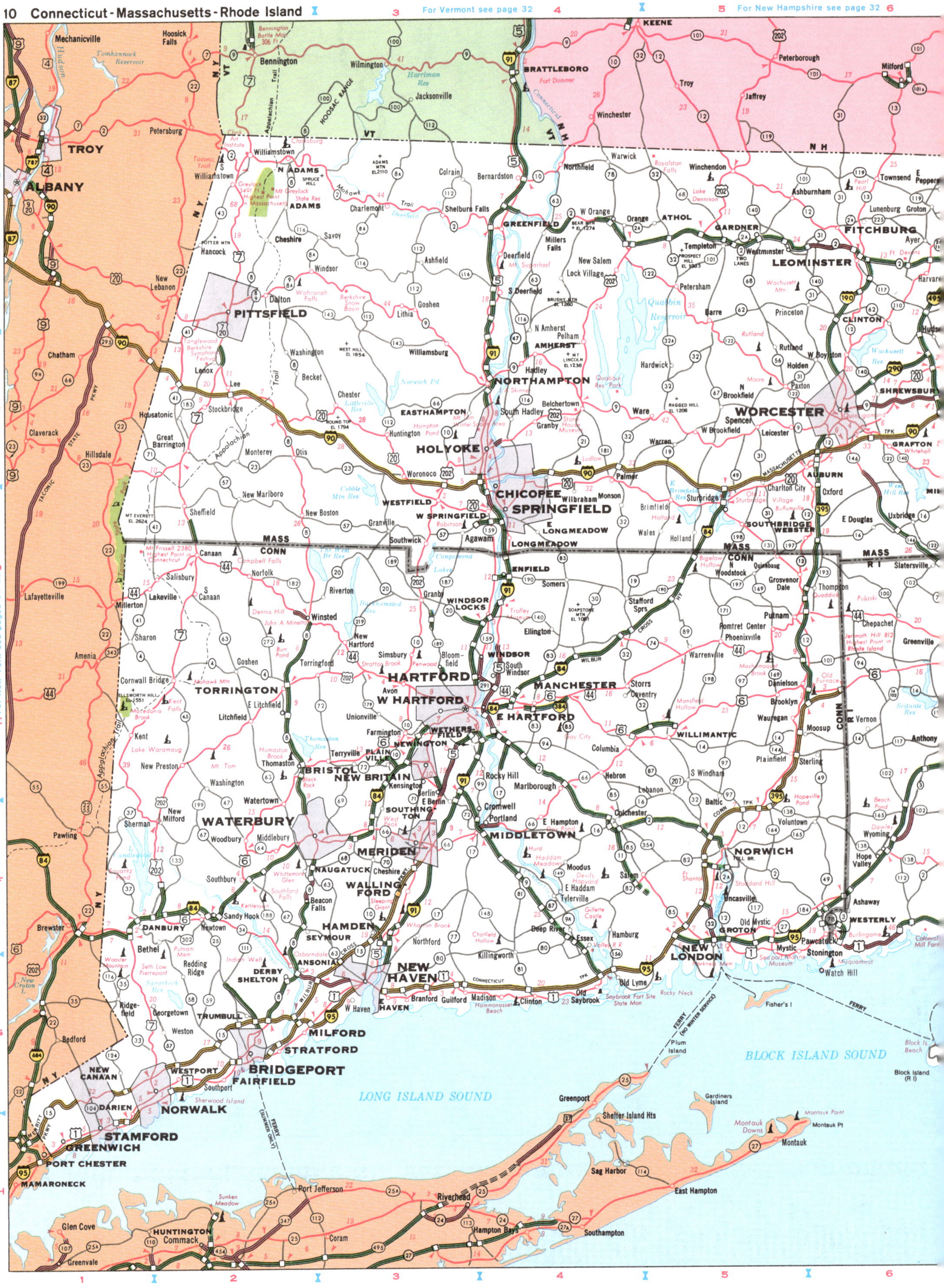

CONNECTICUT

Population: 3,107,576
(1980 Census)
Land Area: 4,872 Sq. Mi.
Capital: Hartford

Cities and Towns

Ansonia..........G-2
Avon..........E-3
Beacon Falls..........F-2
Bethel..........F-2
Branford..........G-3
Bridgeport..........G-2
Bristol..........E-3
Brooklyn..........E-5
Canaan..........D-2
Clinton..........G-4
Colchester..........F-4
Cornwall Bridge..........E-2
Cromwell..........F-4
Danbury..........F-1
Danielson..........E-5
Darien..........H-1
Deep River..........F-4
Derby..........G-2
E. Hartford..........E-4
E. Haven..........G-3
Enfield..........D-4
Essex..........F-4
Fairfield..........G-2
Farmington..........E-3
Georgetown..........G-2
Goshen..........E-2
Granby..........D-3
Greenwich..........H-1
Groton..........F-5
Guilford..........G-3
Hamden..........F-3
Hartford..........E-3
Lakeville..........D-1
Lebanon..........E-5
Litchfield..........E-2
Manchester..........E-4
Marlboro..........E-4
Meriden..........F-3
Middlebury..........F-2
Middletown..........F-4
Milford..........G-2
Moodus..........F-4
Moosup..........E-6
Mystic..........F-5
Naugatuck..........F-2
New Britain..........E-3
New Canaan..........G-1
New Hartford..........D-3
New Haven..........G-3
Newington..........E-3
New London..........F-5
New Milford..........F-2
New Preston..........E-2
Norwalk..........G-2
Norwich..........F-5
Old Lyme..........G-4
Old Saybrook..........G-4
Pawcatuck..........F-6
Plainfield..........E-5
Plainville..........E-3
Portland..........F-4
Putnam..........D-5
Ridgefield..........G-1
Salisbury..........D-2
Sandy Hook..........F-2
Seymour..........F-2
Shelton..........G-2
Simsbury..........E-3
Somers..........D-4
S. Canaan..........D-2
Southington..........F-3
Stafford Sprs..........D-4
Stamford..........H-1
Storrs..........E-4
Stratford..........G-2
Terryville..........E-3
Thomaston..........E-2
Torrington..........E-2
Trumbull..........G-2
Unionville..........E-3
Voluntown..........F-6
Wallingford..........F-3
Waterbury..........F-2
Watertown..........F-2
W. Hartford..........E-3
Westport..........G-2
Wethersfield..........E-3
Willimantic..........E-5
Windsor..........E-4
Windsor Locks..........D-4
Winsted..........D-2

MASSACHUSETTS

Population: 5,737,081
(1980 Census)
Land Area: 7,826 Sq. Mi.
Capital: Boston

Cities and Towns

Adams..........B-2
Agawam..........D-3
Amesbury..........A-8
Amherst..........C-4
Andover..........B-7
Ashburnham..........B-5
Athol..........B-5
Attleboro..........D-7
Auburn..........C-6
Ayer..........B-6
Barre..........B-5
Bedford..........B-7
Beverly..........B-8
Boston..........C-7
Braintree..........C-8
Brockton..........D-7
Brookline..........C-7
Buzzards Bay..........E-9
Cambridge..........C-7
Centerville..........E-9
Charlton City..........C-5
Chatham..........E-10
Chicopee..........D-4
Clinton..........B-6
Cohasset..........C-8
Concord..........B-7
Dalton..........B-2
Danvers..........B-8
Dedham..........C-7
Deerfield..........B-4
Duxbury..........D-8
Eastham..........E-10
Easthampton..........C-3
E. Longmeadow..........D-4
E. Pepperell..........B-6
Edgartown..........F-9
Essex..........B-8
Everett..........C-7
Fairhaven..........E-8
Fall River..........E-7
Falmouth..........F-9
Fitchburg..........B-6
Forge Village..........B-6
Foxboro..........D-7
Framingham..........C-6
Gardner..........B-5
Gloucester..........B-8
Grafton..........C-6
Great Barrington..........C-2
Greenfield..........B-4
Groton..........B-6
Harwich Port..........E-10
Haverhill..........A-7
Hingham..........C-8
Holyoke..........C-4
Housatonic..........C-2
Hudson..........C-6
Hyannis..........E-9
Ipswich..........A-8
Lawrence..........A-7
Lenox..........C-2
Leominster..........B-6
Lexington..........B-7
Longmeadow..........D-4
Lowell..........B-7
Lynn..........B-8
Lynnfield Center..........B-7
Mansfield..........D-7
Marblehead..........B-8
Marion..........E-8
Marlborough..........C-6
Marshfield..........D-8
Mattapoisett..........E-8
Methuen..........A-7
Middleboro..........D-8
Middleton..........B-7
Milford..........D-6
Millers Falls..........B-4
Nantucket..........G-10
Natick..........C-7
New Bedford..........E-8
Newburyport..........A-8
Newton..........C-7
N. Adams..........A-2
Northampton..........C-4
N. Andover..........A-7
N. Attleboro..........D-7
N. Dartmouth..........E-8
Northfield..........A-4
Norwood..........C-7
Oak Bluffs..........F-9
Orange..........B-4
Osterville..........E-9
Palmer..........C-4
Peabody..........B-8
Petersham..........B-5
Pittsfield..........B-2
Plymouth..........D-8
Princeton..........B-6
Provincetown..........D-10
Quincy..........C-8
Randolph..........C-8
Revere..........B-8
Rockland..........D-8
Rockport..........B-8
Rutland..........C-5
Salem..........B-8
Salisbury..........A-8
Salisbury Beach..........A-8
Sandwich..........E-9
Saugus..........B-7
Sharon..........D-7
Shelburne Falls..........B-3
Shrewsbury..........C-6
Somerset..........E-7
Southbridge..........D-5
S. Deerfield..........B-4
S. Hadley..........C-4
Spencer..........C-5
Springfield..........D-4
Stoneham..........B-7
Stoughton..........D-7
Sturbridge..........D-5
Sudbury Center..........C-6
Swampscott..........B-8
Taunton..........D-7
Townsend..........B-6
Truro..........D-10
Uxbridge..........D-6
Vineyard Haven..........F-9
Wakefield..........B-7
Walpole..........C-7
Waltham..........C-7
Ware..........C-5
Wareham..........E-8
Warren..........C-5
Webster..........D-5
Wellesley..........C-7
Wellfleet..........D-10
W. Boylston..........C-6
W. Bridgewater..........D-7
W. Brookfield..........C-5
W. Dennis..........E-10
Westfield..........D-3
Westminster..........B-5
W. Springfield..........D-4
Weymouth..........C-8
Whitman..........D-8
Winchendon..........A-5
Woburn..........B-7
Worcester..........C-6
Wrentham..........D-7

RHODE ISLAND

Population: 947,154
(1980 Census)
Land Area: 1,054 Sq. Mi.
Capital: Providence

Cities and Towns

Allenton..........F-6
Bristol..........E-7
Central Falls..........D-7
Cranston..........E-6
E. Providence..........E-7
E. Greenwich..........E-6
Hope Valley..........F-6
Jamestown..........F-7
Kingston..........F-6
Middletown..........F-7
Narragansett..........F-6
Newport..........F-7
Pawtucket..........E-7
Portsmouth..........F-7
Providence..........E-6
Tiverton..........E-7
Wakefield..........F-6
Warwick..........E-7
Westerly..........F-6
W. Warwick..........E-6
Wickford..........F-6
Woonsocket..........D-6

COLORADO

Population: 2,889,735
(1980 Census)
Land Area: 103,598 Sq. Mi.
Capital: Denver

Cities and Towns

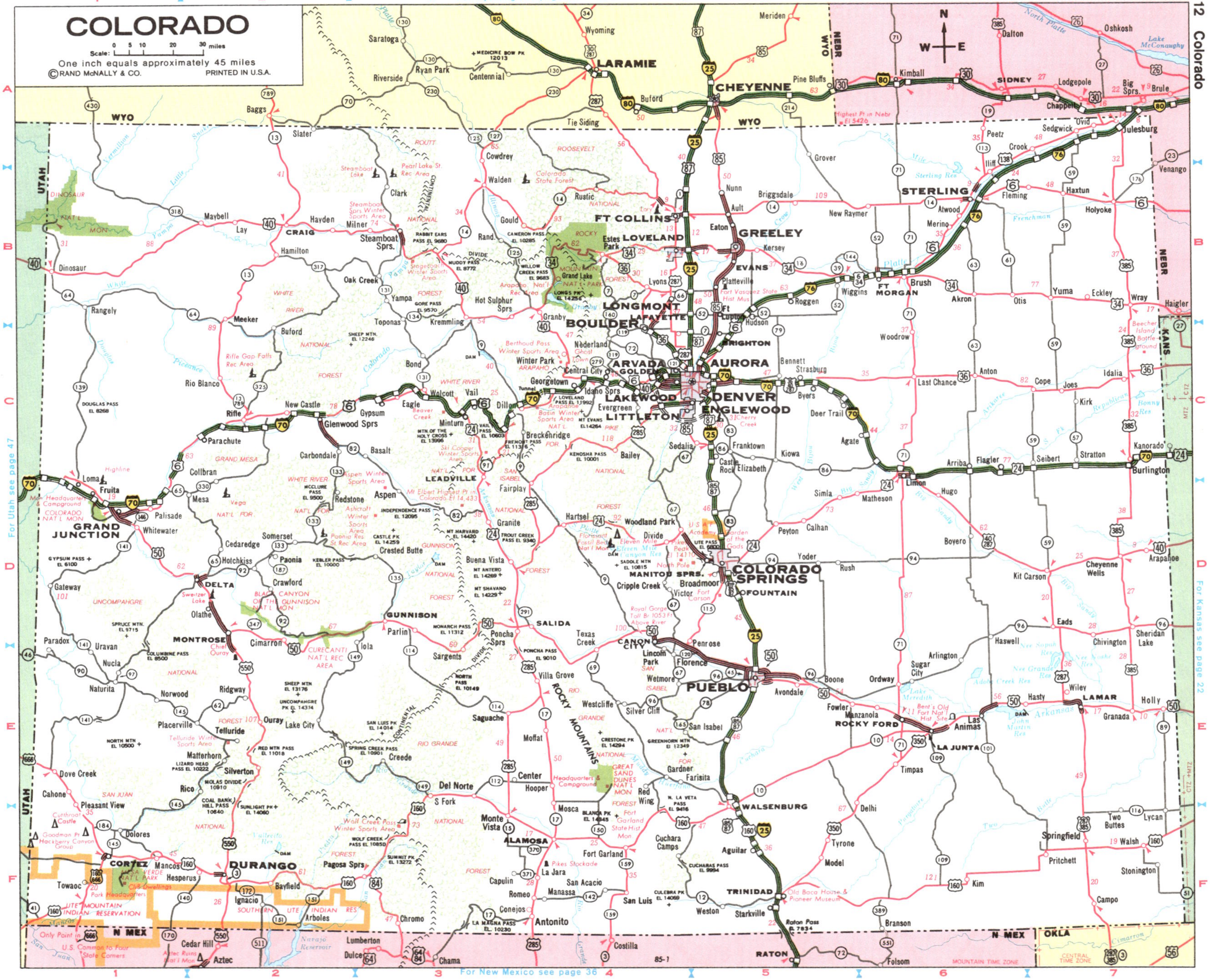

For Pennsylvania see pages 44-45

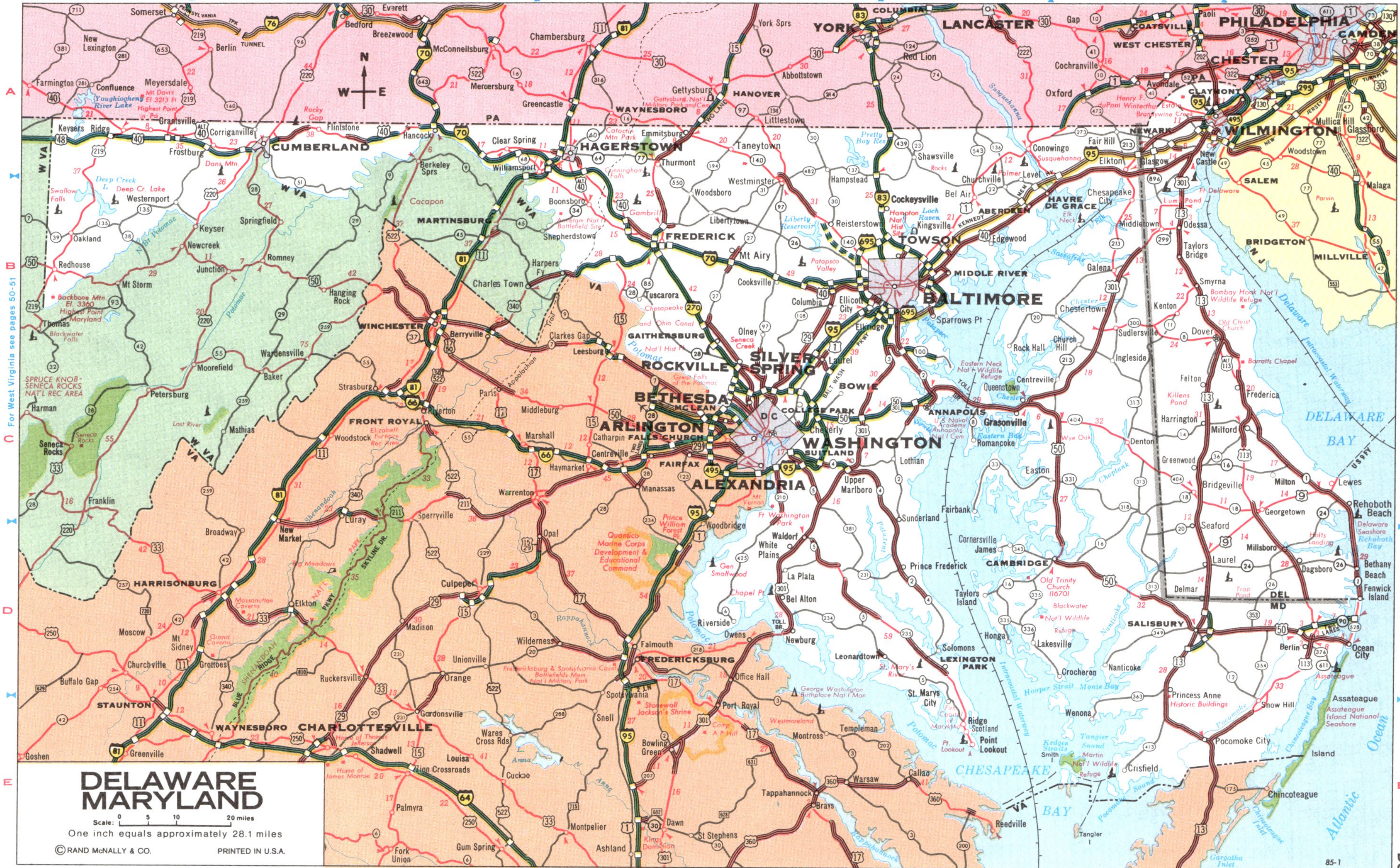

DELAWARE MARYLAND

Scale: 0 5 10 20 miles

One inch equals approximately 28.1 miles

For West Virginia see pages 50-51

For New Jersey see page 33

For Virginia see pages 50-51

MARYLAND

Population: 4,216,941
(1980 Census)
Land Area: 9,838 Sq. Mi.
Capital: Annapolis

Cities and Towns

DELAWARE

Population: 594,317
(1980 Census)
Land Area: 1,933 Sq. Mi.
Capital: Dover

Cities and Towns

DISTRICT OF COLUMBIA

Population: 638,432
(1980 Census)
Land Area: 63 Sq. Mi.

Cities and Towns

FLORIDA

Population: 9,746,421
(1980 Census)
Land Area: 54,157 Sq. Mi.
Capital: Tallahassee

Cities and Towns

For Tennessee see pages 20-21
For North Carolina see pages 38-39

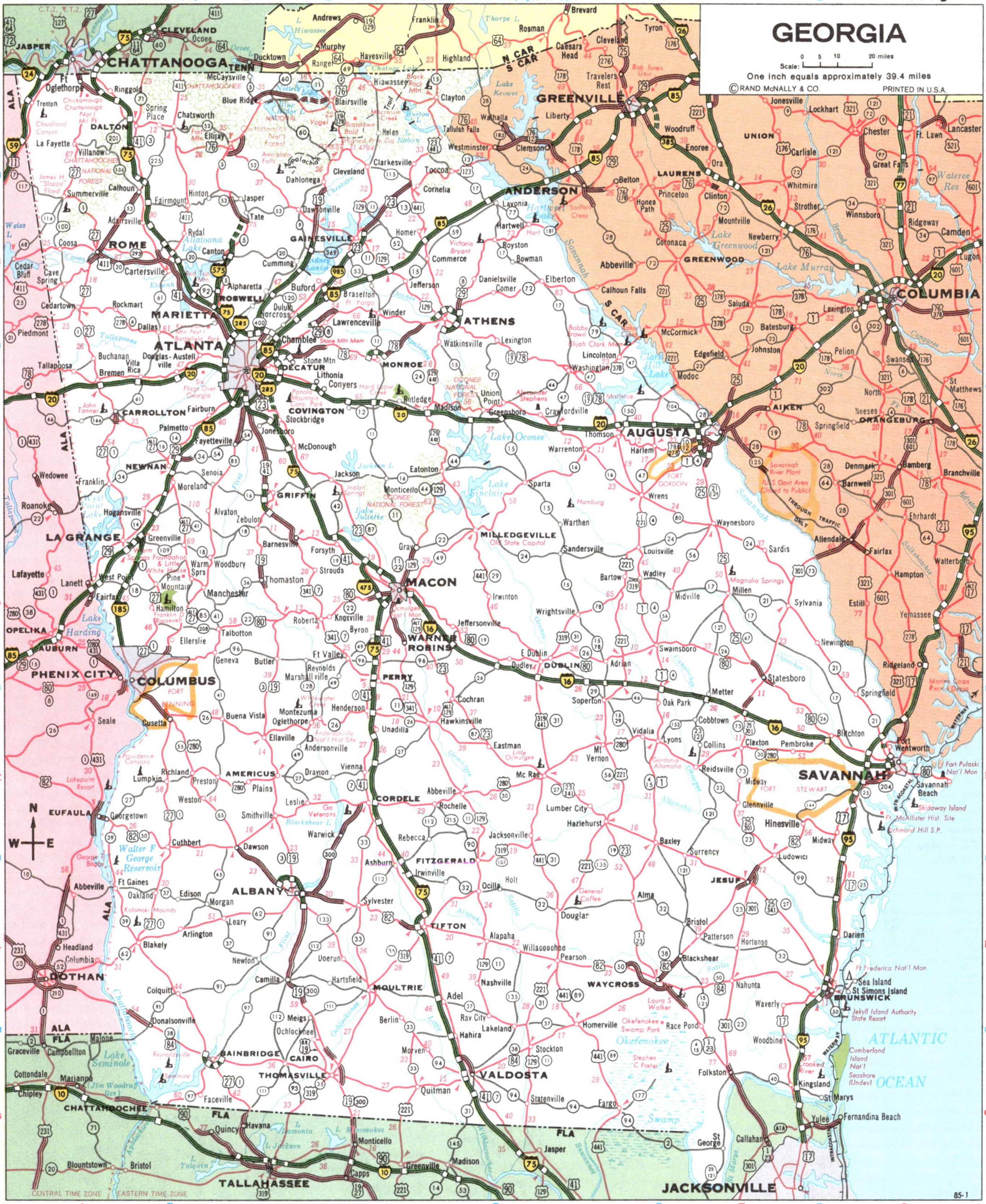

For South Carolina see pages 38-39
For Alabama see page 4
For Florida see page 14

GEORGIA

Population: 5,463,087
(1980 Census)
Land Area: 58,060 Sq. Mi.
Capital: Atlanta

Cities and Towns

IDAHO

Population: 944,038
(1980 Census)
Land Area: 82,413 Sq. Mi.
Capital: Boise

Cities and Towns

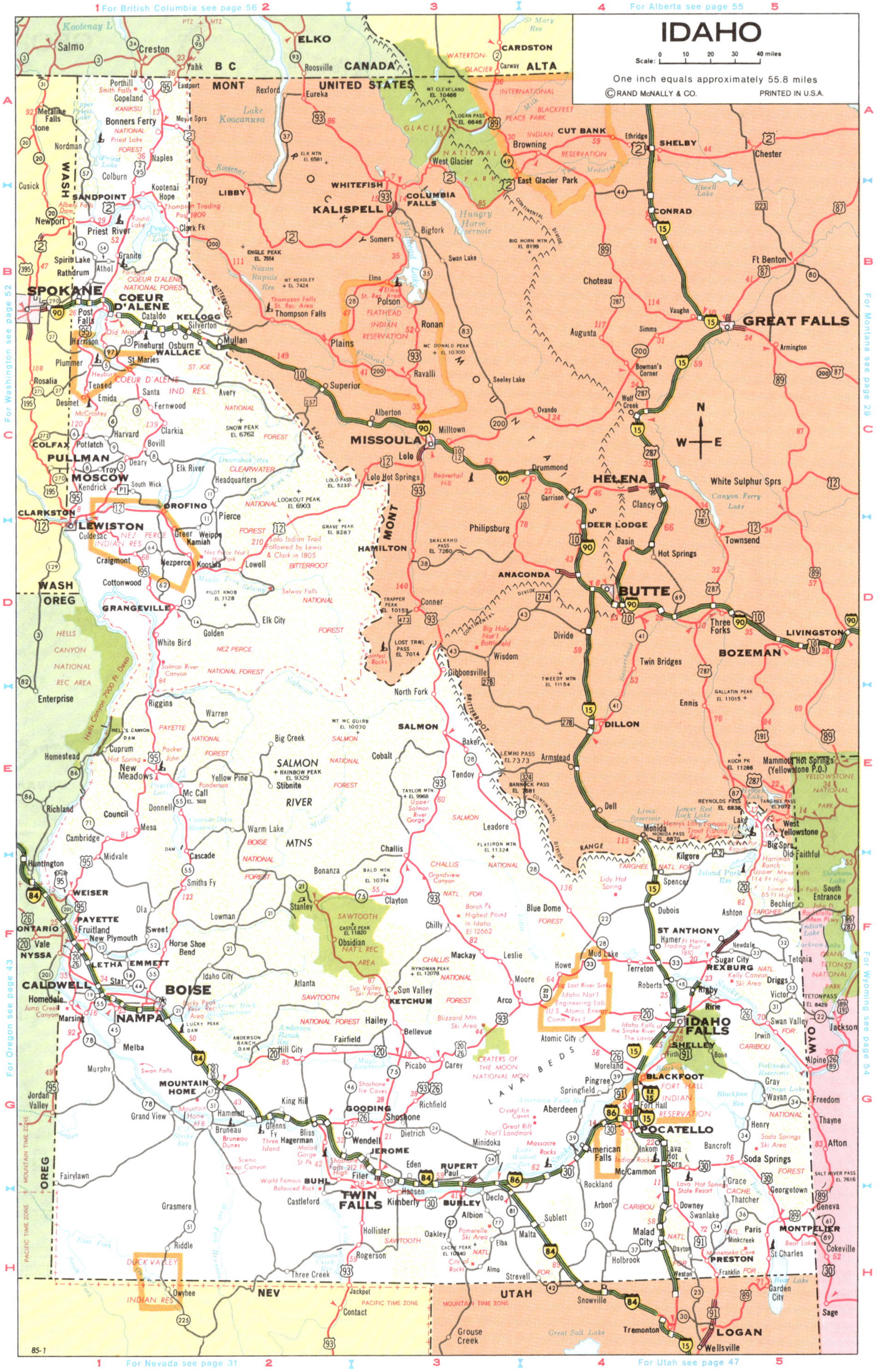

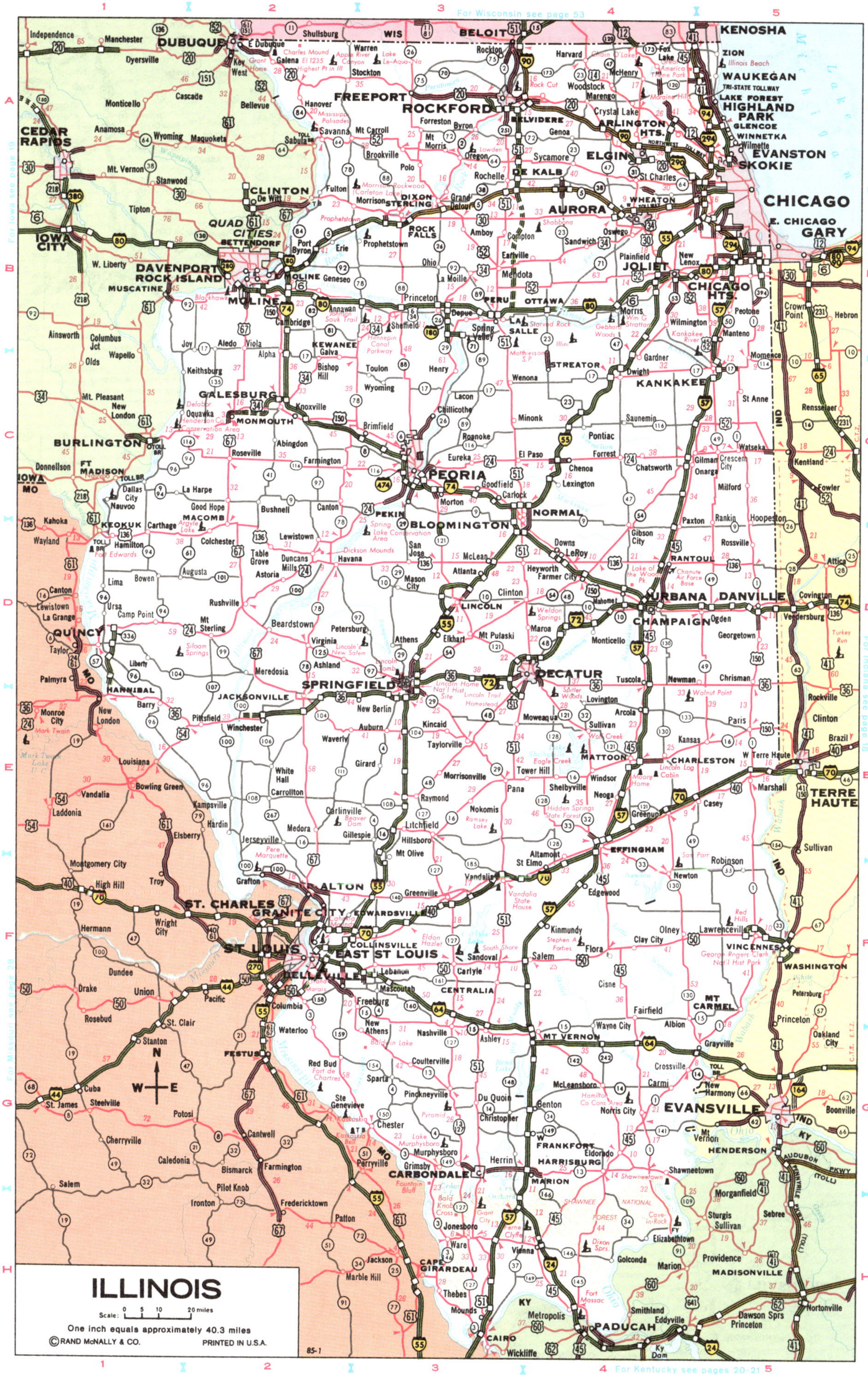

ILLINOIS

Population: 11,427,414
(1980 Census)
Land Area: 55,646 Sq. Mi.
Capital: Springfield

Cities and Towns

Abingdon..........C-2
Albion.............F-4
Aledo..............B-2
Altamont...........E-4
Alton..............F-2
Amboy..............B-3
Arcola.............E-4
Arlington Hts......A-4
Atlanta............D-3
Auburn.............E-3
Aurora.............B-4
Belleville.........F-2
Belvidere..........A-3
Benton.............G-4
Bloomington........D-3
Cairo..............H-3
Carbondale.........G-3
Carmi..............G-4
Centralia..........F-3
Champaign..........D-4
Charleston.........E-4
Chatsworth.........C-4
Chenoa.............C-4
Chicago............B-5
Chicago Heights....B-5
Chillicothe........C-3
Collinsville.......F-2
Columbia...........F-2
Danville...........D-5
Decatur............D-4
De Kalb............A-4
Dixon..............B-3
Earlville..........B-4
East Moline........B-2
East St. Louis.....F-2
Edwardsville.......F-2
Effingham..........E-4
Elgin..............A-4
El Paso............C-3
Erie...............B-2
Eureka.............C-3
Evanston...........A-5
Farmington.........C-2
Forrest............C-4
Forreston..........A-3
Freeburg...........F-3
Freeport...........A-3
Fulton.............B-2
Galena.............A-2
Galesburg..........C-2
Galva..............C-2
Geneseo............B-2
Genoa..............A-4
Gilman.............C-5
Girard.............E-3
Glencoe............A-5
Grafton............F-2
Granite City.......F-2
Harrisburg.........G-4
Harvard............A-4
Havana.............D-2
Henry..............C-3
Highland Park......A-5
Jacksonville.......E-2
Joliet.............B-4
Kankakee...........C-5
Kewanee............B-3
Kincaid............E-3
Lacon..............C-3
Lake Forest........A-5
La Salle...........B-3
Lexington..........C-4
Lincoln............D-3
McHanry............A-4
McLeansboro........G-4
Macomb.............D-2
Manteno............B-5
Marion.............G-4
Marshall...........E-5
Mascoutah..........F-3
Mattoon............E-4
Mendota............B-3
Milford............C-5
Minonk.............C-3
Moline.............B-2
Momence............C-5
Monmouth...........C-2
Monticello.........D-4
Morris.............B-4
Morrison...........B-2
Mt. Carroll........A-2
Mt. Morris.........A-3
Mt. Sterling.......D-2
Mt. Vernon.........G-3
Moweaqua...........E-3
Nashville..........G-3
New Athens.........G-3
Newton.............F-4
Normal.............C-4
Onarga.............C-5
Ottawa.............B-4
Pekin..............C-3
Peoria.............C-3
Peotone............B-5
Peru...............B-3
Pittsfield.........E-2
Pontiac............C-4
Princeton..........B-3
Prophetstown.......B-3
Quincy.............D-1
Rantoul............D-4
Roanoke............C-3
Robinson...........F-5
Rock Falls.........B-3
Rockford...........A-3
Rock Island........B-2
Roseville..........C-2
St. Anne...........C-5
Sandwich...........B-4
Savanna............A-2
Sheffield..........B-3
Skokie.............A-5
Sparta.............G-3
Springfield........D-3
Sterling...........B-3
Stockton...........A-2
Streator...........C-4
Taylorville........E-3
Urbana.............D-4
Vandalia...........F-3
Waterloo...........G-2
Watseka............C-5
Waukegan...........A-5
W. Frankfort.......G-4
Wheaton............B-4
Wilmington.........B-4
Winchester.........E-2
Winnetka...........A-5
Woodstock..........A-4
Zion...............A-5

INDIANA

Population: 5,490,260
(1980 Census)
Land Area: 35,936 Sq. Mi.
Capital: Indianapolis

Cities and Towns

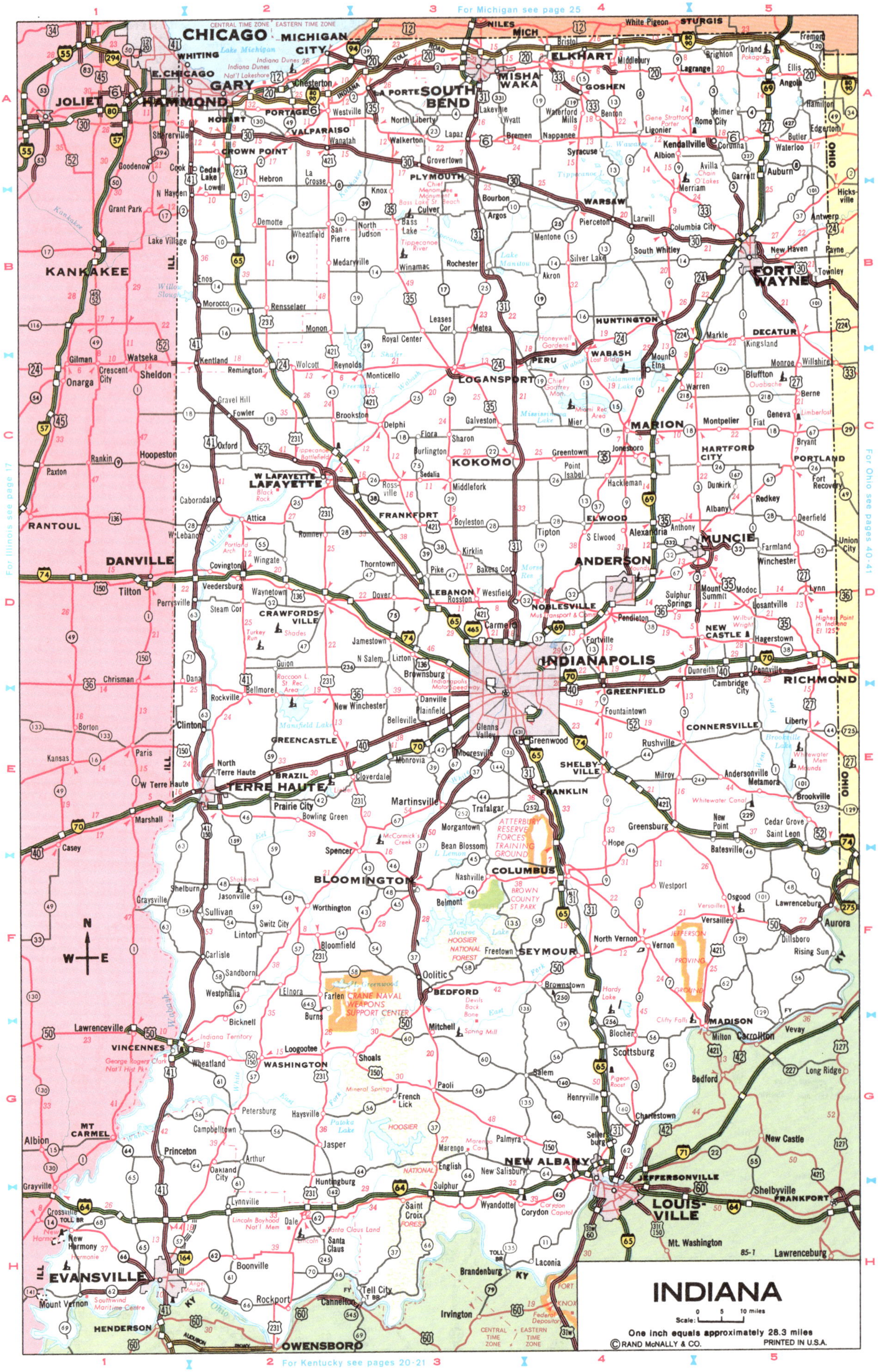

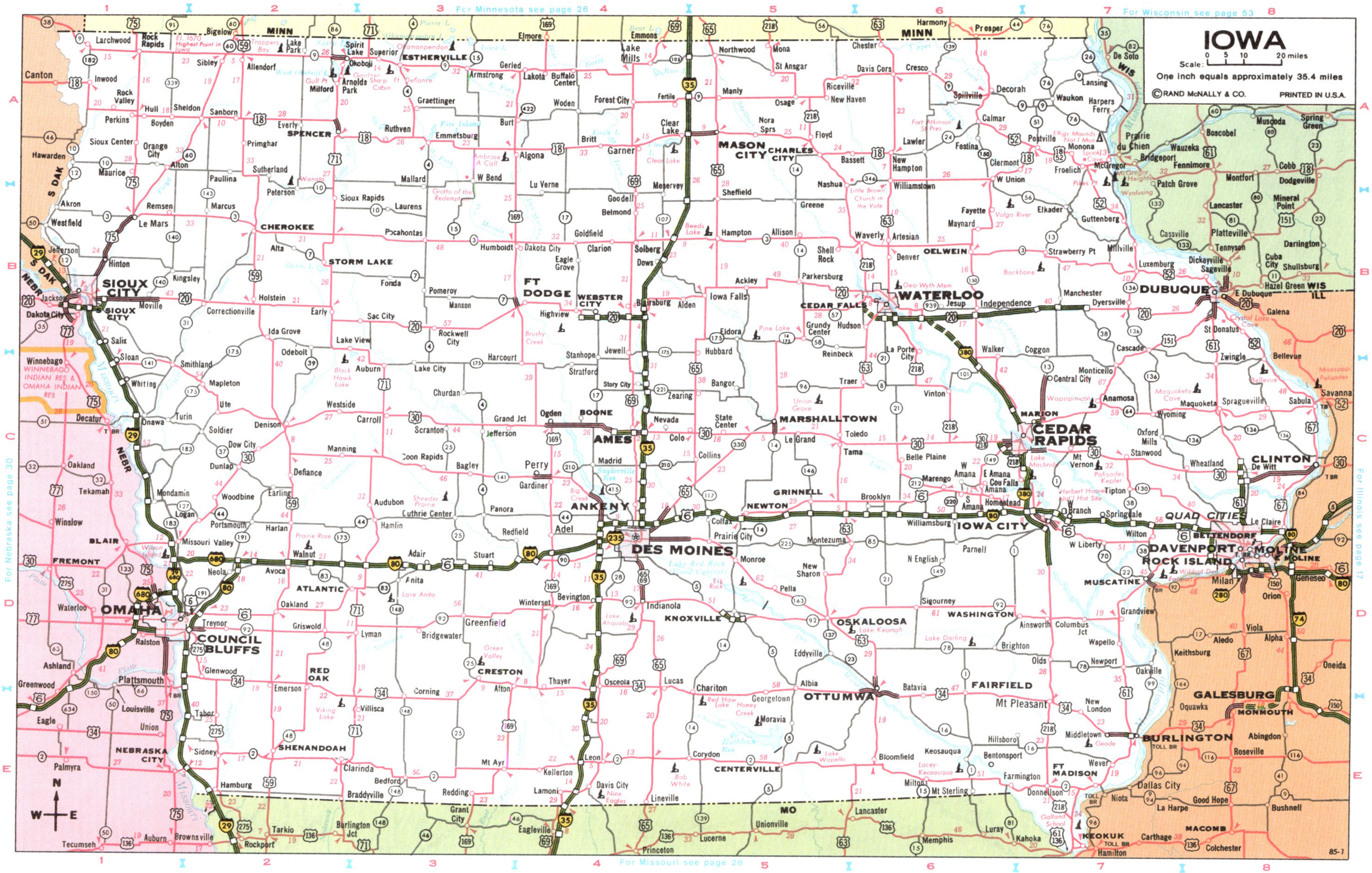

IOWA

Population: 2,913,808
(1980 Census)
Land Area: 55,965 Sq. Mi.
Capital: Des Moines

Cities and Towns

Adel . . . D-4
Albia . . . D-5
Algona . . . A-3
Allison . . . B-5
Ames . . . C-4
Anamosa . . . C-7
Ankeny . . . C-4
Arnolds Park . . . A-2
Atlantic . . . D-2
Audubon . . . C-3
Bedford . . . E-3
Belmond . . . B-4
Bettendorf . . . D-8
Bloomfield . . . E-6
Boone . . . C-4
Burlington . . . E-7
Carroll . . . C-3
Cascade . . . B-7
Cedar Falls . . . B-6
Cedar Rapids . . . C-7
Centerville . . . E-5
Central City . . . C-7
Chariton . . . D-5
Charles City . . . A-5
Cherokee . . . B-2
Clarinda . . . E-2
Clarion . . . B-4
Clear Lake . . . A-4
Clinton . . . C-8
Corning . . . E-3
Corydon . . . E-5
Council Bluffs . . . D-1
Creston . . . D-3
Davenport . . . D-8
Decorah . . . A-6
Denison . . . C-2
Des Moines . . . D-4
De Witt . . . C-8
Dubuque . . . B-8
Dyersville . . . B-7
Eagle Grove . . . B-4
Eldora . . . B-5
Elkader . . . B-7
Emmetsburg . . . A-3
Estherville . . . A-3
Fairfield . . . D-6
Forest City . . . A-4
Ft. Dodge . . . B-4
Ft. Madison . . . E-7
Garner . . . A-4
Glenwood . . . D-2
Greenfield . . . D-3
Grinnell . . . C-5
Grundy Center . . . B-5
Guthrie Center . . . C-3
Hampton . . . B-5
Harlan . . . D-2
Hawarden . . . A-1
Humboldt . . . B-3
Ida Grove . . . B-2
Independence . . . B-6
Indianola . . . D-4
Iowa City . . . C-7
Iowa Falls . . . B-5
Jefferson . . . C-3
Jesup . . . B-6
Keokuk . . . E-7
Knoxville . . . D-5
Laurens . . . B-3
Le Claire . . . C-8
Le Mars . . . B-1
Logan . . . C-2
Manchester . . . B-7
Manning . . . C-2
Maquoketa . . . C-8
Marengo . . . C-6
Marion . . . C-7
Marshalltown . . . C-5
Mason City . . . A-5
Milford . . . A-2
Monona . . . A-7
Monroe . . . D-5
Montezuma . . . D-5
Monticello . . . C-7
Mt. Ayr . . . E-3
Mt. Pleasant . . . E-7
Mt. Vernon . . . C-7
Muscatine . . . D-7
Nashua . . . A-5
Nevada . . . C-4
New Hampton . . . A-6
New London . . . E-7
Newton . . . C-5
Northwood . . . A-5
Oakland . . . D-2
Oelwein . . . B-6
Onawa . . . C-1
Orange City . . . A-1
Osage . . . A-5
Osceola . . . D-4
Oskaloosa . . . D-5
Ottumwa . . . D-6
Pella . . . D-5
Perry . . . C-4
Pocahontas . . . B-3
Postville . . . A-7
Primghar . . . A-2
Red Oak . . . D-2
Rock Rapids . . . A-1
Rock Valley . . . A-1
Rockwell City . . . B-3
Sac City . . . B-3
Sanborn . . . A-2
Sheldon . . . A-2
Shenandoah . . . E-2
Sibley . . . A-2
Sigourney . . . D-6
Sioux City . . . B-1
Spencer . . . A-2
Spirit Lake . . . A-2
Storm Lake . . . B-2
Tipton . . . C-7
Toledo . . . C-5
Wapello . . . D-7
Washington . . . D-7
Waterloo . . . B-6
Waukon . . . A-7
Waverly . . . B-6
Webster City . . . B-4
W. Branch . . . C-7
W. Liberty . . . D-7
W. Union . . . A-6
Wilton . . . D-7
Winterset . . . D-4
Woodbine . . . C-2

For Illinois see page 17
For Indiana see page 18
For Missouri see page 28
For Arkansas see page 7

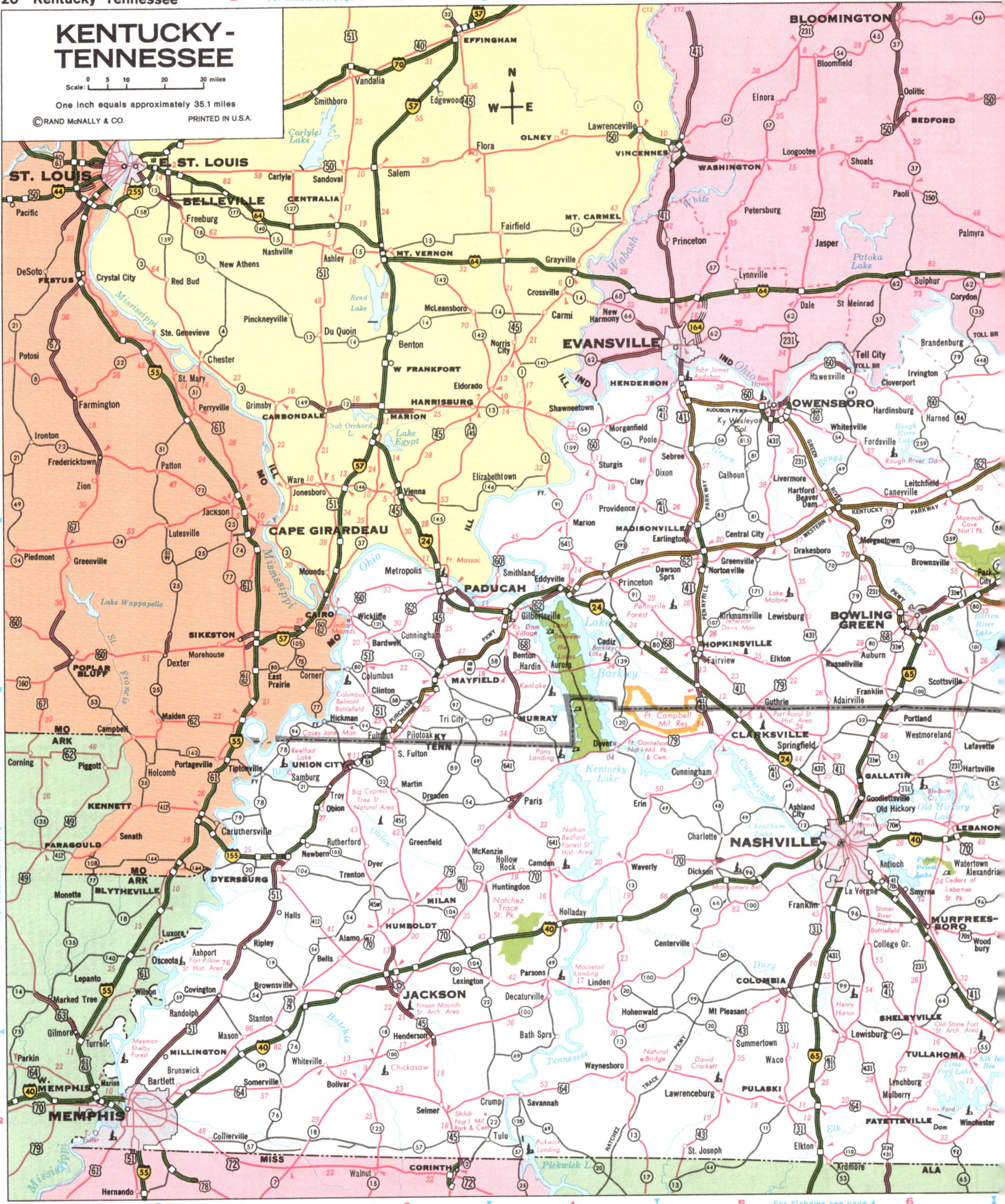

For Mississippi see page 27
For Alabama see page 4

KENTUCKY

Population: 3,660,257
(1980 Census)
Land Area: 39,674 Sq. Mi.
Capital: Frankfort

Cities and Towns

Albany..............E-8
Ashland............B-11
Barbourville........D-9
Bardstown...........C-7
Bardwell............D-3
Beattyville.........C-9
Bedford.............B-7
Benton..............D-4
Berea...............C-9
Booneville..........C-9
Bowling Green.......D-6
Brandenburg.........C-6
Brownsville.........D-6
Burkesville.........D-7
Cadiz...............D-4
Calhoun.............C-5
Campbellsville......D-7
Carlisle............B-9
Clinton.............E-3
Columbia............D-7
Corbin..............D-9
Covington...........A-8
Cynthiana...........B-8
Danville............C-8
Dixon...............C-4
Eddyville...........D-4
Edmonton............D-7
Elizabethtown.......C-7
Flemingsburg........B-9
Florence............A-8
Ft. Thomas..........A-8
Frankfort...........B-8
Georgetown..........B-8
Glasgow.............D-7
Grayson............B-10
Greensburg..........D-7
Greenup............B-10
Greenville..........D-5
Hardinsburg.........C-6
Harlan.............D-10
Harrodsburg.........C-8
Hartford............C-5
Hazard.............D-10
Henderson...........C-5
Hodgenville.........C-7
Hopkinsville........D-5
Hyden..............D-10
Irvington...........C-6
Jamestown...........D-8
Jeffersontown.......B-7
Lancaster...........C-8
Lawrenceburg........B-8
Lebanon.............C-7
Leitchfield.........C-6
Lexington...........B-8
Liberty.............D-8
London..............D-9
Louisville..........B-7
Madisonville........D-5
Manchester..........D-9
Marion..............D-4
Mayfield............D-3
Maysville...........A-9
Middlesboro.........E-9
Morehead...........B-10
Morgantown..........D-6
Mt. Sterling........B-9
Mt. Vernon..........C-8
Munfordville........D-7
Murray..............E-4
Newport.............A-8
Nicholasville.......C-8
Owensboro...........C-5
Owenton.............B-8
Paducah.............D-3
Paintsville........C-10
Paris...............B-9
Pippa Passes.......D-10
Princeton...........D-4
Richmond............C-9
Russellville........D-6
Scottsville.........D-6
Shelbyville.........B-7
Shepherdsville......C-7
Shively.............B-7
Somerset............D-8
Valley Sta..........B-7
Whitesburg.........D-10
Whitley City........E-8
Williamsburg........D-9
Williamstown........B-8
Winchester..........B-9

TENNESSEE

Population: 4,591,120
(1980 Census)
Land Area: 41,154 Sq. Mi.
Capital: Nashville

Cities and Towns

Alamo...............F-

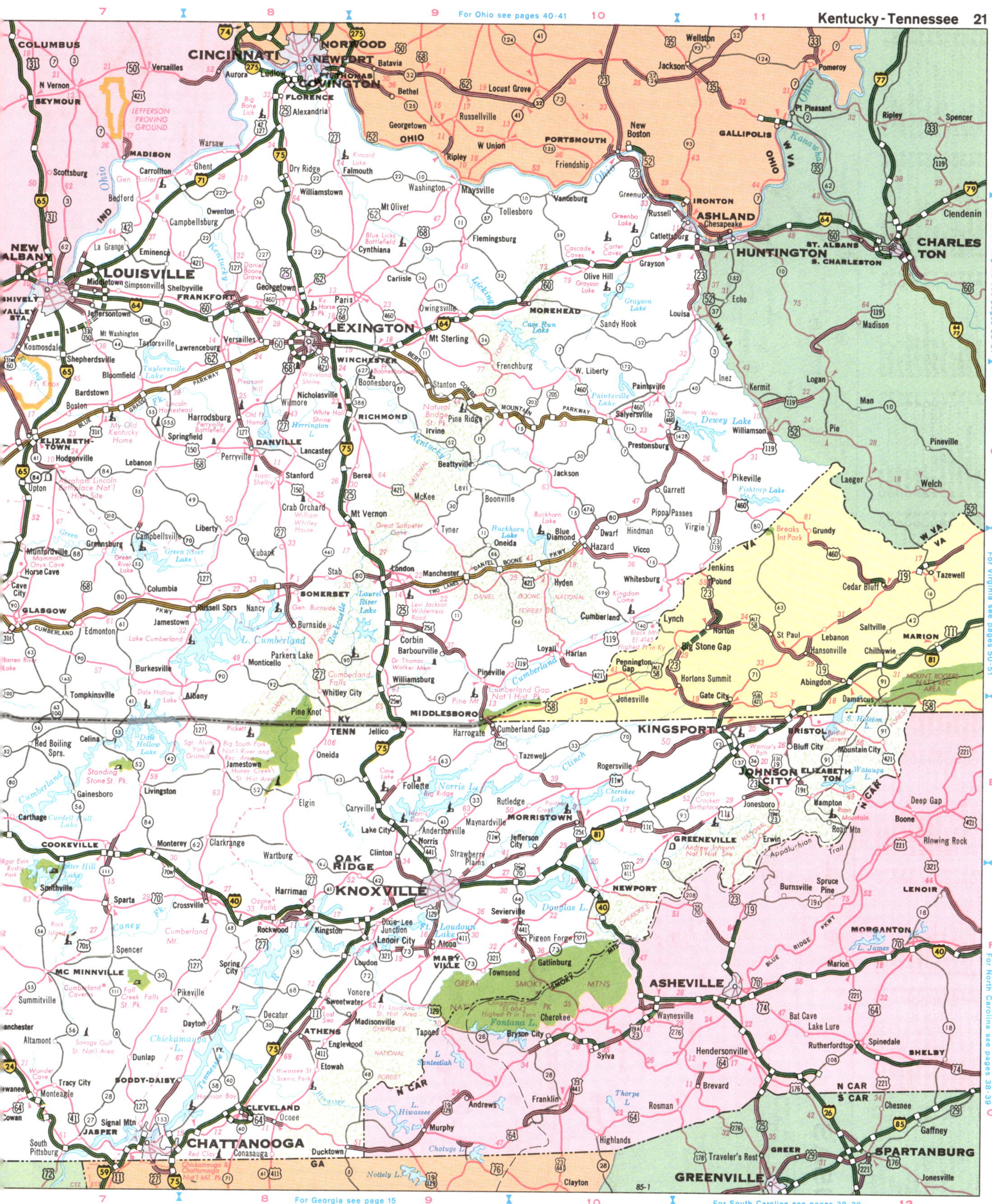
For Ohio see pages 40-41
For West Virginia see pages 50-51
For Virginia see pages 50-51
For North Carolina see pages 38-39
For Georgia see page 15
For South Carolina see pages 38-39
CINCINNATI
LOUISVILLE
LEXINGTON
FRANKFORT
HUNTINGTON
CHARLESTON
ASHLAND
KINGSPORT
JOHNSON CITY
KNOXVILLE
OAK RIDGE
CHATTANOOGA
ASHEVILLE
GREENVILLE
SPARTANBURG

KANSAS

Population: 2,364,236
(1980 Census)
Land Area: 81,783 Sq. Mi.
Capital: Topeka

Cities and Towns

Abilene........C-6
Anthony........E-5
Arkansas City........E-6
Ashland........E-3
Atchison........B-8
Atwood........A-2
Augusta........D-6
Baldwin City........C-8
Baxter Springs........E-8
Belleville........A-5
Beloit........B-5
Blue Rapids........B-6
Burlington........D-7
Caldwell........E-5
Caney........E-7
Chanute........D-7
Cherryvale........E-7
Chetopa........E-8
Cimarron........D-2
Clay Center........B-6
Coffeyville........E-7
Colby........B-2
Columbus........E-8
Concordia........B-5
Cottonwood Falls........C-6
Council Grove........C-6
Dighton........C-2
Dodge City........D-3
El Dorado........D-6
Elkhart........E-1
Ellinwood........C-4
Ellis........C-3
Ellsworth........C-5
Elwood........B-8
Emporia........C-7
Erie........D-8
Eureka........D-7
Ft. Scott........D-8
Fredonia........D-7
Frontenac........D-8
Garden City........D-2
Garnett........C-8
Girard........D-8
Goessel........C-5
Goodland........B-1
Great Bend........C-4
Greensburg........D-3
Harper........E-5
Hays........C-3
Herington........C-6
Hiawatha........A-7
Hill City........B-3
Hillsboro........C-6
Hoisington........C-4
Holton........B-7
Horton........B-7
Hoxie........B-2
Hugoton........E-1
Humboldt........D-7
Hutchinson........D-5
Independence........E-7
Iola........D-7
Johnson........D-1
Junction City........B-6
Kansas City........B-8
Kingman........D-5
Kinsley........D-3
Kiowa........E-4
La Crosse........C-3
Lakin........D-1
Larned........D-4
Lawrence........C-8
Leavenworth........B-8
Leoti........C-1
Liberal........E-2
Lincoln........B-5
Lindsborg........C-5
Lyndon........C-7
Lyons........C-5
McPherson........C-5
Manhattan........B-6
Mankato........B-5
Marion........C-6
Marysville........A-6
Meade........E-2
Medicine Lodge........E-4
Minneapolis........B-5
Mulvane........D-6
Neodesha........E-7
Ness City........C-3
Newton........D-5
Norton........A-3
Oakley........B-2
Oberlin........A-2
Olathe........C-8
Osage City........C-7
Osawatomie........C-8
Osborne........B-4
Oswego........E-8
Ottawa........C-8
Paola........C-8
Parsons........E-8
Peabody........D-6
Phillipsburg........B-3
Pittsburg........D-8
Plainville........B-3
Pratt........D-4
Russell........C-4
Sabetha........A-7
St. Francis........A-1
St. John........D-4
St. Marys........B-7
Salina........C-5
Scott City........C-2
Sedan........E-7
Seneca........A-7
Sharon Sprs.........C-1
Smith Center........B-4
Stafford........D-4
Sterling........D-4
Stockton........B-3
Sublette........D-2
Syracuse........D-1
Tonganoxie........B-8
Topeka........B-7
Tribune........C-1
Troy........A-8
Ulysses........D-1
WaKeeney........B-3
Wamego........B-6
Washington........A-6
Wellington........E-5
Wichita........D-5
Winfield........E-6
Yates Center........D-7

For Nebraska see page 30

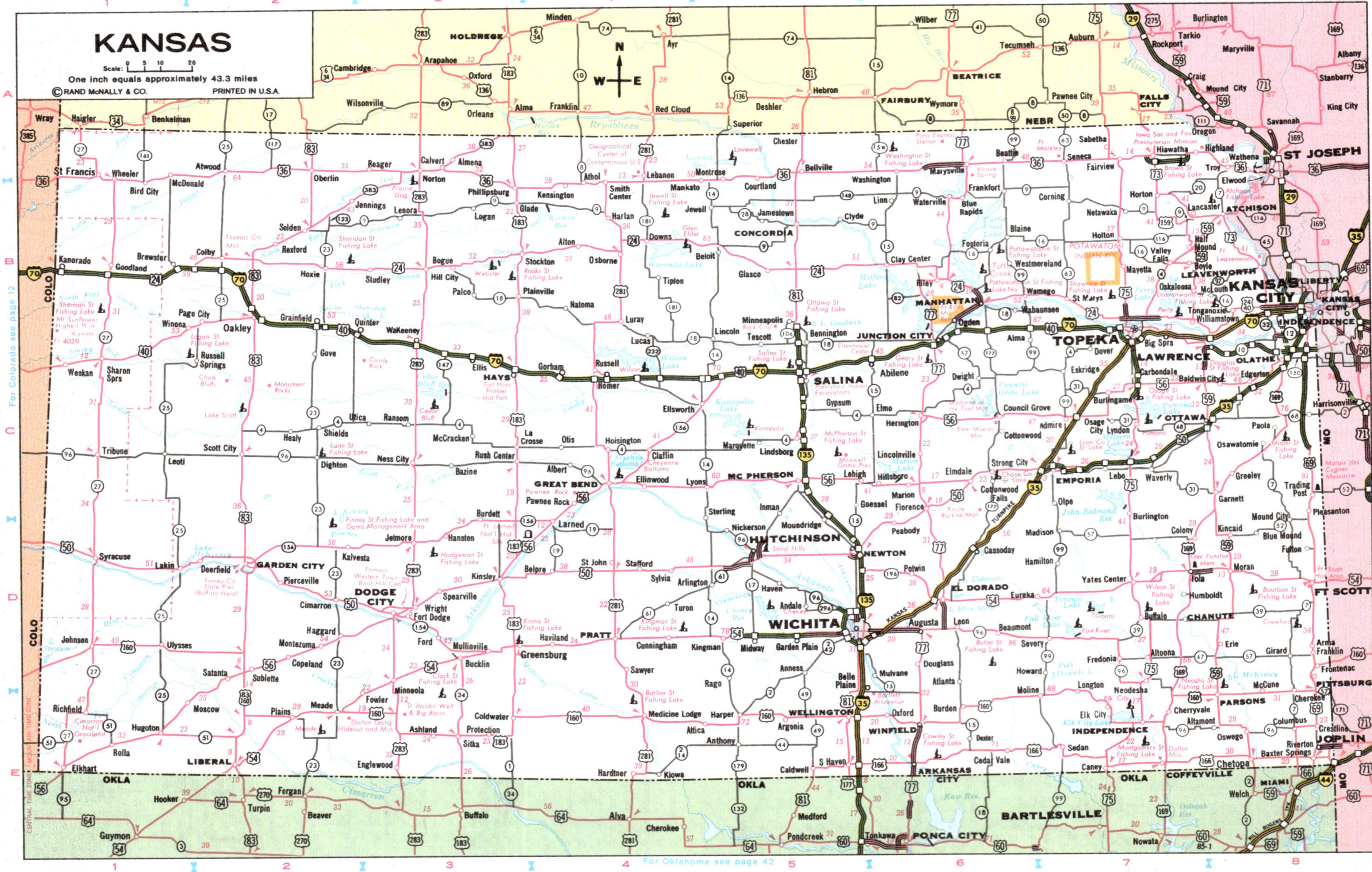

For Colorado see page 12
For Missouri see page 28
For Oklahoma see page 42

LOUISIANA

Population: 4,206,098
(1980 Census)
Land Area: 44,520 Sq. Mi.
Capital: Baton Rouge

Cities and Towns

MAINE

Population: 1,125,030
(1980 Census)
Land Area: 30,995 Sq. Mi.
Capital: Augusta

Cities and Towns

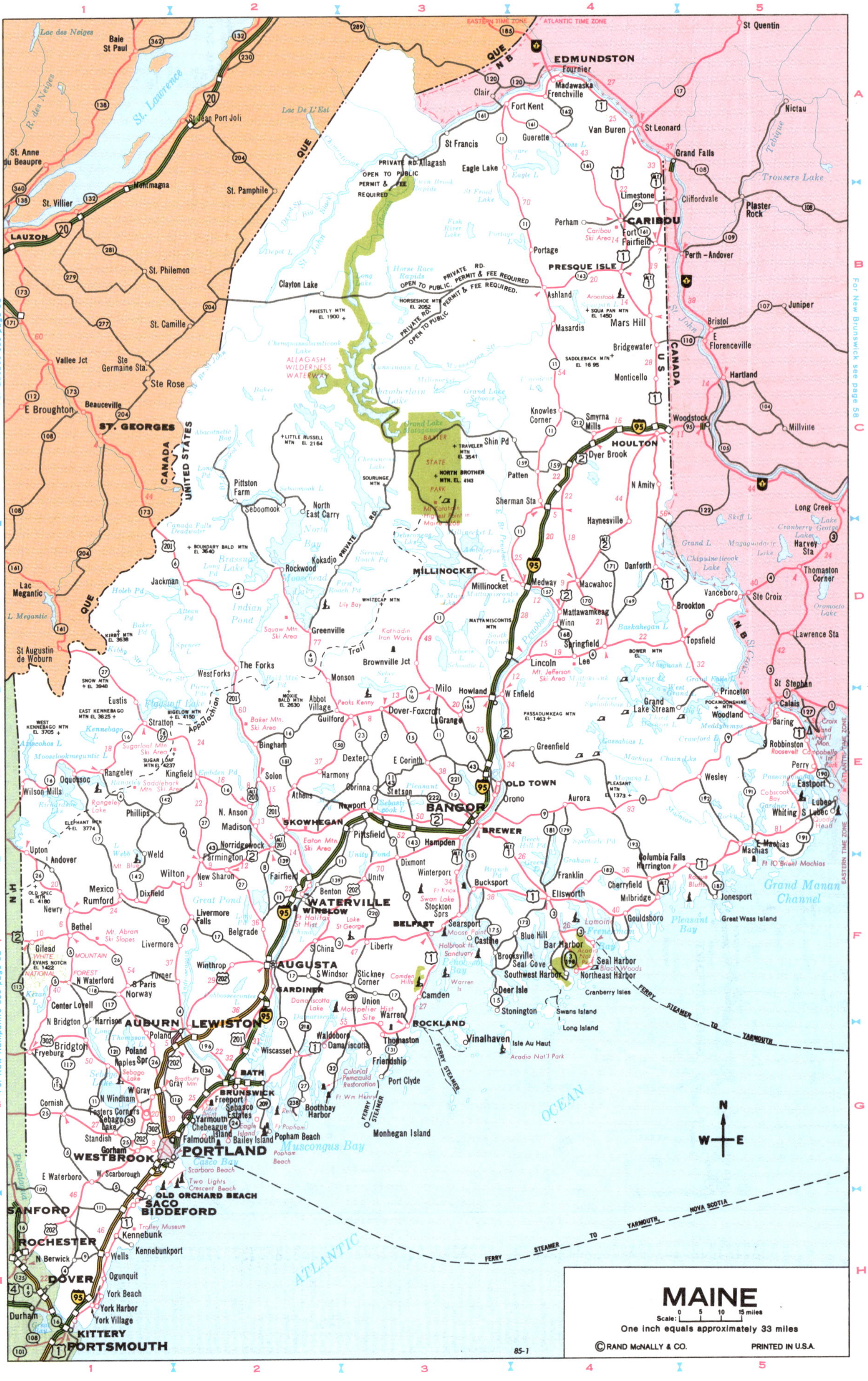

MICHIGAN

Population: 9,262,070
(1980 Census)
Land Area: 56,959 Sq. Mi.
Capital: Lansing

Cities and Towns

MINNESOTA

Population: 4,075,970
(1980 Census)
Land Area: 79,548 Sq. Mi.
Capital: St. Paul

Cities and Towns

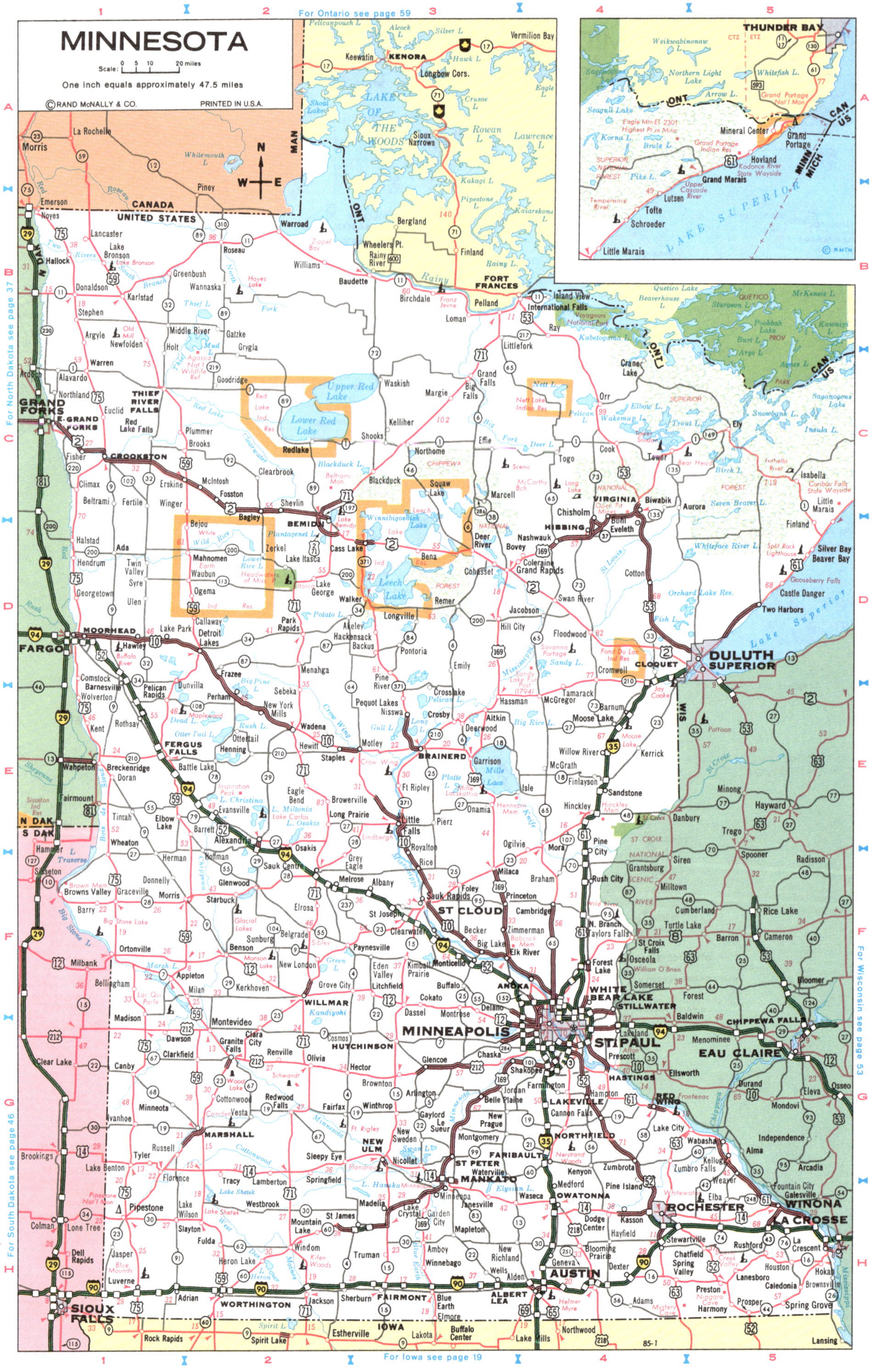

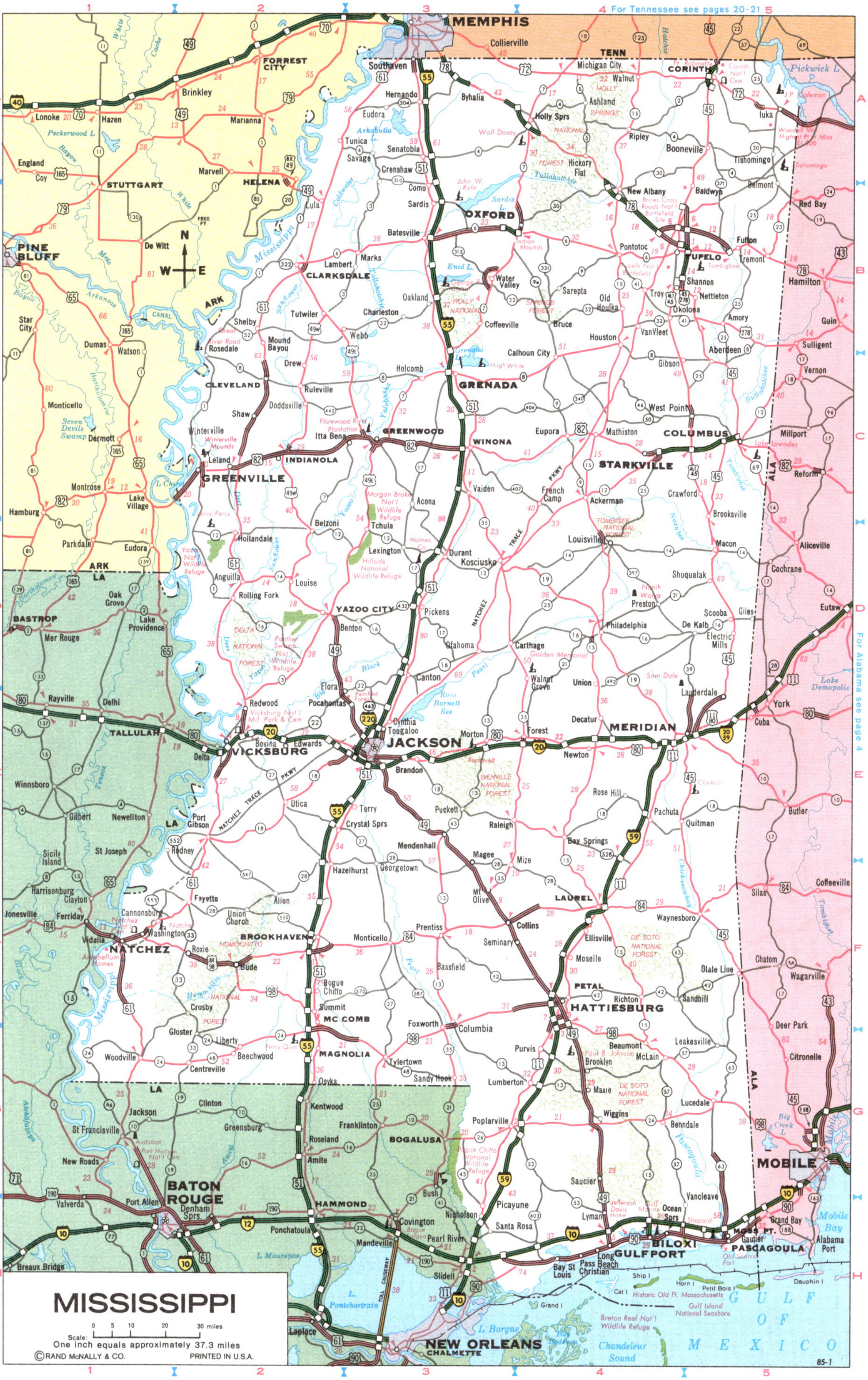

MISSISSIPPI

Population: 2,520,631
(1980 Census)
Land Area: 47,234 Sq. Mi.
Capital: Jackson

Cities and Towns

MISSOURI

Population: 4,916,759
(1980 Census)
Land Area: 68,945 Sq. Mi.
Capital: Jefferson City

Cities and Towns

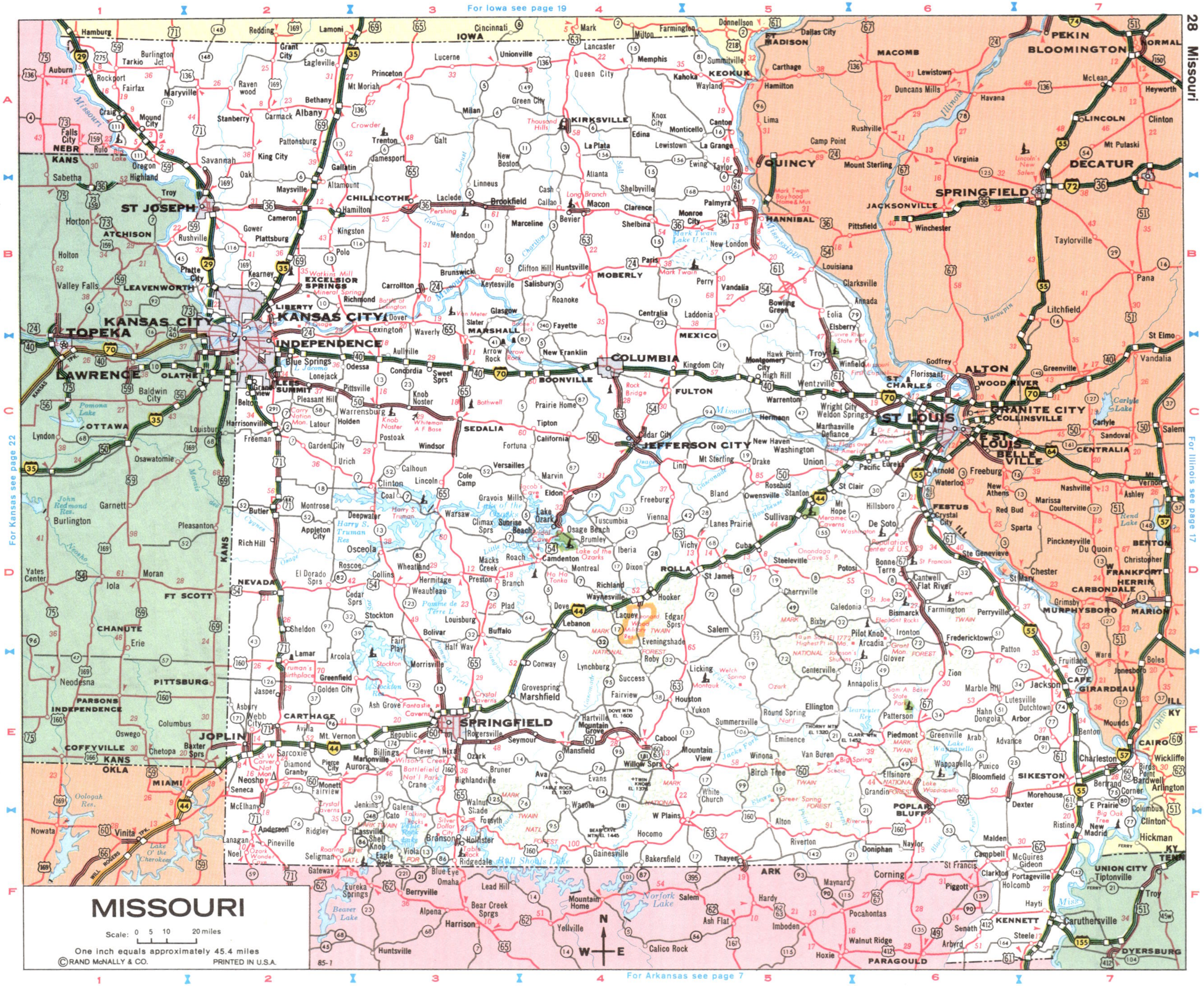

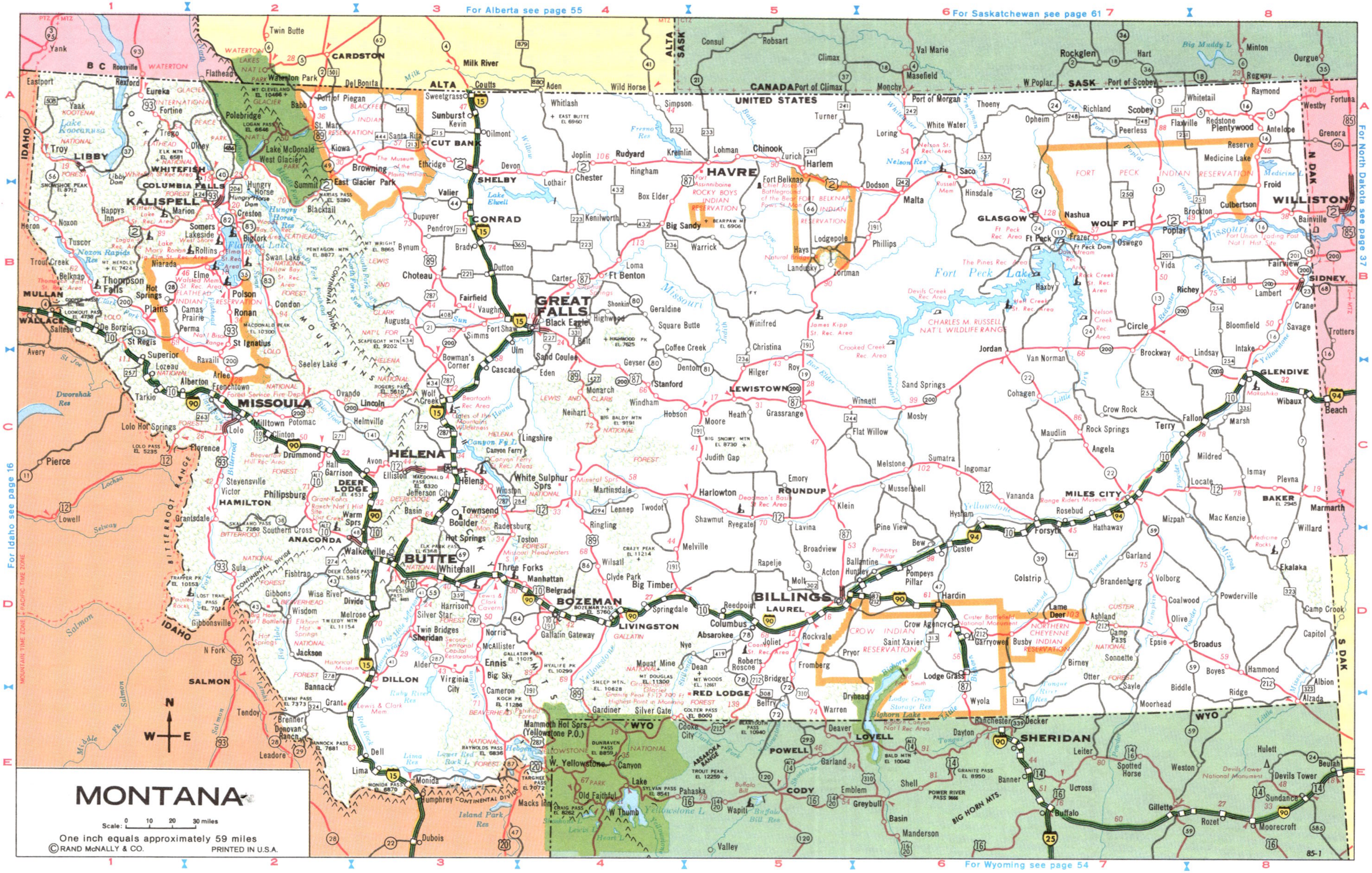

MONTANA

Population: 786,690
(1980 Census)
Land Area: 145,388 Sq. Mi.
Capital: Helena

Cities and Towns

Absarokee	D-5
Alberton	C-2
Anaconda	D-2
Ashland	D-7
Augusta	B-3
Avon	C-3
Bainville	B-8
Baker	C-8
Ballantine	D-6
Belfry	E-5
Belgrade	D-4
Belt	B-4
Big Sandy	B-4
Big Timber	D-4
Billings	D-5
Black Eagle	B-4
Boulder	D-3
Bozeman	D-4
Bridger	D-5
Broadus	D-8
Browning	A-3
Butte	D-3
Cascade	C-3
Chester	A-4
Chinook	A-5
Choteau	B-3
Circle	B-7
Clyde Park	D-4
Columbia Falls	A-2
Columbus	D-5
Conrad	B-3
Crow Agency	D-6
Culbertson	B-8
Cut Bank	A-3
Deer Lodge	C-3
Denton	C-4
Dillon	D-3
Dodson	A-6
Drummond	C-2
East Glacier Park	A-2
E. Helena	C-3
Ekalaka	D-8
Ennis	D-3
Eureka	A-1
Fairfield	B-3
Fairview	B-8
Flaxville	A-7
Forsyth	C-7
Ft. Belknap	A-5
Ft. Benton	B-4
Ft. Peck	B-7
Froid	A-8
Geraldine	B-4
Geyser	C-4
Glasgow	B-7
Glendive	C-8
Grantsdale	C-2
Grassrange	C-5
Great Falls	B-4
Hamilton	C-2
Hardin	D-6
Harlem	A-5
Harlowton	C-5
Havre	A-5
Hays	B-5
Helena	C-3
Hindsdale	A-6
Hot Springs	B-1
Hysham	C-6
Joliet	D-5
Joplin	A-4
Jordon	B-6
Kalispell	B-2
Kremlin	A-4
Laurel	D-5
Lewistown	C-5
Libby	A-1
Lima	E-3
Lincoln	C-3
Livingston	D-4
Lodge Grass	D-6
Malta	B-6
Manhattan	D-4
Martinsdale	C-4
Medicine Lake	A-8
Miles City	C-7
Milltown	C-2
Missoula	C-2
Nashua	B-7
Opheim	A-7
Philipsburg	C-2
Plains	B-1
Plentywood	A-8
Polson	B-2
Pompeys Pillar	D-6
Poplar	B-7
Red Lodge	E-5
Rexford	A-1
Richey	B-8
Ronan	B-2
Roundup	C-5
Roy	C-5
Rudyard	A-4
Ryegate	C-5
Saco	A-6
St. Ignatius	B-2
St. Regis	B-1
Scobey	A-7
Seeley Lake	C-2
Shelby	A-3
Sheridan	D-3
Sidney	B-8
Simms	B-3
Somers	B-2
Stanford	C-4
Sunburst	A-3
Superior	C-1
Terry	C-7
Thompson Falls	B-1
Three Forks	D-3
Toston	D-3
Townsend	C-3
Troy	A-1
Twin Bridges	D-3
Ulm	B-3
Valier	B-3
Walkerville	D-3
Warm Springs	D-3
Whitefish	A-2
Whitehall	D-3
White Sulphur Sprs.	C-4
Wolf Pt.	B-7

NEBRASKA

Population: 1,569,825
(1980 Census)
Land Area: 76,639 Sq. Mi.
Capital: Lincoln

Cities and Towns

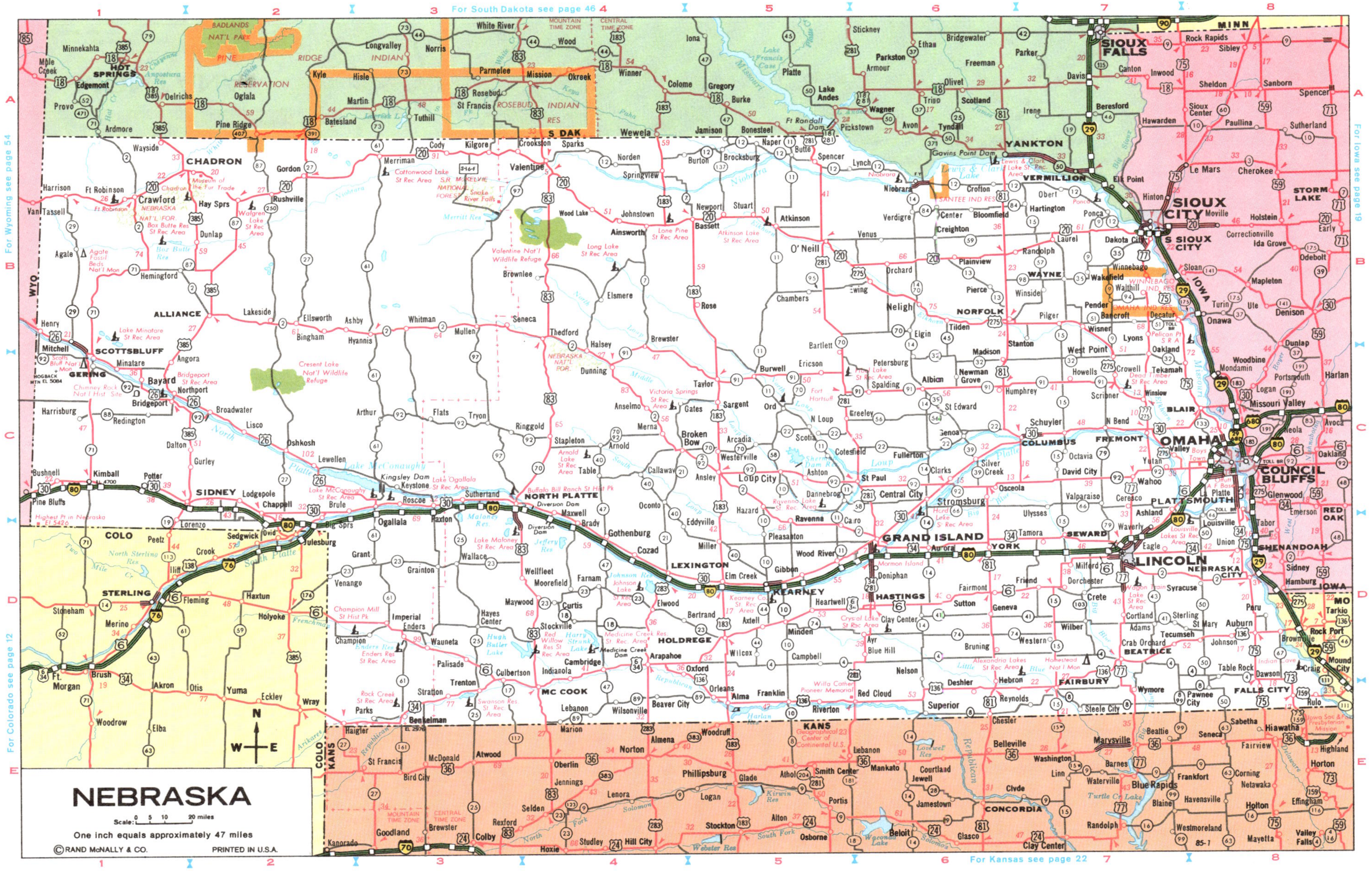

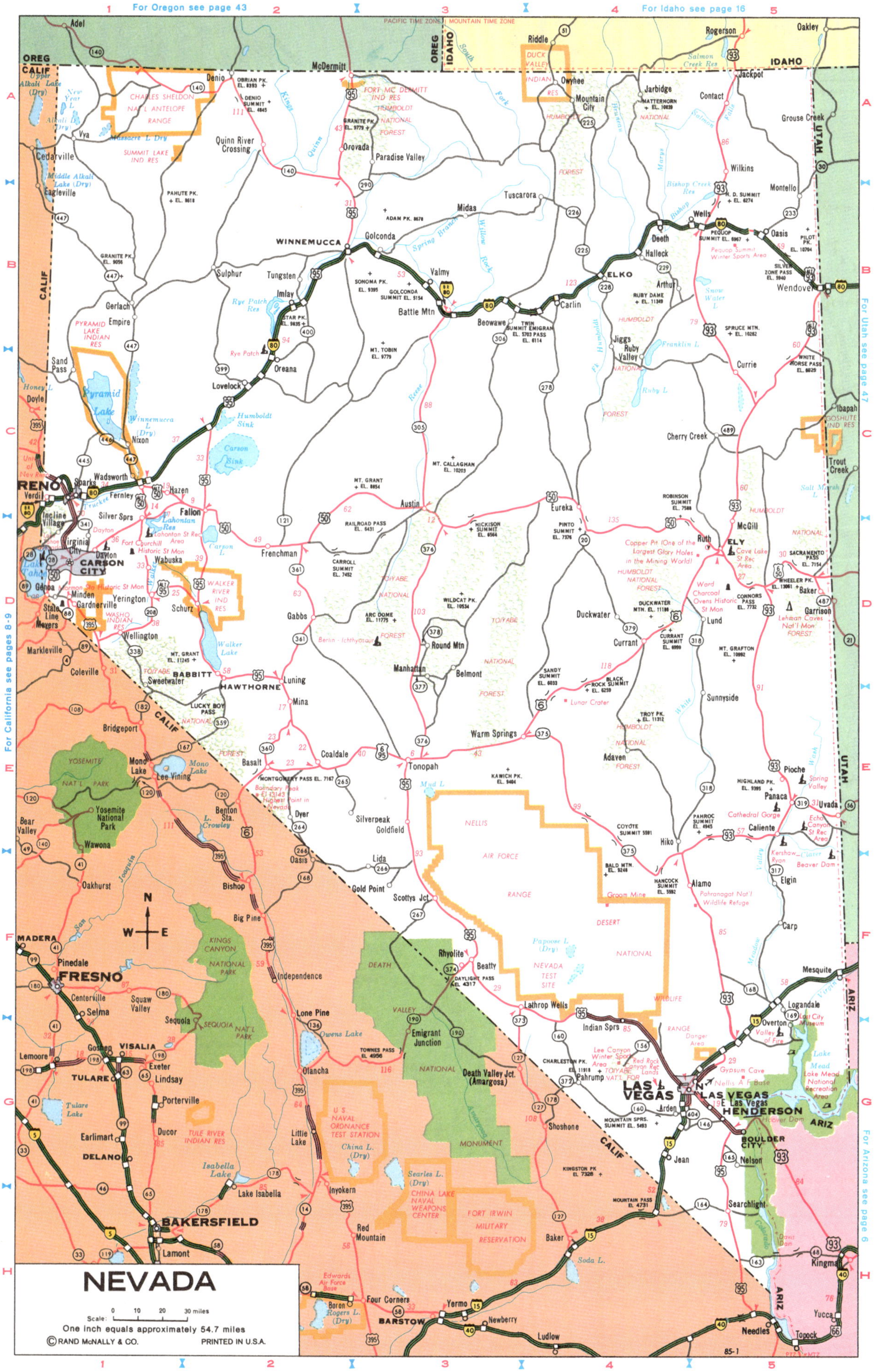

NEVADA

Population: 800,493
(1980 Census)
Land Area: 109,895 Sq. Mi.
Capital: Carson City

Cities and Towns

Adaven............E-4
Alamo............F-4
Arthur............B-4
Austin............C-3
Babbitt............D-2
Baker............D-5
Basalt............E-2
Battle Mtn............B-3
Beatty............F-3
Belmont............D-3
Beowawe............B-3
Boulder City............G-5
Caliente............E-5
Carlin............B-4
Carson City............D-1
Cherry Creek............C-5
Coaldale............E-2
Contact............A-5
Currant............D-4
Currie............C-5
Dayton............D-1
Deeth............B-4
Denio............A-2
Duckwater............D-4
Dyer............E-2
E. Las Vegas............G-5
Elgin............F-5
Elko............B-4
Ely............D-5
Empire............B-1
Eureka............C-4
Fallon............C-2
Fernley............C-1
Frenchman............D-2
Gabbs............D-2
Gardnerville............D-1
Gerlach............B-1
Golconda............B-3
Goldfield............E-3
Gold Point............F-3
Halleck............B-4
Hawthorne............D-2
Hazen............C-1
Henderson............G-5
Hiko............E-4
Imlay............B-2
Incline Village............D-1
Indian Sprs............G-4
Jarbidge............A-4
Jiggs............B-4
Las Vegas............G-4
Lathrop Wells............F-3
Lida............F-3
Logandale............F-5
Lovelock............C-2
Lund............D-5
Luning............D-2
McDermitt............A-2
McGill............D-5
Manhattan............D-3
Mesquite............F-5
Midas............B-3
Mina............E-2
Minden............D-1
Montello............B-5
Mountain City............A-4
Nelson............G-5
Nixon............C-1
N. Las Vegas............G-5
Oasis............B-5
Orovada............A-2
Overton............G-5
Owyhee............A-4
Pahrump............G-4
Panaca............E-5
Paradise Valley............A-3
Pioche............E-5
Quinn River Crossing............A-2
Reno............C-1
Round Mtn............D-3
Ruby Valley............C-4
Ruth............D-5
Sand Pass............C-1
Schurz............D-2
Scottys Jct............F-3
Searchlight............H-5
Silverpeak............E-3
Silver Sprs............C-1
Sparks............C-1
Sulphur............B-2
Sunnyside............E-5
Tonopah............E-3
Tungsten............B-2
Tuscarora............B-4
Valmy............B-3
Verdi............C-1
Virginia City............D-1
Vya............A-1
Wabuska............D-1
Wadsworth............C-1
Warm Sprs............E-3
Wellington............D-1
Wells............B-5
Wendover............B-5
Wilkins............A-5
Winnemucca............B-2
Yerington............D-1

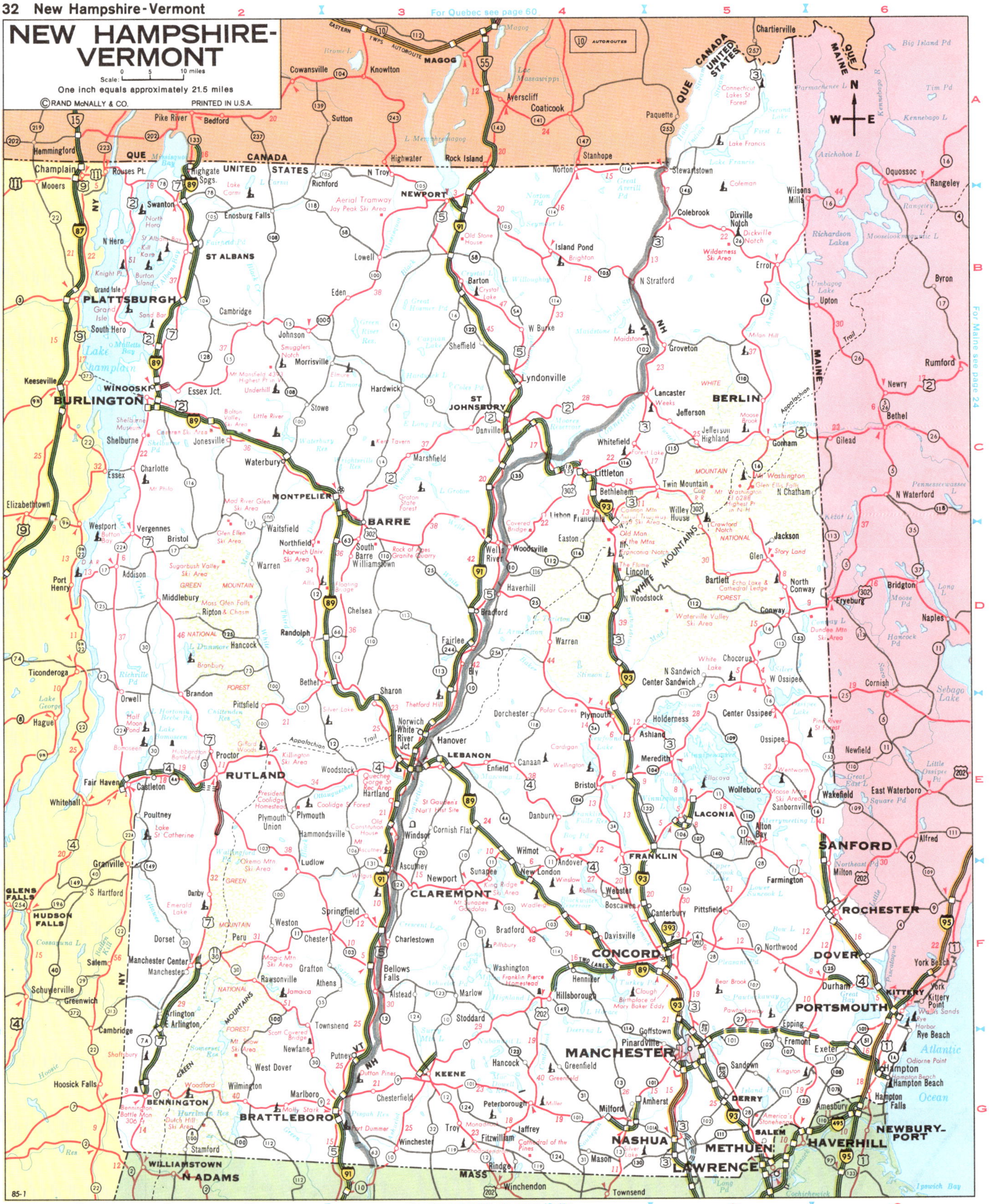

N. HAMPSHIRE

Population: 920,610
(1980 Census)
Land Area: 8,992 Sq. Mi.
Capital: Concord

Cities and Towns

Ashland	E-4
Berlin	C-5
Bristol	E-4
Canaan	E-4
Center Ossipee	E-5
Charlestown	F-3
Chocorua	D-5
Claremont	F-3
Colebrook	B-5
Concord	F-5
Conway	D-5
Derry	G-5
Dover	F-6
Epping	F-5
Franklin	E-4
Glen	D-5
Gorham	C-5
Groveton	B-5
Hampton	G-6
Hampton Beach	G-6
Hanover	E-3
Haverhill	D-4
Henniker	F-4
Hillsborough	F-4
Jaffrey	G-4
Keene	G-3
Laconia	E-5
Lancaster	C-5
Lebanon	E-4
Lincoln	D-4
Littleton	C-4
Manchester	G-5
Meredith	E-5
Milford	G-4
Nashua	G-5
Newport	F-3
North Conway	D-5
N. Stratford	B-4
N. Woodstock	D-4
Peterborough	G-4
Pittsfield	F-5
Plymouth	E-4
Portsmouth	F-6
Rochester	F-6
Rye Beach	G-6
Salem	G-5
Troy	G-3
Twin Mountain	C-5
Whitefield	C-4
Winchester	G-3
Woodsville	D-4

VERMONT

Population: 511,456
(1980 Census)
Land Area: 9,273 Sq. Mi.
Capital: Montpelier

Cities and Towns

Arlington	F-1
Barre	C-3
Barton	B-3
Bellows Falls	F-3
Bennington	G-1
Bethel	D-2
Brandon	D-2
Brattleboro	G-3
Bristol	D-2
Burlington	C-1
Cambridge	B-2
Chester	F-3
Enosburg Falls	B-2
Essex Jct.	C-2
Fair Haven	E-1
Grafton	F-3
Hardwick	C-3
Highgate Sprs.	A-2
Island Pond	B-4
Ludlow	F-2
Lyndonville	C-4
Middlebury	D-1
Montpelier	C-3
Morrisville	C-3
Newport	B-3
Norwich	E-3
Poultney	E-1
Randolph	D-2
Richford	A-2
Rutland	E-2
St. Albans	B-2
St. Johnsbury	C-4
Shelburne	C-1
Springfield	F-3
Swanton	B-2
Vergennes	D-1
Waterbury	C-2
Wells River	D-4
W. Burke	B-4
White River Jct.	E-3
Windsor	E-3
Winooski	C-1
Woodstock	E-3

NEW JERSEY

Population: 7,365,011
(1980 Census)
Land Area: 7,468 Sq. Mi.
Capital: Trenton

Cities and Towns

NEW YORK
Scale: 0 5 10 20 miles
One inch equals approximately 29.2 miles
©RAND McNALLY & CO.
PRINTED IN U.S.A.
LAKE ONTARIO
LAKE ERIE
CANADA
UNITED STATES
PA
TORONTO
HAMILTON
OSHAWA
PETERBOROUGH
KINGSTON
BELLEVILLE
TRENTON
BARRIE
ORILLIA
LINDSAY
GUELPH
BRAMPTON
ST CATHARINES
NIAGARA FALLS
WELLAND
BUFFALO
LACKAWANNA
CHEEKTOWAGA
LOCKPORT
BATAVIA
ROCHESTER
SYRACUSE
AUBURN
GENEVA
ITHACA
CORTLAND
ELMIRA
CORNING
HORNELL
OLEAN
JAMESTOWN
DUNKIRK
ERIE
BINGHAMTON
OSWEGO
FULTON
WATERTOWN
For Ontario see page 59
NEW YORK
JERSEY CITY
NEWARK
PATERSON
CLIFTON
YONKERS
MT VERNON
NEW ROCHELLE
WHITE PLAINS
STAMFORD
NORWALK
LONG ISLAND SOUND
ATLANTIC OCEAN
©R. McN. & CO.

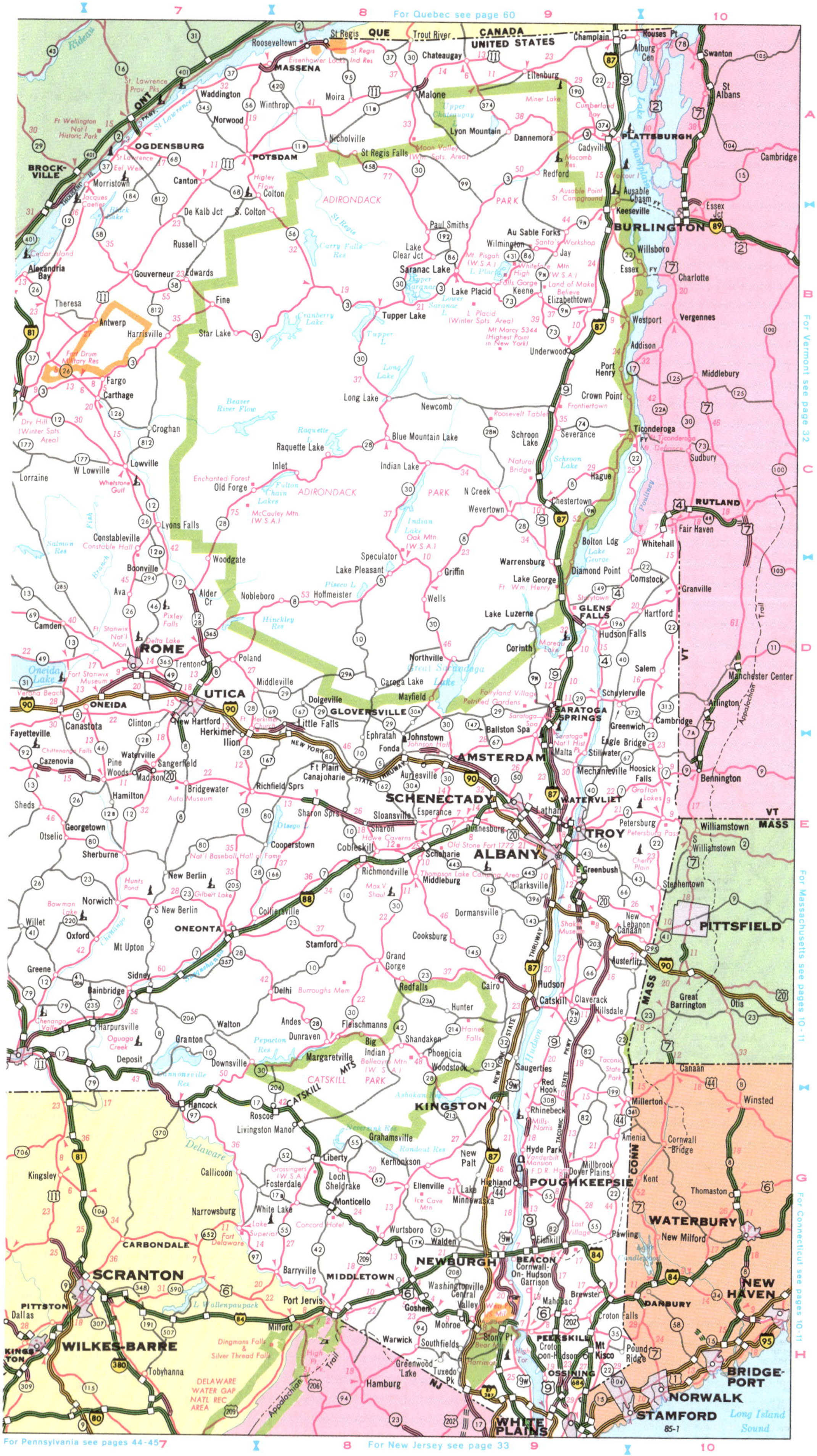

NEW YORK

Population: 17,558,072
(1980 Census)
Land Area: 47,379 Sq. Mi.
Capital: Albany

Cities and Towns

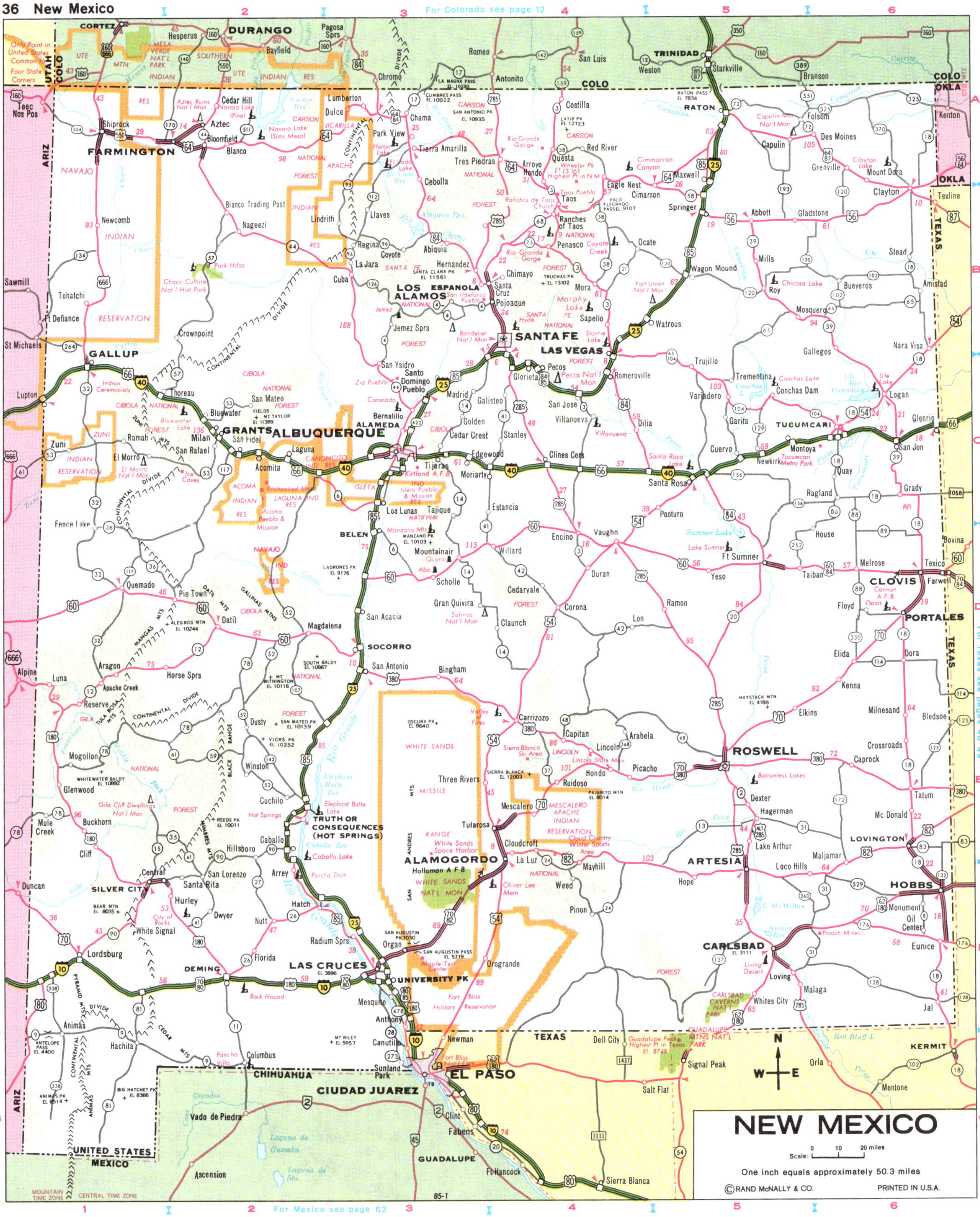

NEW MEXICO

Population 1,303,445
(1980 Census)
Land Area: 121,336 Sq. Mi.
Capital: Santa Fe

Cities and Towns

Abiquiu..........B-3
Alameda..........C-3
Alamogordo..........E-4
Albuquerque..........C-3
Alcalde..........B-4
Anthony..........F-3
Arroyo Hondo..........A-4
Artesia..........F-5
Aztec..........A-2
Belen..........D-3
Bernalillo..........C-3
Blanco..........A-2
Bloomfield..........A-2
Bluewater..........C-2
Capitan..........E-4
Carlsbad..........F-5
Carrizozo..........E-4
Cedar Crest..........C-3
Central..........F-1
Chama..........A-3
Cimarron..........A-5
Clayton..........B-6
Cloudcroft..........E-4
Clovis..........D-6
Crown Point..........B-2
Cuba..........B-3
Deming..........F-2
Des Moines..........A-6
Dexter..........E-5
Dulce..........A-3
Eagle Nest..........A-4
Elida..........D-6
Espanola..........B-3
Estancia..........C-4
Eunice..........F-6
Farmington..........A-2
Ft. Sumner..........D-5
Gallup..........C-1
Grants..........C-2
Hagerman..........E-5
Hatch..........F-2
Hobbs..........F-6
Hondo..........E-4
Hurley..........F-2
Lake Arthur..........E-5
Las Cruces..........F-3
Las Vegas..........B-4
Logan..........C-6
Lordsburg..........F-1
Los Alamos..........B-3
Los Lunas..........C-3
Loving..........F-5
Lovington..........E-6
Magdalena..........D-2
Mescalero..........E-4
Moriarty..........C-4
Mosquero..........B-6
Mountainair..........D-3
Penasco..........B-4
Polvadera..........D-3
Portales..........D-6
Quemado..........D-1
Questa..........A-4
Ranches of Taos..........B-4
Raton..........A-5
Reserve..........E-1
Roswell..........E-5
Roy..........B-5
Ruidoso..........E-4
San Antonio..........D-3
San Jon..........C-6
San Jose..........C-4
San Lorenzo..........F-2
San Mateo..........C-2
San Rafael..........C-2
Santa Fe..........B-4
Santa Rita..........F-2
Santa Rosa..........C-5
Santo Domingo Pueblo..........C-3
Shiprock..........A-1
Silver City..........F-1
Socorro..........D-3
Springer..........B-5
Taos..........B-4
Tatum..........E-6
Thoreau..........C-2
Tierra Amarilla..........A-3
Tohatchi..........B-1
Truth or Consequences..........E-2
Tucumcari..........C-6
Tularosa..........E-4
Vaughn..........D-4
Yeso..........D-5
Zuni..........C-1

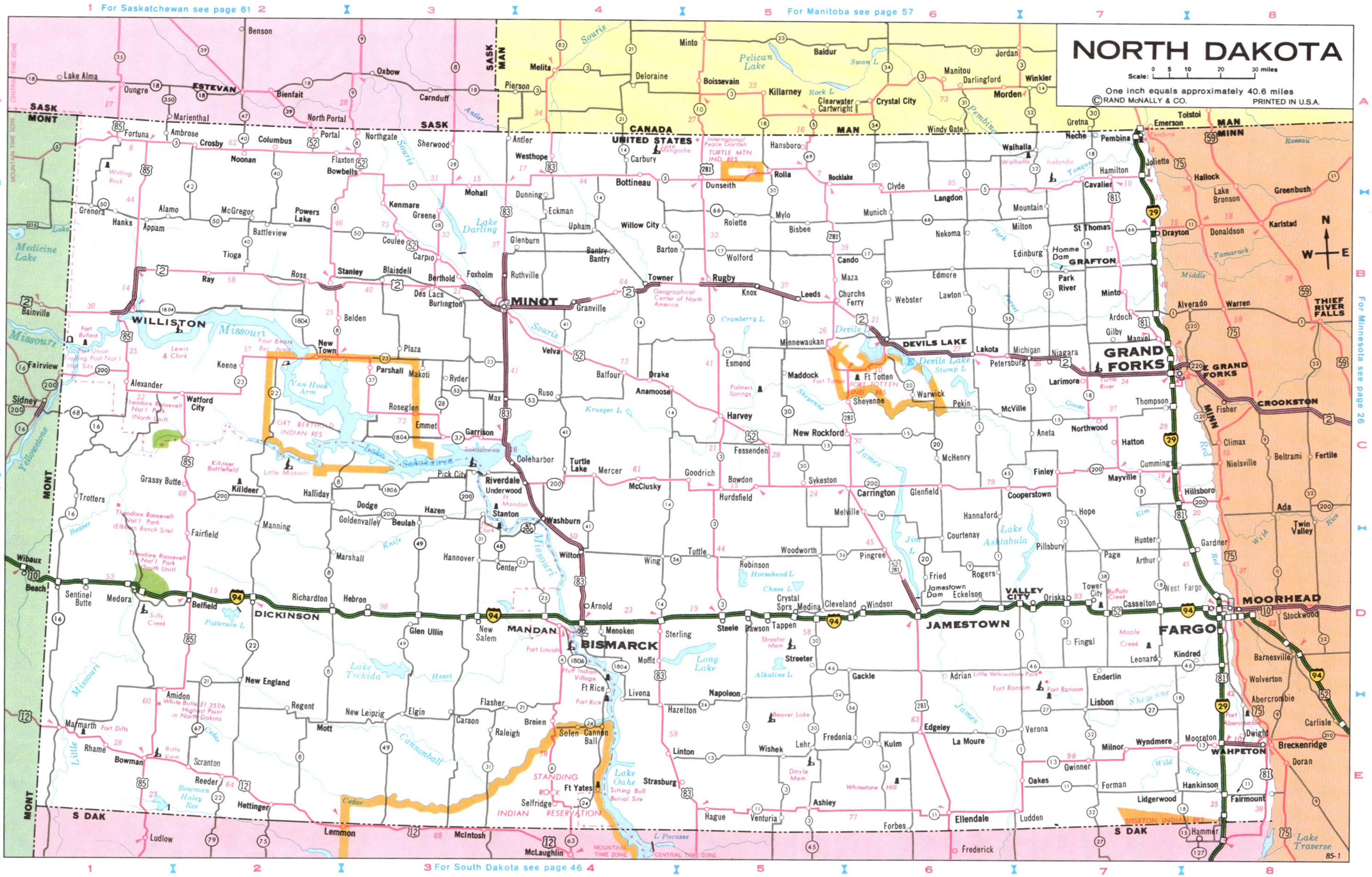

NORTH DAKOTA

Population: 652,717
(1980 Census)
Land Area: 69,299 Sq. Mi.
Capital: Bismarck

Cities and Towns

Anamoose..........C-4
Aneta..........C-7
Ashley..........E-5
Beach..........D-1
Belfield..........D-2
Berthold..........B-3
Beulah..........D-3
Bisbee..........B-5
Bismarck..........D-4
Bottineau..........A-4
Bowbells..........A-3
Bowman..........E-1
Cando..........B-5
Cannon Ball..........E-4
Carrington..........C-6
Casselton..........D-7
Cavalier..........A-7
Center..........D-3
Columbus..........A-2
Cooperstown..........C-6
Crosby..........A-2
Devils Lake..........B-6
Dickinson..........D-2
Drake..........C-4
Dunseith..........A-5
Edgeley..........E-6
Edmore..........B-6
Ellendale..........E-6
Enderlin..........D-7
Esmond..........B-5
Fairmount..........E-8
Fargo..........D-8
Fessenden..........C-5
Finley..........C-7
Flasher..........E-3
Flaxton..........A-2
Forman..........E-7
Ft. Yates..........E-4
Gackle..........D-6
Garrison..........C-3
Glen Ullin..........D-3
Goodrich..........C-5
Grafton..........B-7
Grand Forks..........C-7
Grenora..........B-1
Halliday..........C-2
Hankinson..........E-8
Harvey..........C-5
Hatton..........C-7
Hazelton..........E-4
Hazen..........C-3
Hettinger..........E-2
Hillsboro..........C-7
Hope..........C-7
Hunter..........D-7
Jamestown..........D-6
Kenmare..........B-3
Killdeer..........C-2
Kindred..........D-8
Kulm..........E-6
Lakota..........B-6
La Moure..........E-6
Langdon..........B-6
Larimore..........C-7
Leeds..........B-5
Lidgerwood..........E-7
Linton..........E-4
Lisbon..........E-7
McClusky..........C-4
McVille..........C-6
Maddock..........C-5
Mandan..........D-4
Max..........C-3
Mayville..........C-7
Medina..........D-5
Medora..........D-1
Milnor..........E-7
Minnewaukan..........B-5
Minot..........B-3
Minto..........B-7
Mohall..........B-3
Mott..........E-2
Napoleon..........E-5
Neche..........A-7
New England..........D-2
New Leipzig..........E-3
New Rockford..........C-5
New Salem..........D-3
New Town..........C-2
Noonan..........A-2
Northwood..........C-7
Oakes..........E-7
Page..........D-7
Park River..........B-7
Parshall..........C-3
Pembina..........A-7
Powers Lake..........B-2
Ray..........B-2
Regent..........E-2
Richardton..........D-2
Riverdale..........C-3
Rolette..........B-5
Rolla..........A-5
Rugby..........B-5
Ryder..........C-3
St. Thomas..........B-7
Selfridge..........E-4
Sherwood..........A-3
Sheyenne..........C-6
Solen..........E-4
Stanley..........B-2
Stanton..........C-3
Steele..........D-5
Strasburg..........E-5
Streeter..........D-5
Sykeston..........C-5
Tappen..........D-5
Tioga..........B-2
Towner..........B-4
Tower City..........D-7
Turtle Lake..........C-4
Underwood..........C-4
Valley City..........D-7
Velva..........B-4
Wahpeton..........E-8
Walhalla..........A-7
Warwick..........C-6
Washburn..........C-4
Watford City..........C-2
West Fargo..........D-8
Westhope..........A-4
Williston..........B-1
Willow City..........B-4
Wilton..........D-4
Wishek..........E-5

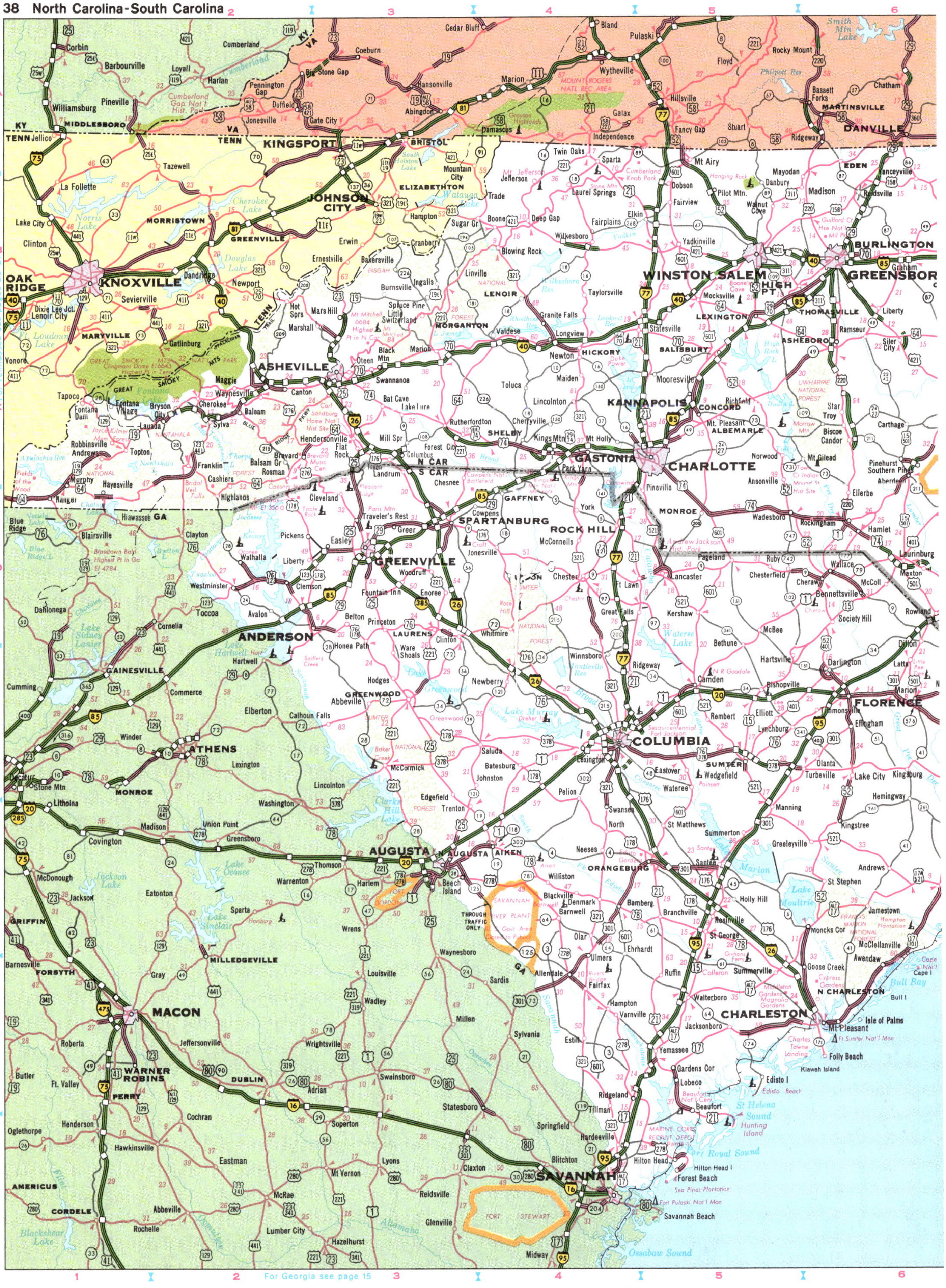

For Tennessee see pages 20-21

For Georgia see page 15

NORTH CAROLINA

Population: 5,881,385
(1980 Census)
Land Area: 48,843 Sq. Mi.
Capital: Raleigh

Cities and Towns

SOUTH CAROLINA

Population: 3,122,814
(1980 Census)
Land Area: 30,207 Sq. Mi.
Capital: Columbia

Cities and Towns

For Michigan see page 25

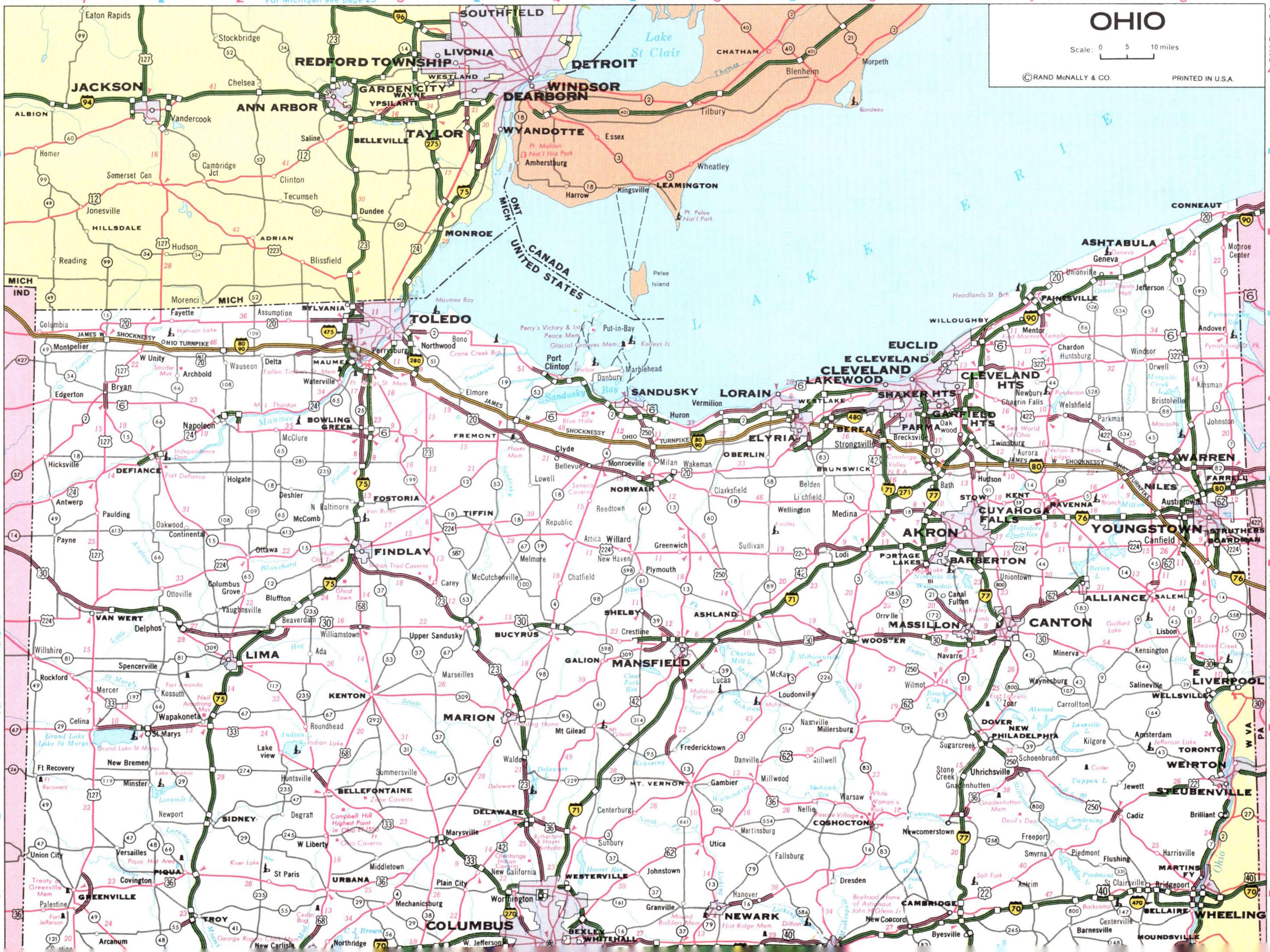

For Indiana see page 18

For Pennsylvania see pages 44-45

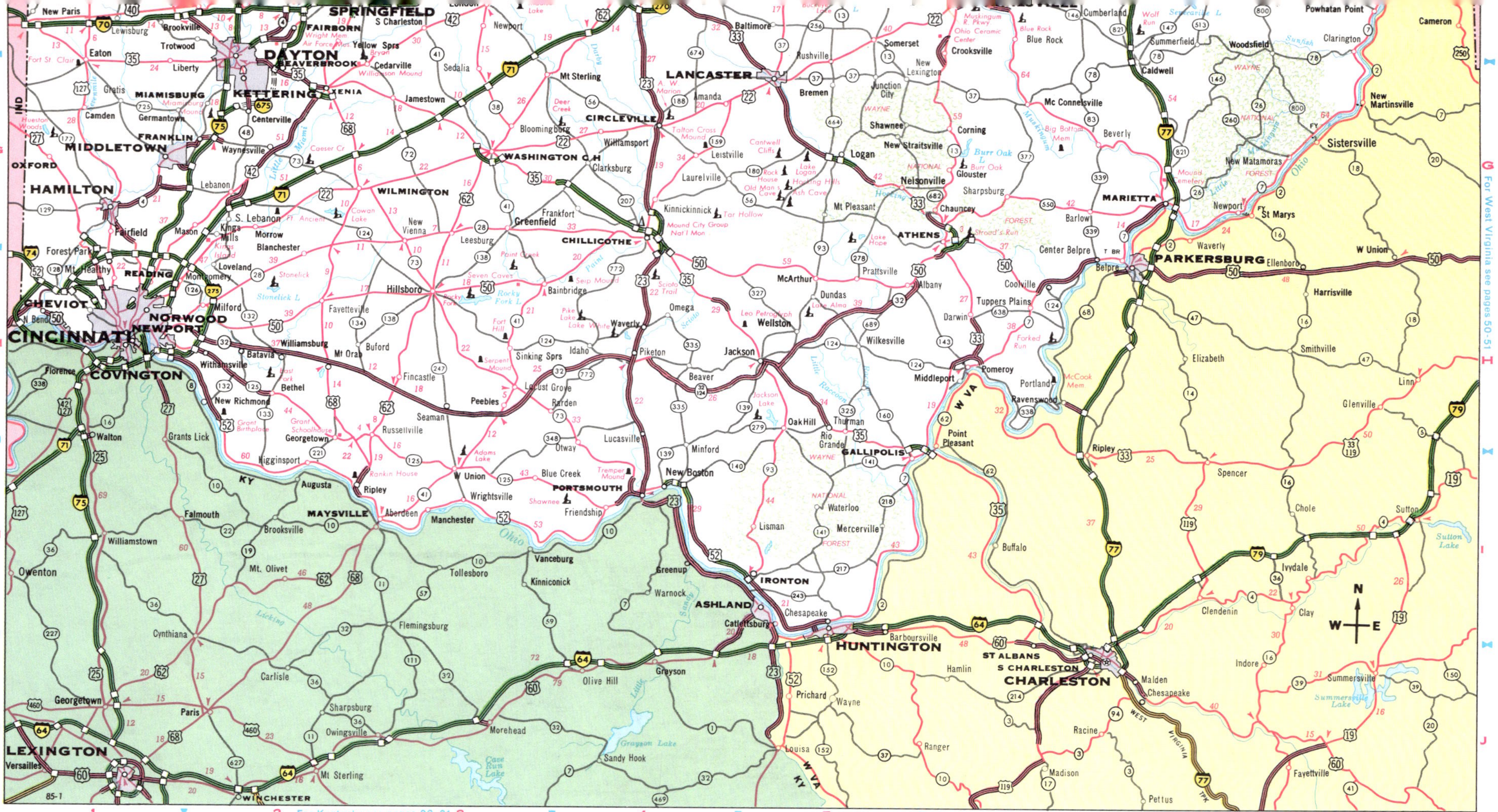

For Kentucky see pages 20-21

For West Virginia see pages 50-51

OHIO

Population: 10,797,624
(1980 Census)
Land Area: 41,004 Sq. Mi.
Capital: Columbus

Cities and Towns

OKLAHOMA

Population: 3,025,495
(1980 Census)
Land Area: 68,656 Sq. Mi.
Capital: Oklahoma City

Cities and Towns

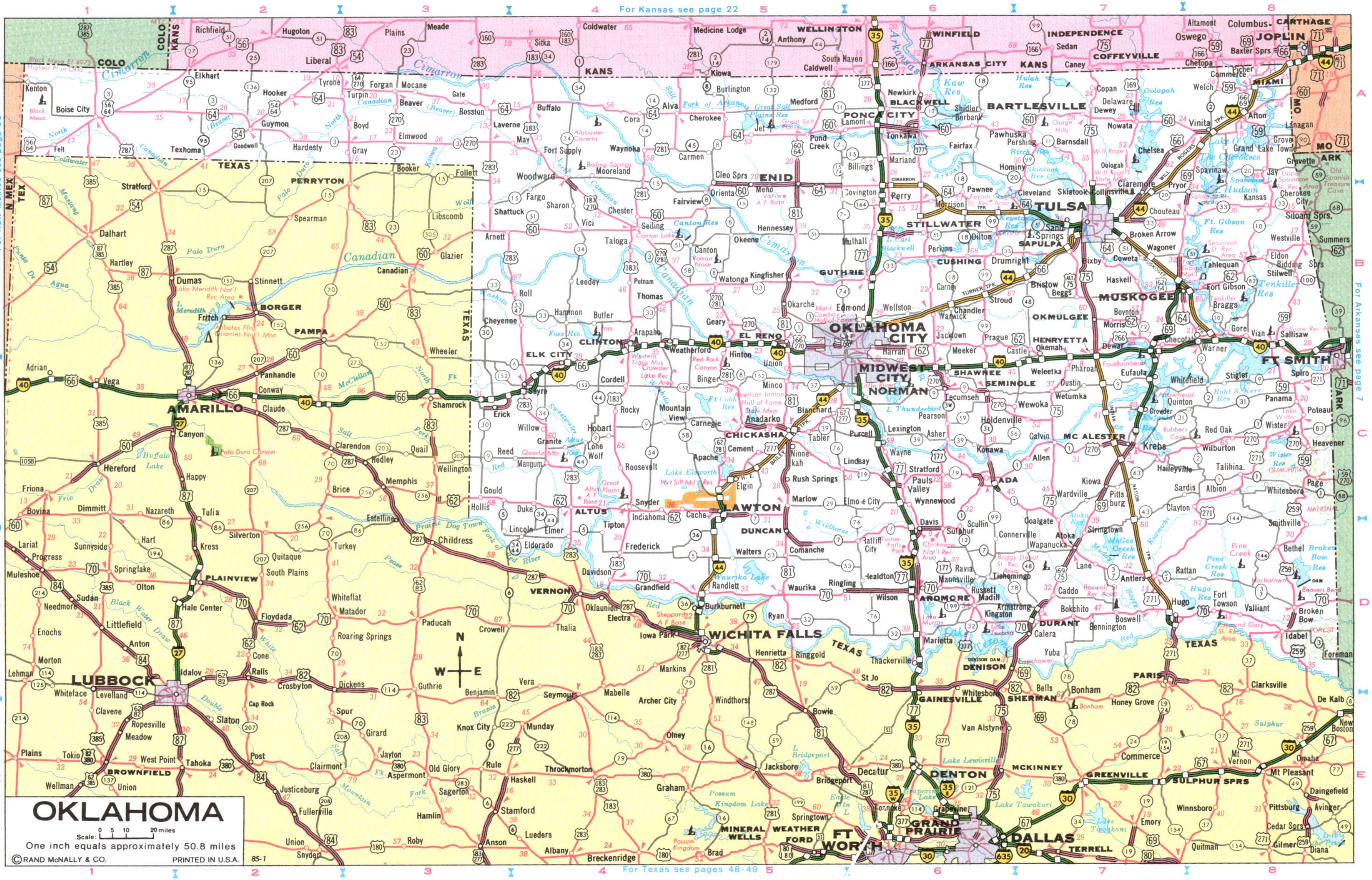

OREGON

Population: 2,633,149
(1980 Census)
Land Area: 96,187 Sq. Mi.
Capital: Salem

Cities and Towns

Albany........C-2
Ashland........F-2
Astoria........A-1
Athena........A-6
Baker........B-6
Bandon........D-1
Bay City........A-1
Bend........C-3
Bonneville........B-3
Brookings........F-1
Bunker Hill........D-1
Burns........D-5
Canby........B-2
Canyon City........C-5
Canyonville........E-2
Carlton........B-2
Cave Junction........F-1
Central Point........E-2
Chiloquin........E-3
Clatskanie........A-2
Condon........B-4
Coos Bay........D-1
Coquille........D-1
Corvallis........C-2
Cottage Grove........D-2
Dallas........B-2
Drain........D-2
Elgin........B-6
Enterprise........B-7
Estacada........B-3
Eugene........C-2
Florence........C-1
Forest Grove........B-2
Fossil........B-4
Four Corners........B-2
Garibaldi........A-1
Gladstone........B-3
Gold Beach........E-1
Grants Pass........E-2
Heppner........B-5
Hermiston........A-5
Hillsboro........B-2
Hood River........A-3
Junction City........C-2
Klamath Falls........F-3
La Grande........B-6
Lakeside........D-1
Lakeview........F-4
Lebanon........C-2
Lincoln City........B-1
McMinnville........B-2
Madras........C-4
Mapleton........C-1
Medford........E-2
Mill City........B-2
Milton-Freewater........A-6
Molalla........B-2
Myrtle Creek........E-2
Myrtle Point........D-1
Newberg........B-2
Newport........C-1
North Bend........D-1
Nyssa........C-7
Oakridge........D-2
Ontario........C-7
Oregon City........B-2
Pacific City........B-1
Pendleton........A-6
Philomath........C-2
Pilot Rock........B-5
Portland........B-2
Port Orford........E-1
Powers........E-1
Prineville........C-4
Rainier........A-2
Redmond........C-4
Reedsport........D-1
Roseburg........D-2
St. Helens........A-2
Salem........B-2
Sandy........B-3
Seaside........A-1
Silverton........B-2
Springfield........C-2
Stayton........B-2
Sutherlin........D-2
Sweet Home........C-2
The Dalles........B-4
Tigard........B-2
Tillamook........B-1
Toledo........C-1
Union........B-6
Vale........C-7
Vernonia........A-2
Waldport........C-1
Wallowa........A-7
Winston........D-2
Woodburn........B-2

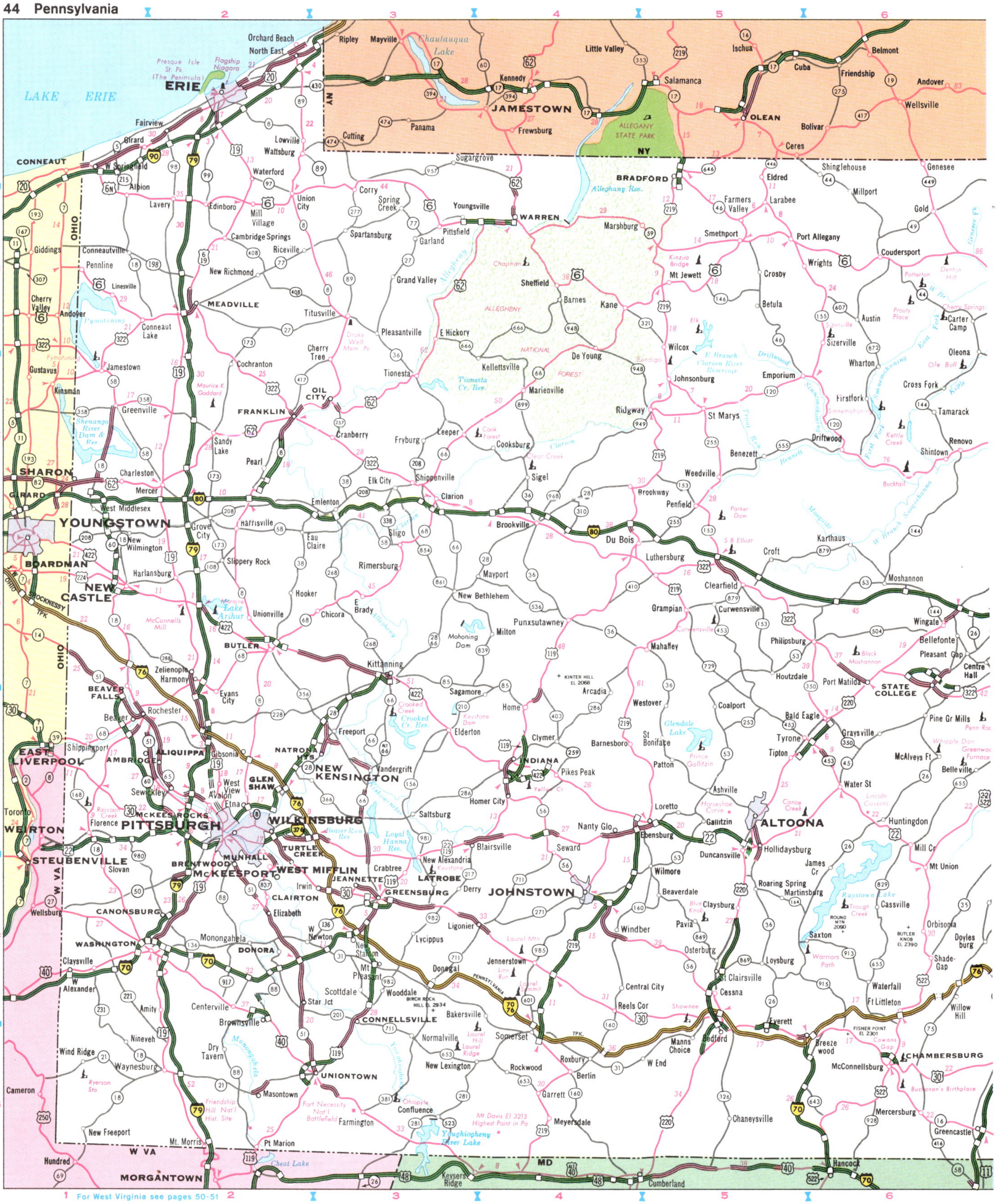

PENNSYLVANIA

Population: 11,864,751
(1980 Census)
Land Area: 44,892 Sq. Mi.
Capital: Harrisburg

Cities and Towns

Akron........F-9
Aliquippa........E-1
Allentown........E-11
Altoona........E-5
Ambler........F-11
Ambridge........E-2
Annville........F-9
Avis........C-7
Barnesboro........E-4
Beaver........E-1
Beaver Falls........D-1
Bedford........G-5
Bellefonte........D-6
Belleville........E-6
Berwick........D-9
Bethlehem........E-11
Blairsville........E-4
Bloomsburg........D-9
Boyertown........F-11
Bradford........A-5
Brentwood........F-2
Brookville........D-4
Brownsville........F-2
Butler........D-2
Cambridge Springs........B-2
Canton........B-8
Carbondale........B-11
Carlisle........F-7
Catawissa........D-9
Centerville........F-2
Centre Hall........D-6
Chambersburg........G-7
Chester........G-11
Clairton........F-2
Clarion........C-3
Clarks Summit........C-10
Clearfield........D-5
Coaldale........D-10
Coatesville........G-10
Collegeville........F-11
Columbia........F-9
Connellsville........F-3
Cornwall........F-9
Corry........B-3
Coudersport........B-6
Curwensville........D-5
Dallas........C-10
Danville........D-8
Darby........G-11
Dillsburg........F-8
Dowingtown........G-10
Doylestown........F-11
Du Bois........D-4
Duncannon........E-8
Easton........E-11
E. Stroudsburg........D-11
Ebensburg........E-5
Elizabethtown........F-9
Elysburg........D-9
Emporium........C-5
Ephrata........F-9
Erie........A-2
Etna........E-2
Everett........G-5
Fairview........A-2
Forest City........B-11
Ft. Washington........F-11
Franklin........C-2
Galeton........B-7
Gallitzin........E-5
Gettysburg........G-7
Girard........A-1
Glenshaw........E-2
Greensburg........F-3
Greenville........C-1
Grove City........D-2
Hamburg........E-10
Hanover........G-8
Harmony........D-2
Harrisburg........F-8
Haverford........G-11
Hazleton........D-10
Hershey........F-8
Hollidaysburg........E-5
Honesdale........B-11
Horsham........F-11
Hughesville........C-8
Huntingdon........E-6
Indiana........E-4
Jeannette........F-3
Jenkintown........F-11
Jersey Shore........C-7
Jim Thorpe........D-10
Johnsonburg........C-5
Johnstown........F-4
Kane........B-4
King of Prussia........F-11
Kingston........C-10
Kittanning........D-3
Kutztown........E-10
Lafayette Hill........F-11
Lancaster........F-9

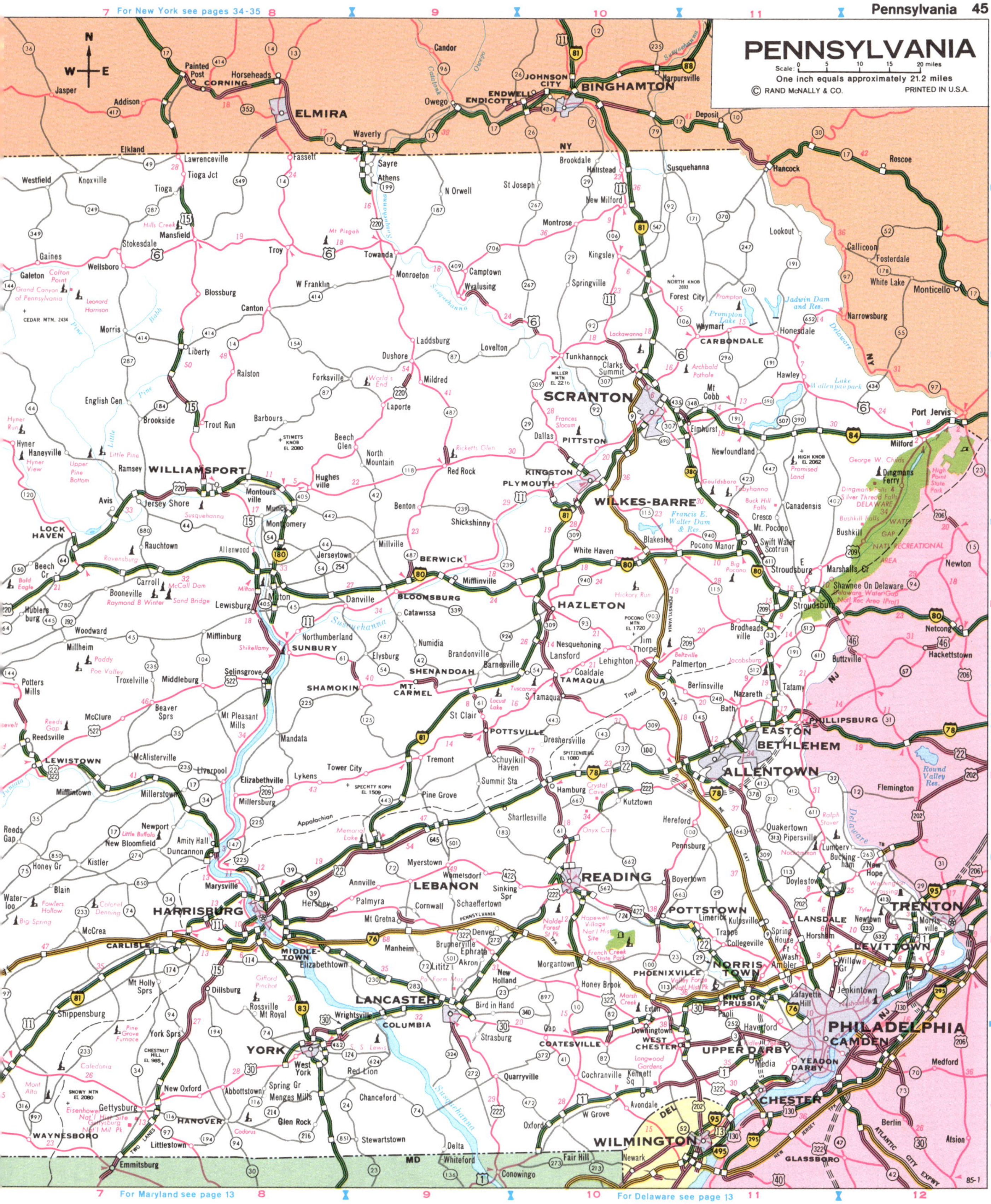

Lansdale F-11	Meadville B-2	Morrisville F-12	Norristown F-11	Pottstown F-10	Scranton C-10	Tamaqua D-10	Waynesboro G-7
Lansford D-10	Media G-11	Mt. Carmel D-9	Oil City C-3	Pottsville E-9	Selinsgrove D-8	Titusville B-3	Waynesburg G-2
Lebanon F-9	Mercer C-2	Muncy C-8	Oxford G-10	Punxsutawney D-4	Shamokin D-9	Towanda B-9	Wellsboro B-7
Lehighton D-10	Meyersdale G-4	Munhall E-2	Palmerton D-10	Quakertown E-11	Sharon C-1	Tower City E-9	West Chester G-11
Lewisburg D-8	Middleburg E-8	Myerstown F-9	Palmyra F-9	Reading F-10	Shenandoah D-9	Troy B-8	West Mifflin F-2
Lewistown E-7	Middletown F-8	Nanty Glo E-4	Patton E-5	Red Lion G-8	Shickshinny D-9	Tunkhannock C-10	W. Newton F-2
Ligonier F-3	Mifflinburg D-8	Nazareth E-11	Philadelphia G-11	Renovo C-6	Sinking Spr. F-10	Turtle Creek E-2	Wilkes-Barre C-10
Lock Haven D-7	Milford C-12	Nesquehoning D-10	Philipsburg D-6	Ridgway C-5	Smethport B-5	Tyrone E-5	Wilkinsburg E-2
McConnellsburg G-6	Millersburg E-8	New Castle D-1	Pine Grove E-9	Roaring Spring F-5	Somerset G-4	Union City B-2	Williamsport C-8
McKeesport F-2	Milton D-8	New Holland F-9	Pittsburgh E-2	Rochester E-2	Spring City F-11	Uniontown G-3	Willow Grove F-11
McKees Rocks E-2	Monongahela F-2	New Kensington E-3	Pittston C-10	St. Clair E-9	State College D-6	Upper Darby G-11	Windber F-4
Manheim F-9	Montgomery D-8	New Oxford G-8	Pleasant Gap D-6	St. Marys C-5	Stroudsburg D-11	Vandergrift E-3	Yeadon G-11
Mansfield B-8	Montoursville C-8	Newport E-7	Plymouth C-10	Sayre A-9	Sunbury D-8	Warren B-4	York G-8
Masontown G-2	Montrose B-10	Newtown F-12	Port Allegany B-5	Scottdale F-3	Susquehanna A-11	Washington F-1	Zelienople D-2

SOUTH DAKOTA

Population: 690,768
(1980 Census)
Land Area: 75,956 Sq. Mi.
Capital: Pierre

Cities and Towns

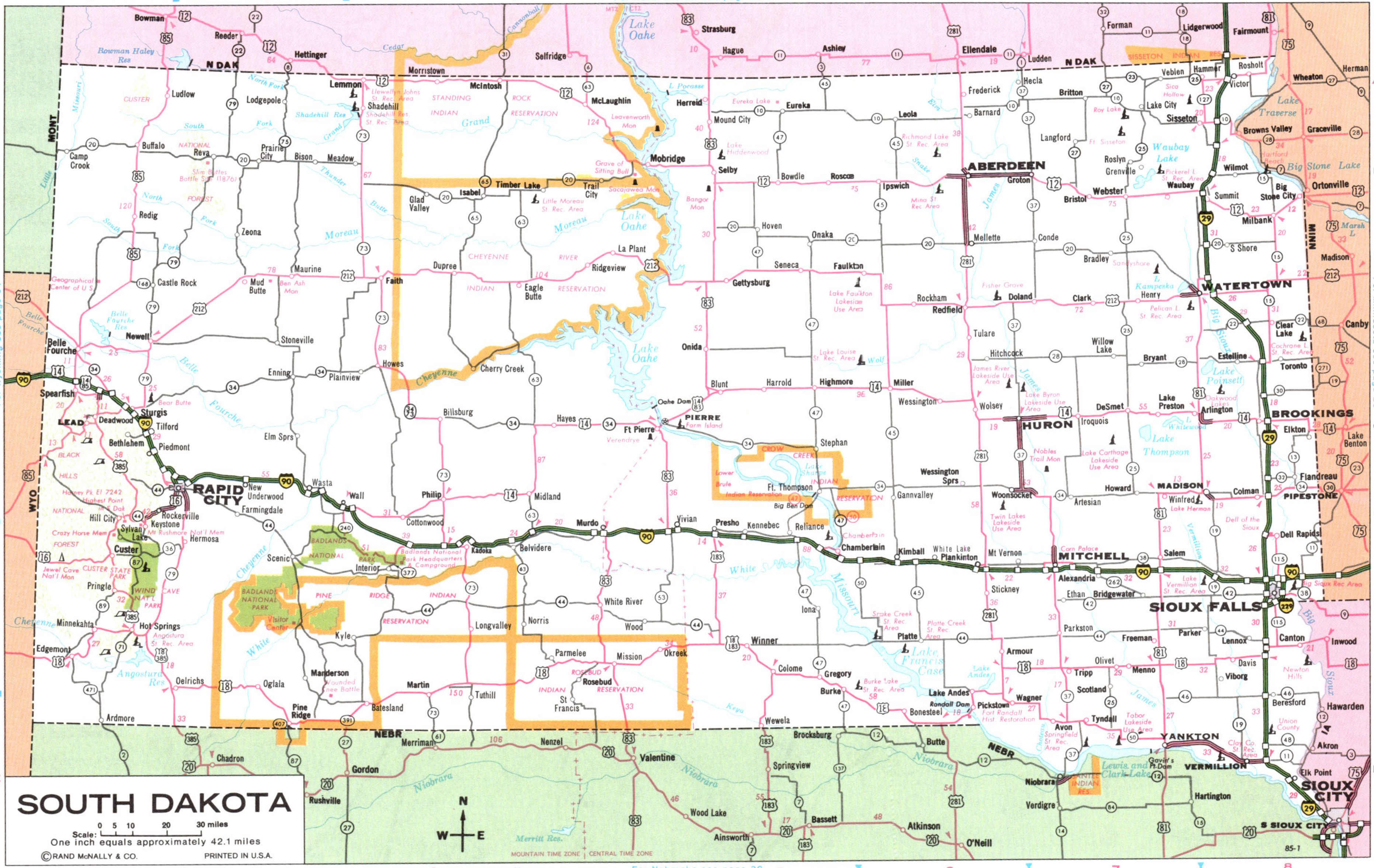

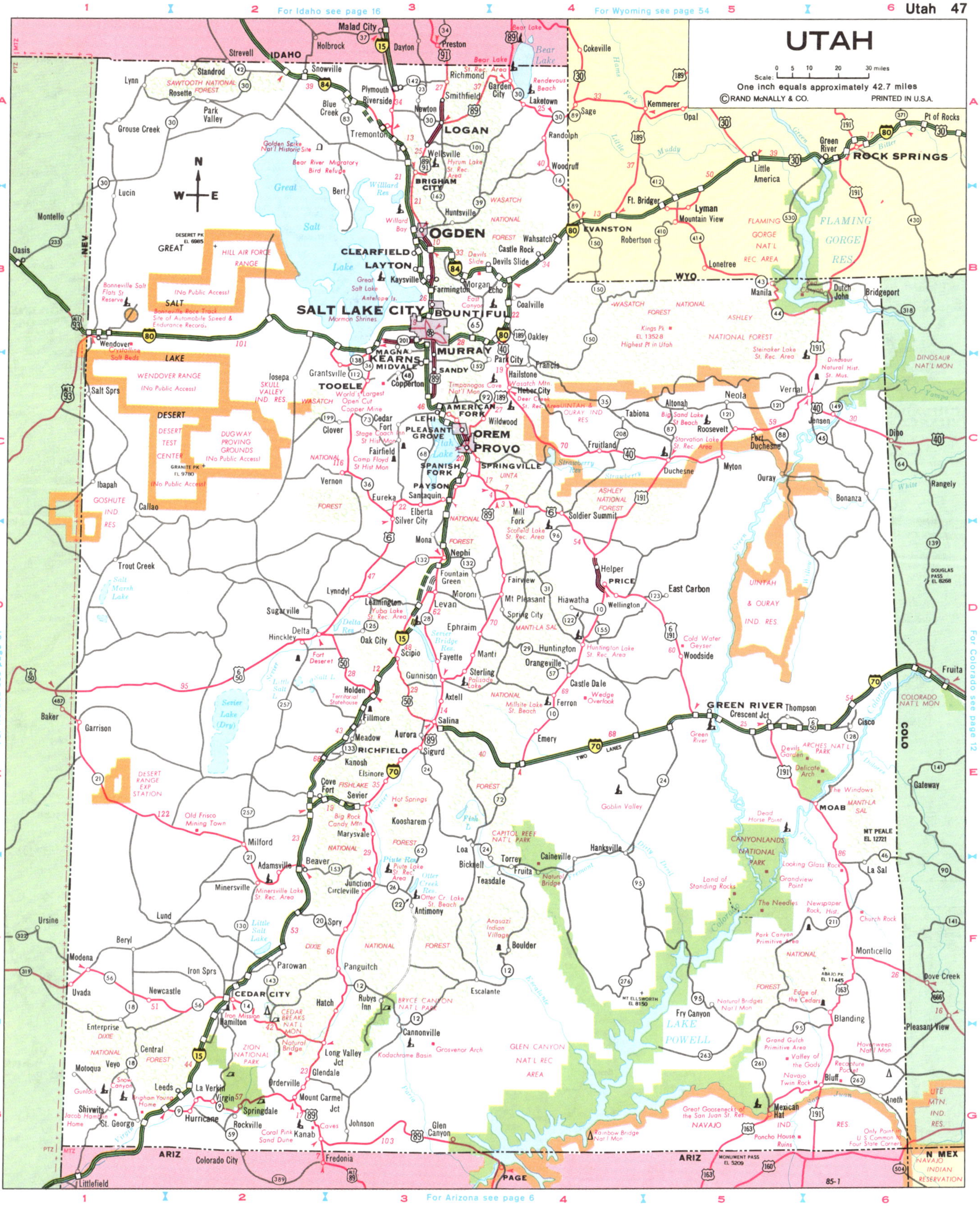

UTAH

Population: 1,461,037
(1980 Census)
Land Area: 82,076 Sq. Mi.
Capital: Salt Lake City

Cities and Towns

For New Mexico see page 36
For continuation see inset

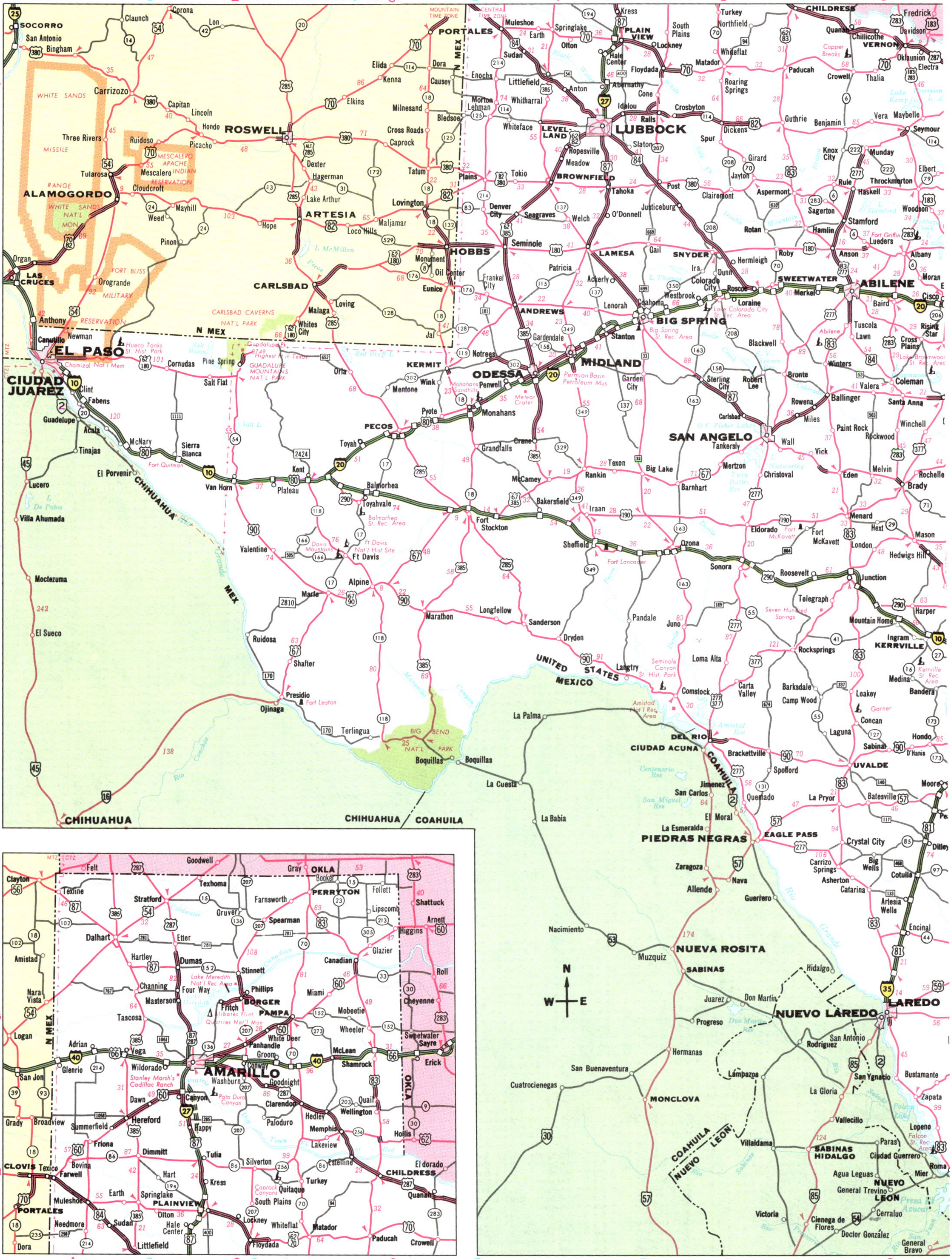

For continuation see main map
For Mexico see page 62

TEXAS

Population: 14,227,574
(1980 Census)
Land Area: 262,015 Sq. Mi.
Capital: Austin

Cities and Towns

For Ohio see pages 40-41

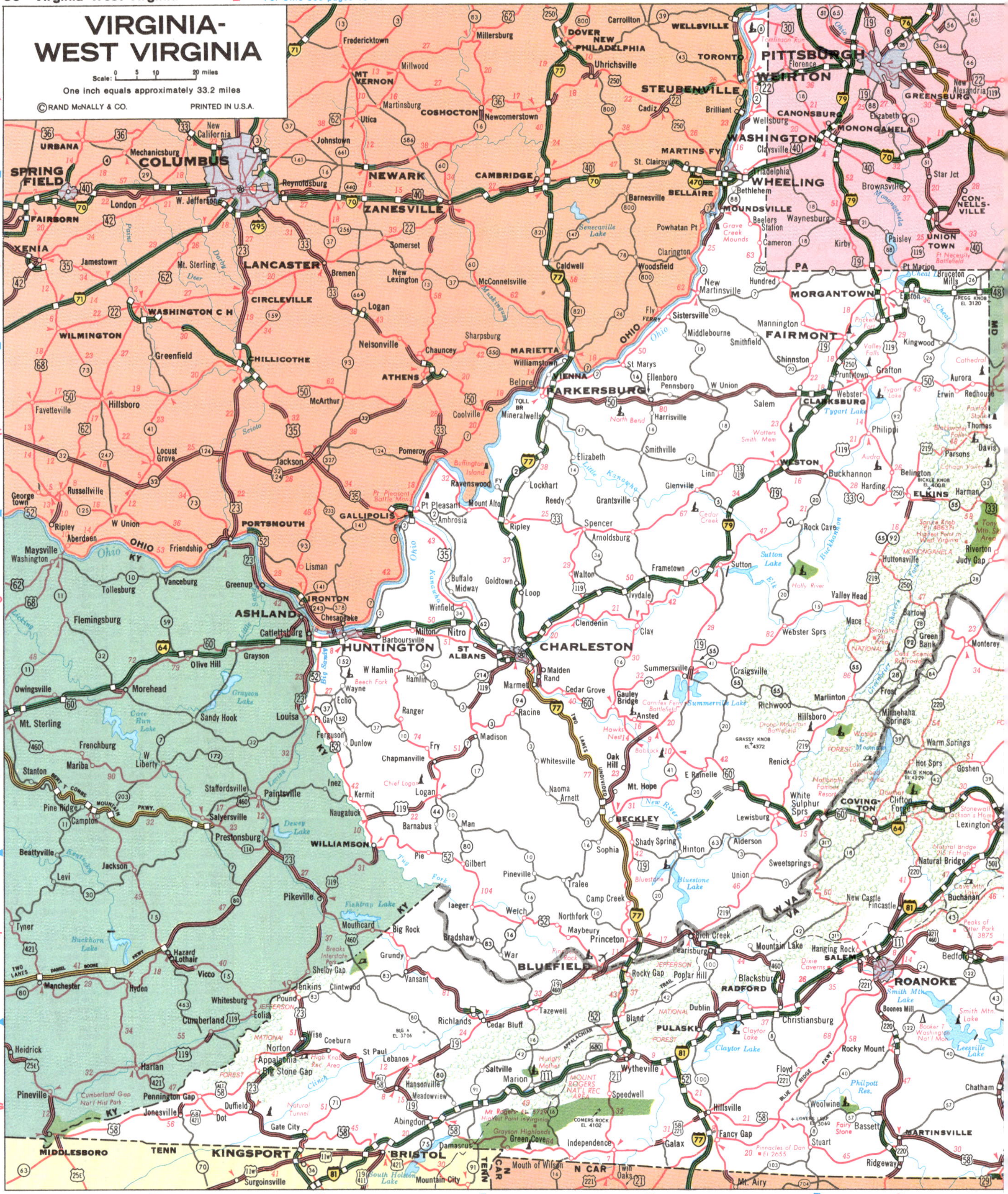

VIRGINIA

Population: 5,346,797
(1980 Census)
Land Area: 39,700 Sq. Mi.
Capital: Richmond

Cities and Towns

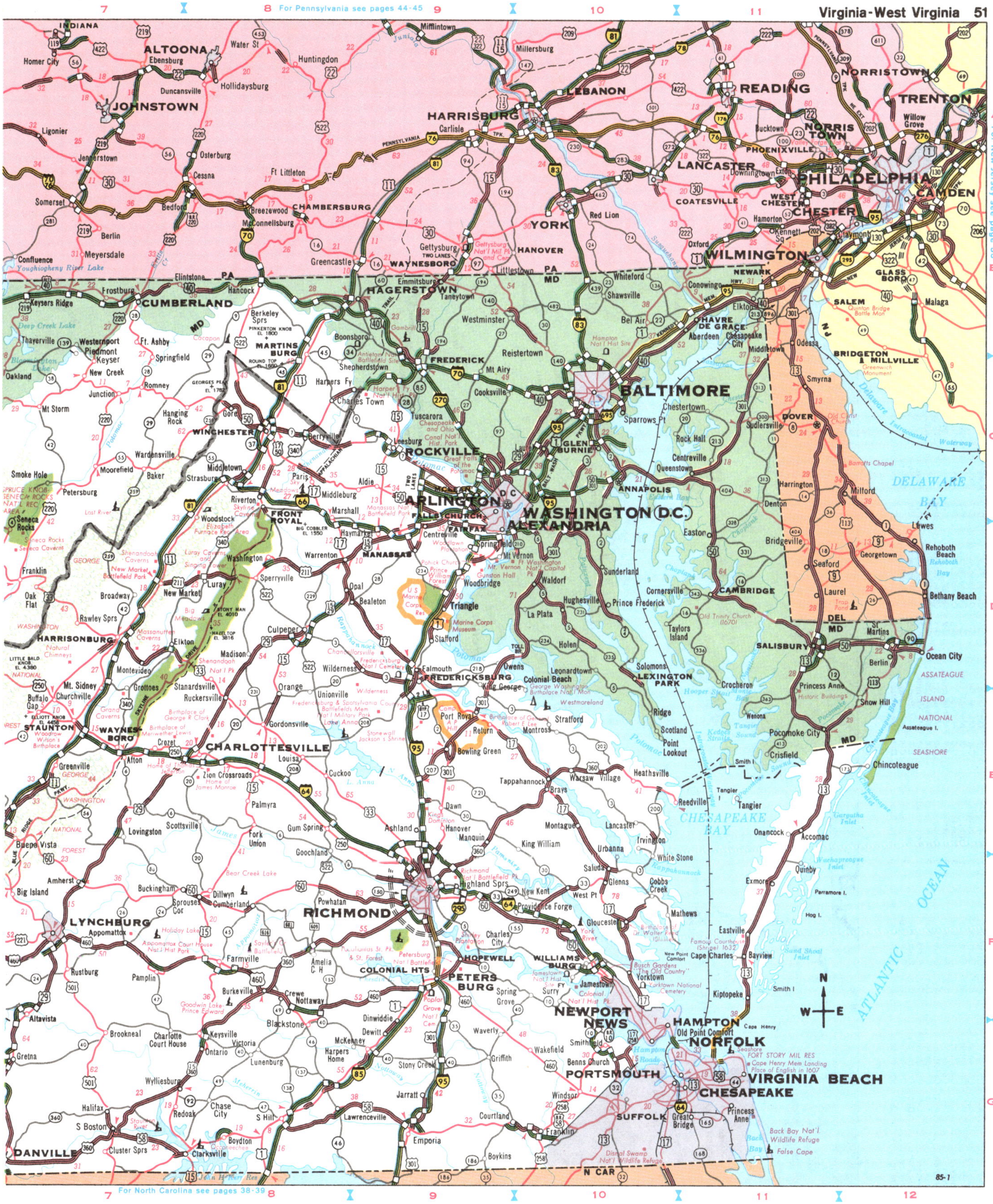

S. Hill........G-8	Winchester........C-8	Ansted........E-4	Clendenin........D-4	Kingwood........B-6	Nitro........D-3	Ripley........D-4	War........F-4
Staunton........E-7	Woodbridge........D-9	Barboursville........D-3	Elizabeth........C-4	Lewisburg........E-5	Oak Hill........E-4	Romney........C-7	Wayne........E-3
Strasburg........C-8	Woodstock........C-8	Barnabus........E-3	Elkins........C-6	Logan........E-3	Parkersburg........C-4	St. Albans........D-3	Webster Sprs........D-5
Suffolk........G-10	Wytheville........G-4	Beckley........E-4	Fairmont........B-6	Madison........E-3	Parsons........C-6	St. Marys........C-4	Weirton........A-5
Tangier........E-11		Berkeley Sprs........B-8	Franklin........D-7	Mannington........B-5	Pennsboro........C-5	Salem........C-5	Welch........F-4
Tappahannock........E-10	**WEST VIRGINIA**	Bethlehem........B-5	Gilbert........F-3	Marlinton........E-6	Petersburg........C-7	Shinnston........C-5	Wellsburg........A-5
Tazewell........F-4	Population: 1,950,258	Bluefield........F-4	Glenville........C-5	Marmet........E-4	Philippi........C-6	Spencer........D-4	Weston........C-5
Victoria........G-8	(1980 Census)	Bradshaw........F-3	Grafton........C-6	Martinsburg........C-8	Piedmont........B-7	Summersville........D-5	W. Union........C-5
Virginia Beach........G-11	Land Area: 24,124 Sq. Mi.	Buckhannon........C-6	Grantsville........C-4	Milton........D-3	Pineville........F-4	Sutton........D-5	Wheeling........A-5
Warm Springs........E-6	Capital: Charleston	Chapmanville........E-3	Hamlin........D-3	Moorefield........C-7	Pt. Pleasant........C-3	Sweetsprings........F-5	White Sulphur
Waverly........G-9		Charleston........D-4	Harpers Fy........C-9	Morgantown........B-6	Princeton........F-4	Triadelphia........A-5	Sprs........E-5
Waynesboro........E-7	**Cities and Towns**	Charles Town........C-8	Hinton........E-5	Moundsville........B-5	Rand........D-4	Union........F-5	Whitesville........E-4
White Stone........F-10		Clarksburg........C-5	Huntington........D-3	Mt. Hope........E-4	Ravenswood........C-4	Valley Head........D-6	Williamson........E-3
Williamsburg........F-10	Alderson........E-5	Clay........D-4	Keyser........C-7	New Martinsville........B-5	Richwood........E-5	Vienna........C-4	Winfield........D-3

WASHINGTON

Population: 4,132,204
(1980 Census)
Land Area: 66,512 Sq. Mi.
Capital: Olympia

Cities and Towns

For British Columbia see page 56

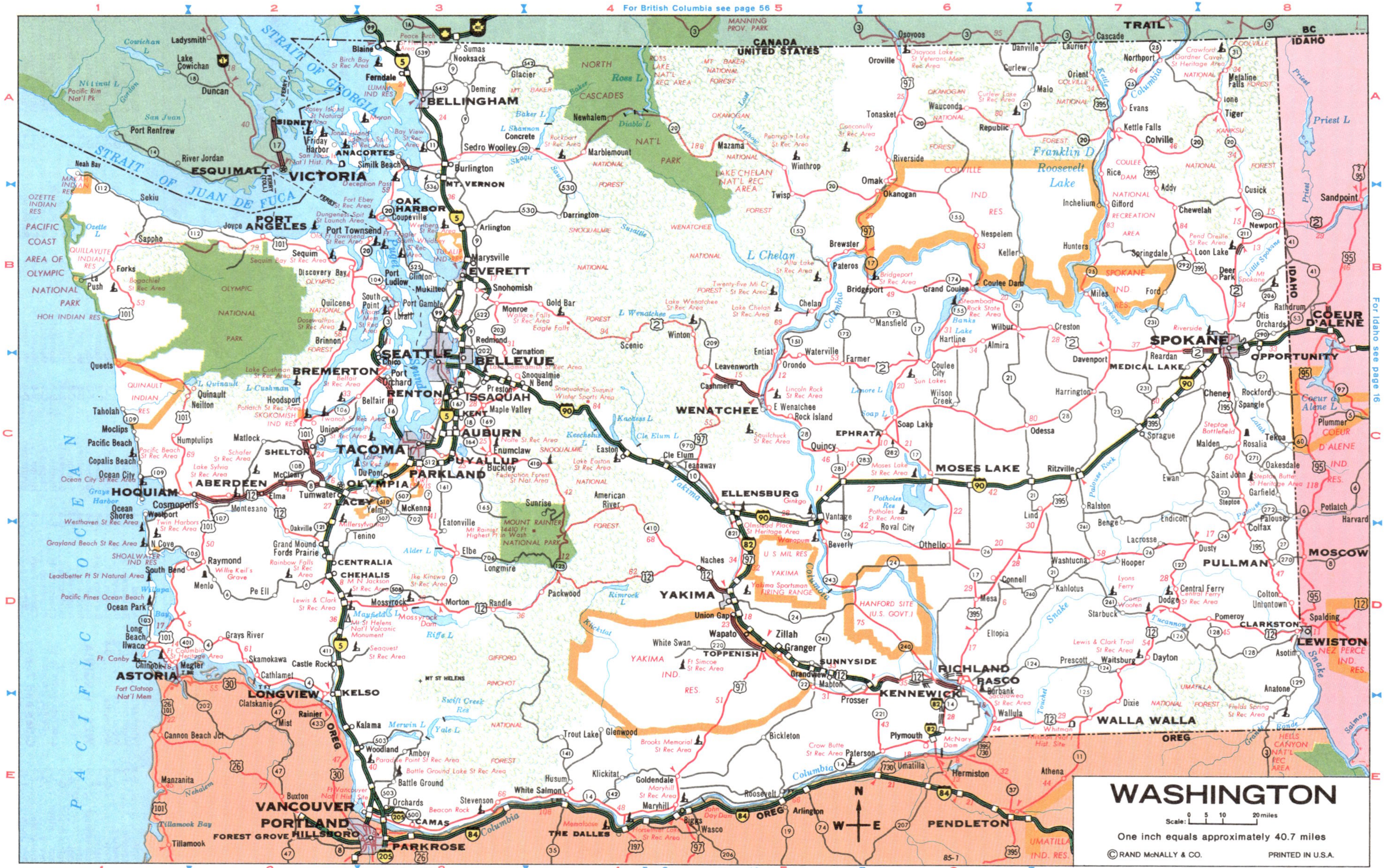

For Idaho see page 16

For Oregon see page 43

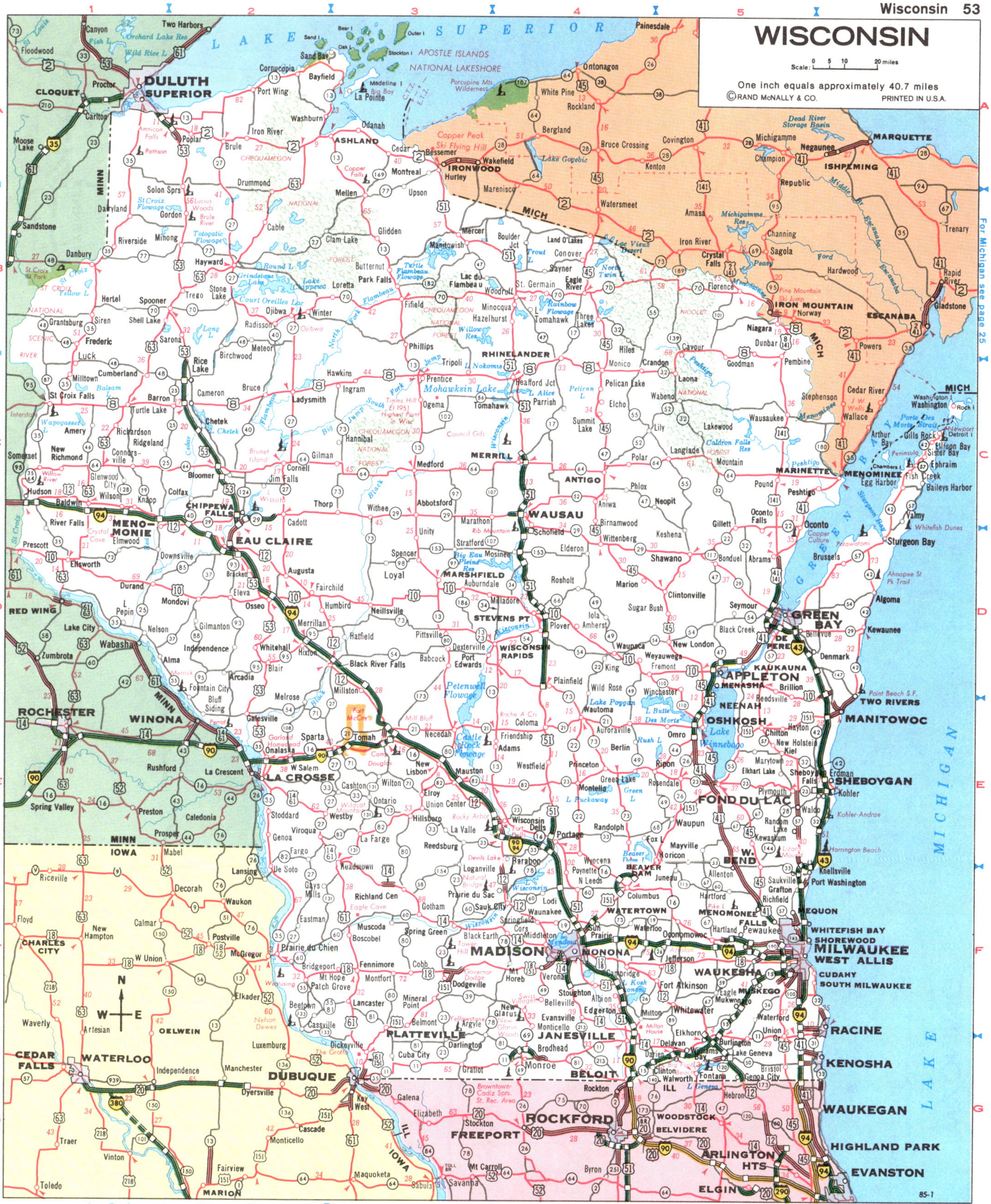

WISCONSIN

Population: 4,705,642
(1980 Census)
Land Area: 54,424 Sq. Mi.
Capital: Madison

Cities and Towns

Alma................D-1
Antigo..............C-4
Appleton............D-5
Ashland.............A-3
Augusta.............D-2
Baraboo.............E 4
Barron..............C-2
Bayfield............A-3
Beaver Dam..........E-5
Beloit..............G-4
Black River Falls...D-3
Chilton.............E-5
Chippewa Falls......C-2
Crandon.............C-4
Darlington..........G-3
Dodgeville..........F-3
Durand..............D-1
Eagle...............F-5
Eagle River.........B-4
Eau Claire..........D-2
Elkhorn.............G-5
Ellsworth...........D-1
Elroy...............E-3
Florence............B-5
Fond Du Lac.........E-5
Grantsburg..........B-1
Green Bay...........D-5
Green Lake..........E-4
Hayward.............B-2
Hudson..............C-1
Hurley..............A-3
Janesville..........G-4
Jefferson...........F-5
Juneau..............F-5
Kaukauna............D-5
Kenosha.............G-6
Keshena.............D-5
Kewaunee............D-6
La Crosse...........E-2
Ladysmith...........C-2
Lancaster...........F-3
Madison.............F-4
Manitowoc...........E-6
Marinette...........C-6
Marshfield..........D-3
Mauston.............E-3
Medford.............C-3
Menasha.............D-5
Menomonee Falls.....F-5
Menomonie...........D-1
Mequon..............F-5
Merrill.............C-4
Milwaukee...........F-5
Monona..............F-4
Monroe..............G-4
Montello............E-4
Muskego.............F-5
Neillsville.........D-3
Oconto..............C-5
Oshkosh.............E-5
Park Falls..........B-3
Phillips............B-3
Portage.............E-4
Port Edwards........D-3
Port Washington.....F-6
Prairie du Chien....F-2
Racine..............F-6
Rhinelander.........B-4
Rice Lake...........C-2
Richland Cen........F-3
Ripon...............E-5
Shawano.............D-5
Sheboygan...........E-6
Shorewood...........F-6
Sparta..............E-3
Spooner.............B-1
Spring Green........F-3
Stevens Pt..........D-4
Sturgeon Bay........D-6
Superior............A-1
Tomah...............E-3
Tomahawk............C-4
Two Rivers..........E-6
Viroqua.............E-2
Washburn............A-2
Watertown...........F-5
Waukesha............F-5
Waupaca.............D-4
Wausau..............C-4
Wautoma.............E-4
West Allis..........F-5
W. Bend.............E-5
Whitefish Bay.......F-5
Whitehall...........D-2
Wisconsin Dells.....E-4
Wisconsin Rapids....D-4

WYOMING

Population: 469,557
(1980 Census)
Land Area: 96,988 Sq. Mi.
Capital: Cheyenne

Cities and Towns

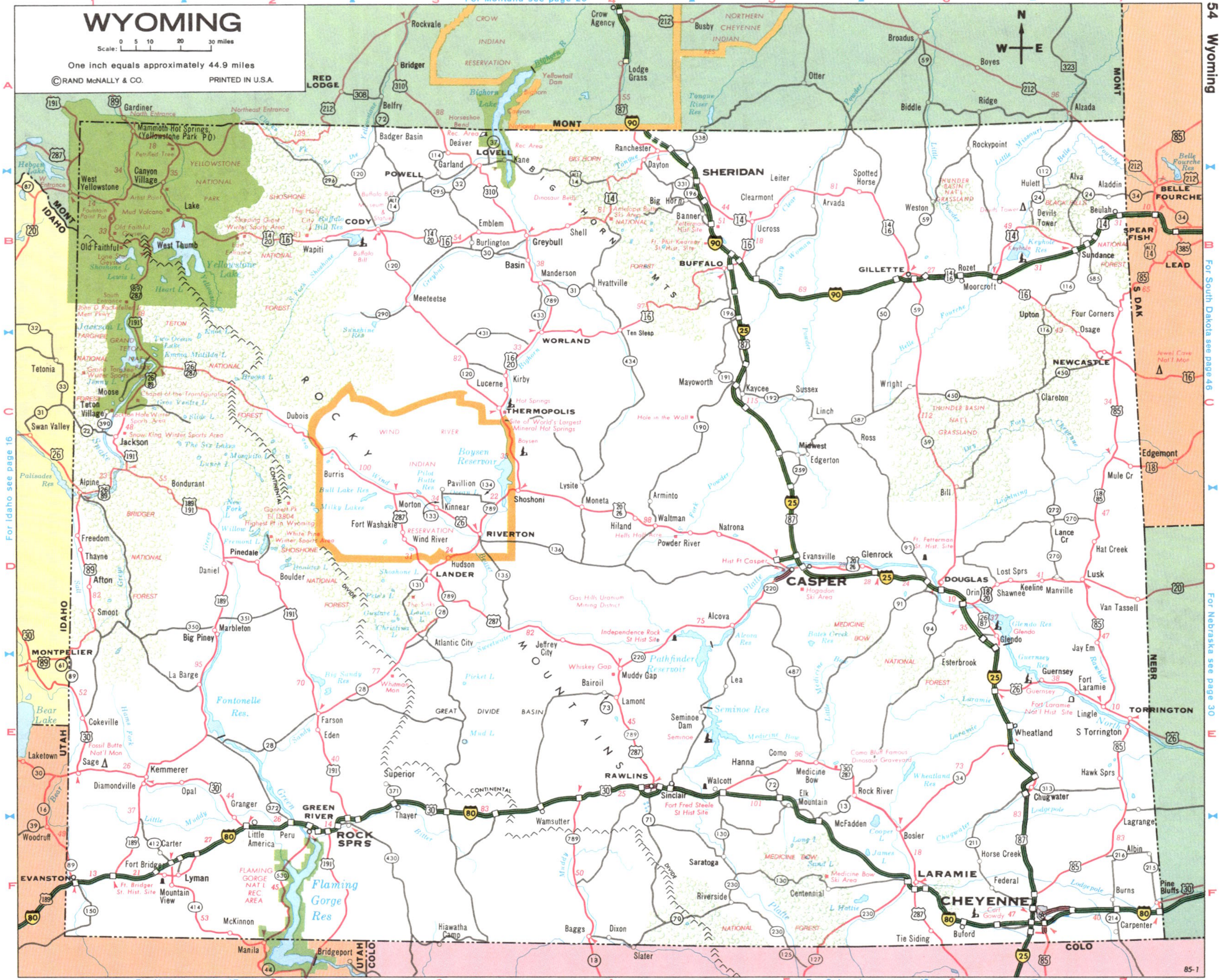

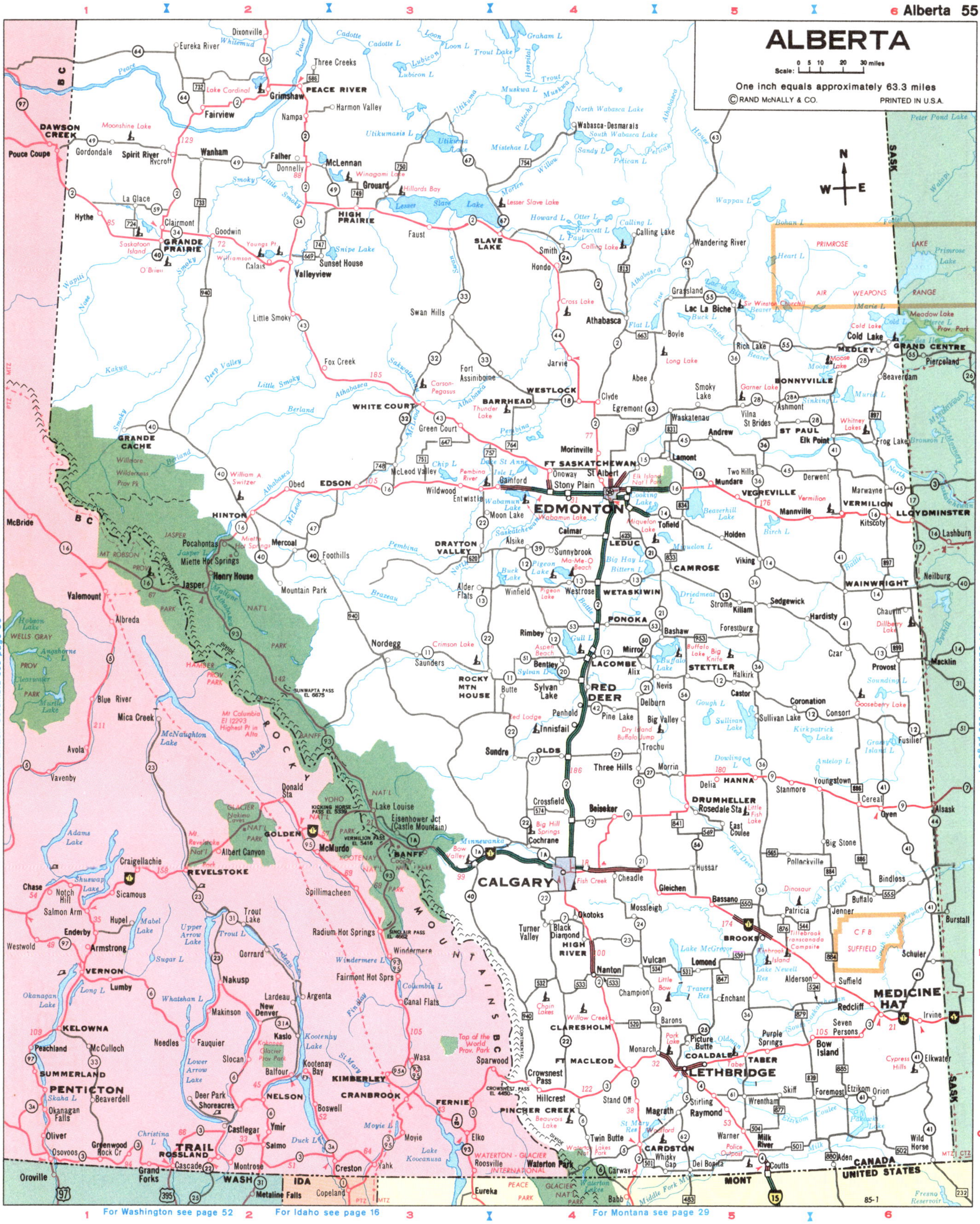

ALBERTA

Population: 2,237,724
(1981 Estimate)
Land Area: 255,285 Sq. Mi.
Capital: Edmonton

Cities and Towns

British Columbia

Population: 2,744,467
(1981 Estimate)
Land Area: 366,255 Sq. Mi.
Capital: Victoria

Cities and Towns

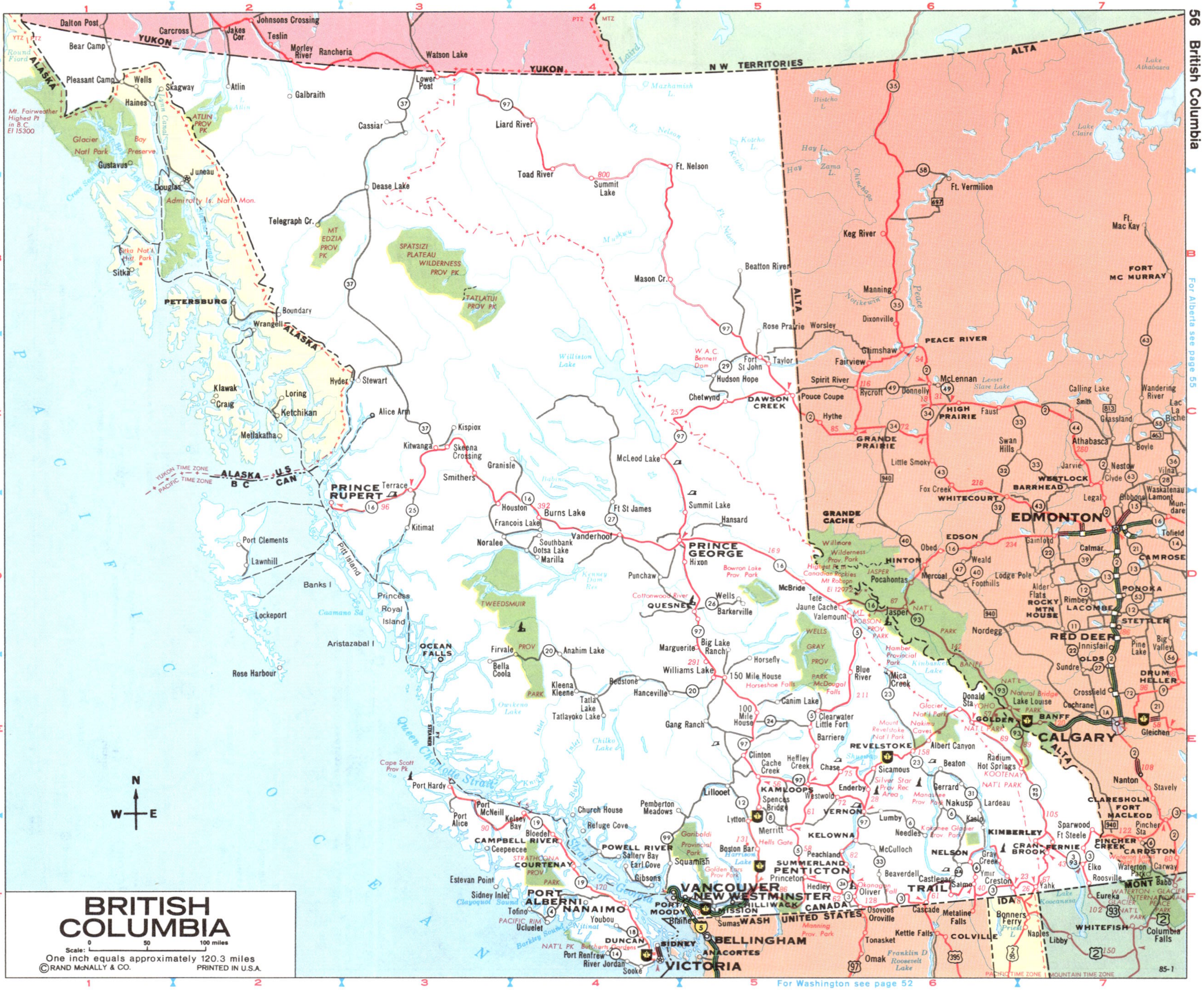

MANITOBA

Population: 1,026,241
(1981 Estimate)
Land Area: 251,000 Sq. Mi.
Capital: Winnipeg

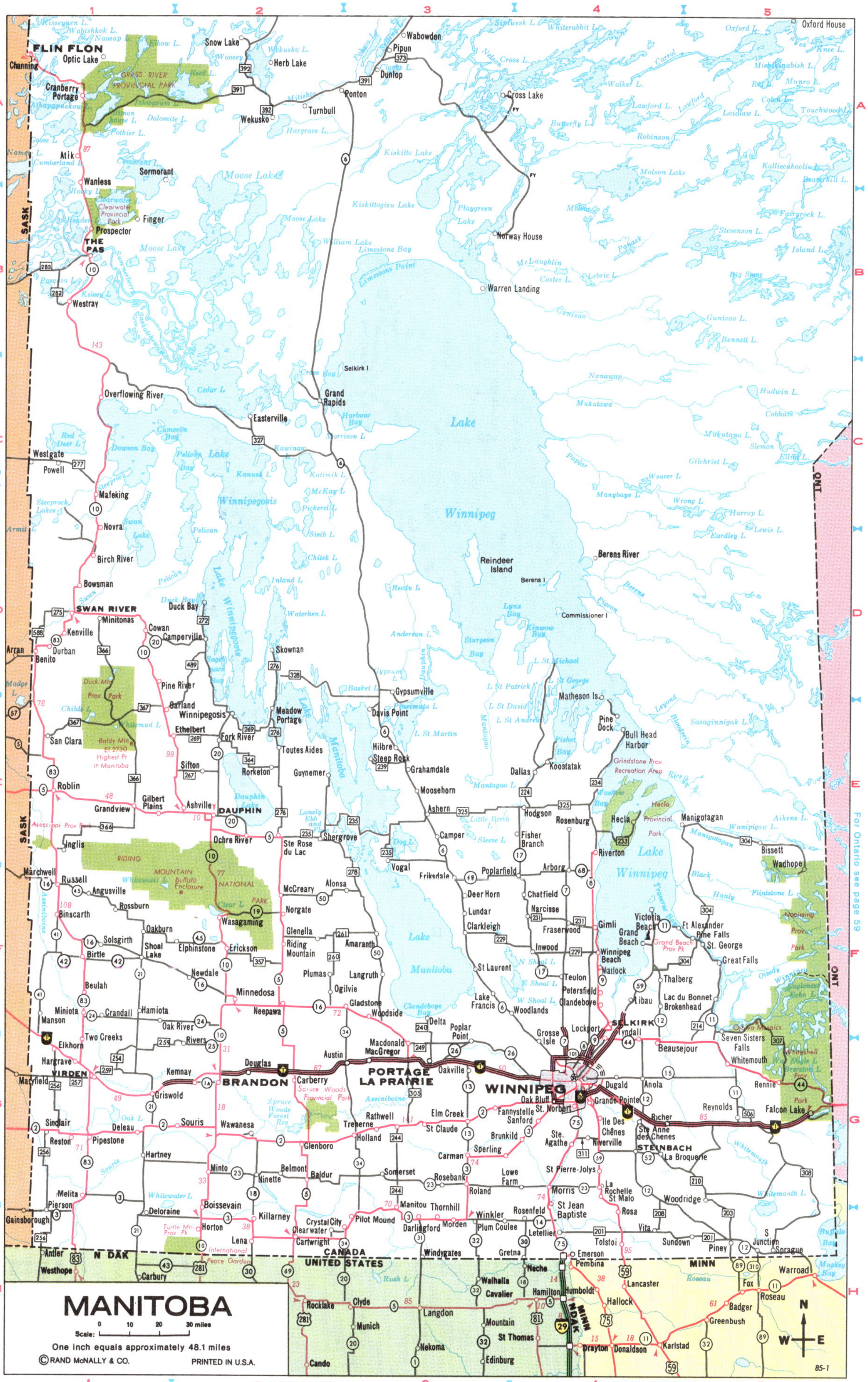

Cities and Towns

NEW BRUNSWICK

Population: 696,403
(1981 Estimate)
Land Area: 28,354 Sq. Mi.
Capital: Fredericton

Cities and Towns

NOVA SCOTIA

Population: 847,442
(1981 Estimate)
Land Area: 21,425 Sq. Mi.
Capital: Halifax

Cities and Towns

PRINCE EDWARD ISLAND

Population: 122,506
(1981 Estimate)
Land Area: 2,184 Sq. Mi.
Capital: Charlottetown

Cities and Towns

NEWFOUNDLAND

Population: 567,681
(1981 Estimate)
Land Area: 156,185 Sq. Mi.
Capital: St. John's

Cities and Towns

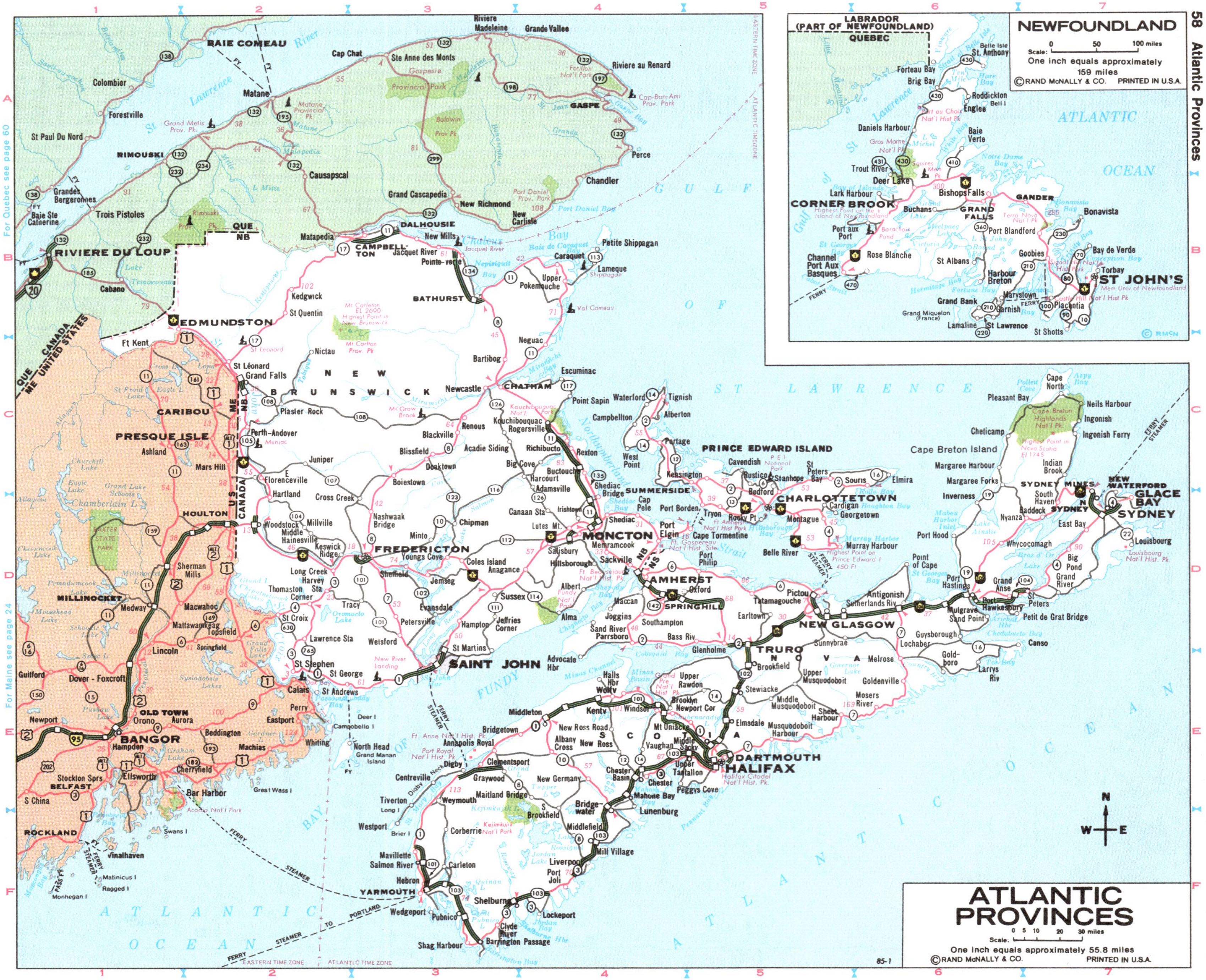

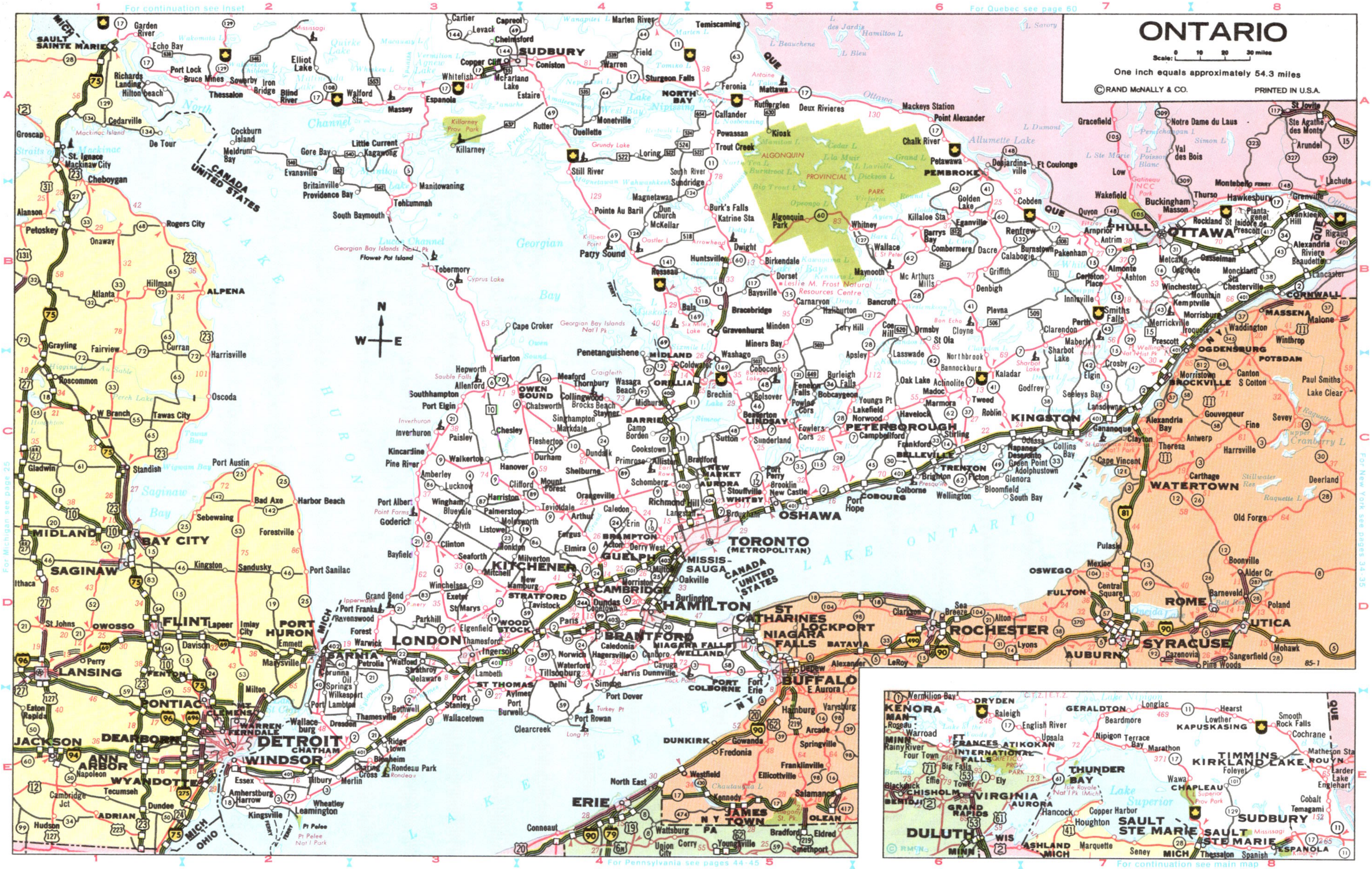

ONTARIO

Population: 8,625,107
(1981 Estimate)
Land Area: 412,582 Sq. Mi.
Capital: Toronto

Cities and Towns

QUEBEC

Population: 6,438,403
(1981 Estimate)
Land Area: 594,860 Sq. Mi.
Capital: Quebec

Cities and Towns

Acton Vale	E-4
Alma	B-4
Amos	A-2
Asbestos	E-4
Baie Comeau	A-7
Baie St. Paul	C-5
Beauport	D-5
Bedford	F-3
Buckingham	E-1
Cabano	C-7
Cap de la Madeleine	D-3
Cap St. Ignace	D-5
Causapscal	F-6
Chambord	B-4
Charlemagne	E-3
Châteauguay	F-3
Chicoutimi	B-5
Coaticook	F-4
Cookshire	F-4
Disraeli	E-5
Donnacona	D-4
Dorion-Vaudreuil	F-2
Drummondville	E-4
E. Angus	F-4
Farnham	F-3
Ferme Neuve	D-1
Gatineau	D-1
Granby	F-3
Grand' Mere	D-3
Hébertville	B-5
Hull	E-1
Huntingdon	F-2
Iberville	F-3
Joliette	E-3
Jonquiere	B-5
Knowlton	F-4
La Baie	B-5
Lac Mégantic	E-5
La Guadeloupe	E-5
La Malbaie	C-6
Laprairie	F-3
L'Ascension	D-2
La Tuque	C-3
Laurentides	E-2
Lennoxville	F-4
Levis	D-5
Loretteville	D-5
Magog	F-4
Maniwaki	D-1
Marieville	F-3
Matane	F-6
Mont Laurier	D-1
Montreal	E-3
Montreal Nord	E-3
Pierreville	E-3
Plessisville	E-4
Pointe Claire	F-2
Portneuf	D-4
Princeville	E-4
Quebec	D-5
Rimouski	B-7
Rivière Bleue	C-7
Rivière du Loup	C-6
Roberval	B-4
Ste. Agathe des Monts	E-2
Ste. Anne de Beaupré	D-5
Ste. Claire	D-5
Ste. Marie	D-5
Ste. Martine	F-2
St. Felicien	A-4
St. Ferdinand	E-4
St. Georges de Champlain	D-4
St. Hyacinthe	E-3
St. Jean Port Joli	C-6
St. Jean-Sur-Richelieu	F-3
St. Jerome	E-2
St. Lambert	F-3
St. Michel des Saints	D-2
St. Pascal	C-6
St. Raymond	D-4
St. Tite	D-4
St. Tite des Capes	C-5
Salaberry-de-Valleyfield	F-2
Scotstown	F-5
Scott Jct.	D-5
Shawinigan	D-3
Sherbrooke	F-4
Sorel	E-3
Thetford Mines	E-5
Trois Rivieres	D-4
Vallée Jonction	D-5
Victoriaville	E-4
Waterloo	F-4
Westmount	F-3
Windsor	E-4

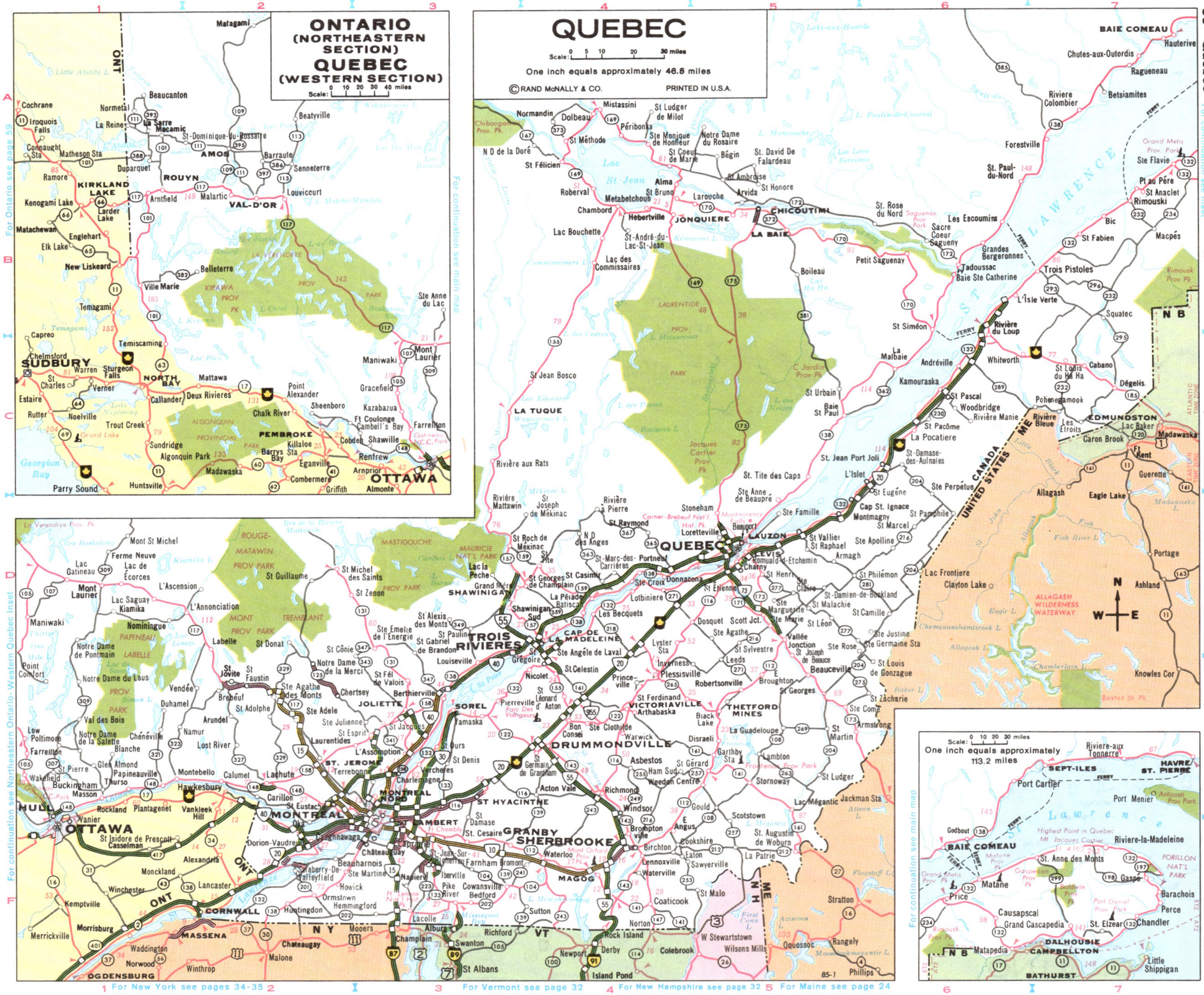

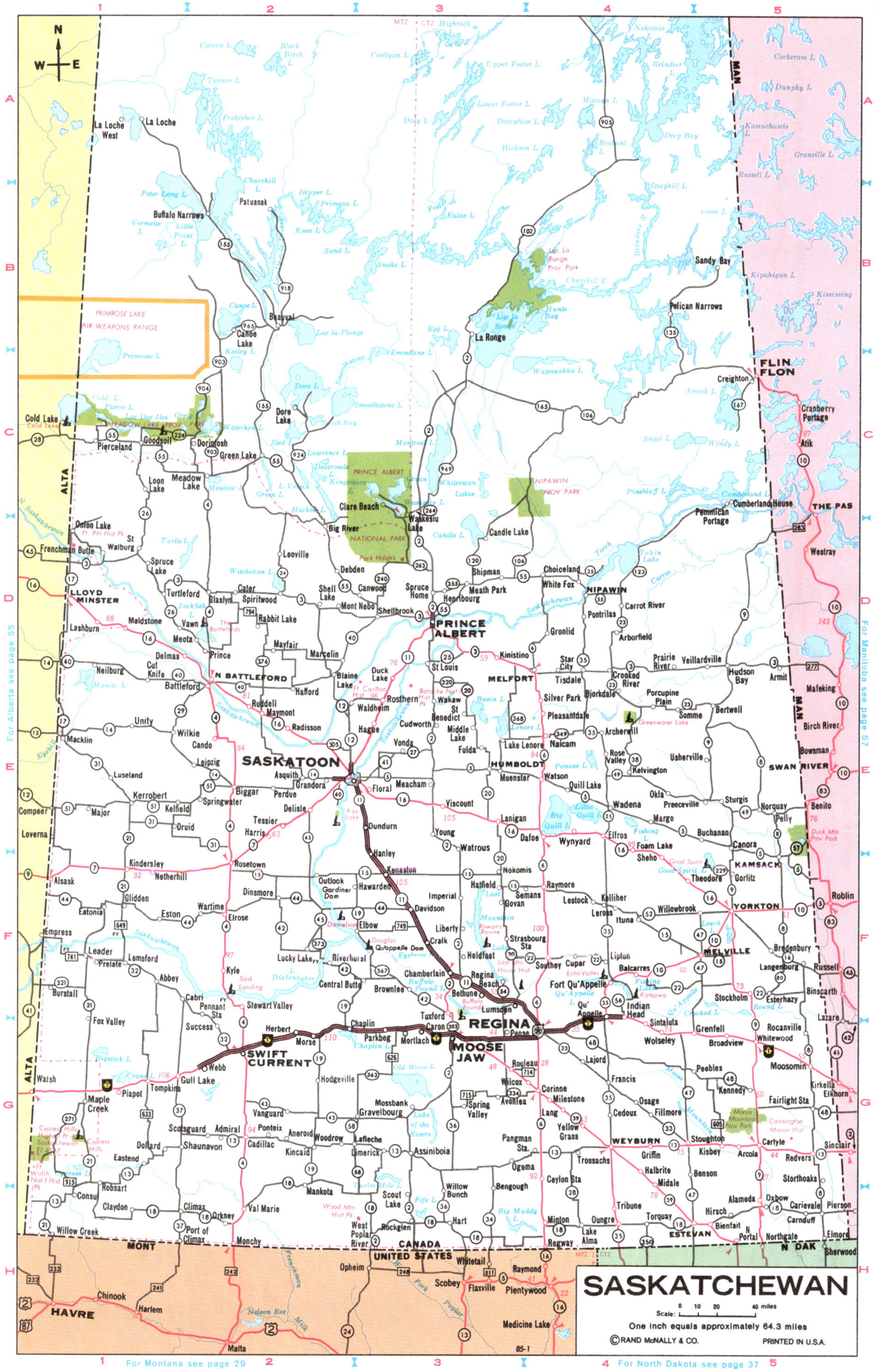

SASKATCHEWAN

Population: 968,313
(1981 Estimate)
Land Area: 251,700 Sq. Mi.
Capital: Regina

Cities and Towns

Abbey.............F-1
Alameda...........H-5
Alsask............F-1
Arborfield........D-4
Archerwill........E-4
Arcola............G-5
Assiniboia........G-3
Avonlea...........G-3
Balcarres.........F-4
Battleford........E-2
Bengough..........H-3
Bienfait..........H-5
Bethune...........F-3
Biggar............E-2
Big River.........C-2
Blaine Lake.......D-2
Bredenbury........F-5
Broadview.........G-5
Buchanan..........E-4
Cabri.............F-1
Canora............E-5
Carievale.........H-5
Carlyle...........G-5
Carnduff..........H-5
Carrot River......D-4
Central Butte.....F-3
Choiceland........D-4
Climax............H-1
Craik.............F-3
Cudworth..........E-3
Cupar.............F-4
Cut Knife.........D-1
Davidson..........F-3
Duck Lake.........D-3
Eastend...........G-1
Eatonia...........F-1
Elrose............F-2
Esterhazy.........F-5
Estevan...........H-4
Eston.............F-1
Fillmore..........G-4
Foam Lake.........E-4
Fort Qu'Appelle....F-4
Fox Valley........F-1
Govan.............F-3
Gravelbourg.......G-3
Grenfell..........G-5
Gull Lake.........G-1
Hafford...........E-2
Herbert...........G-2
Holdfast..........F-3
Hudson Bay........D-5
Humboldt..........E-3
Imperial..........F-3
Indian Head.......G-4
Ituna.............F-4
Kamsack...........F-5
Kelvington........E-4
Kenaston..........F-3
Kennedy...........G-5
Kerrobert.........E-1
Kindersley........F-1
Kinistino.........D-3
Lafléche..........G-2
Lang..............G-4
Langenburg........F-5
Lanigan...........E-3
Lashburn..........D-1
Leader............F-1
Leoville..........D-2
Lloydminster......D-1
Lumsden...........F-3
Luseland..........E-1
Macklin...........E-1
Maidstone.........D-1
Maple Creek.......G-1
Margo.............E-4
Meadow Lake.......C-2
Melfort...........D-4
Melville..........F-5
Midale............G-4
Moose Jaw.........G-3
Moosomin..........G-5
Morse.............G-2
Mossbank..........G-3
Naicam............E-4
Nipawin...........D-4
Norquay...........E-5
N. Battleford.....D-2
Outlook...........F-2
Pense.............G-3
Piapot............G-1
Ponteix...........G-2
Porcupine Plain....E-4
Preeceville.......E-5
Prelate...........F-1
Prince Albert.....D-3
Qu'Appelle........F-4
Quill Lake........E-4
Radisson..........E-2
Raymore...........F-4
Redvers...........G-5
Regina............G-4
Rocanville........G-5
Rockglen..........H-3
Rosetown..........F-2
Rose Valley.......E-4
Rosthern..........E-3
St. Louis.........D-3
St. Walburg.......D-1
Saskatoon.........E-3
Semans............F-4
Shaunavon.........G-1
Sheho.............F-4
Shellbrook........D-2
Spiritwood........D-2
Star City.........D-4
Stoughton.........G-4
Strasbourg Sta.....F-3
Sturgis...........E-5
Swift Current.....G-2
Theodore..........F-4
Tisdale...........D-4
Tompkins..........G-1
Unity.............E-1
Val Marie.........H-2
Vanguard..........G-2
Wadena............E-4
Wakaw.............E-3
Waldheim..........E-2
Watrous...........E-3
Watson............E-4
Weyburn...........G-4
Whitewood.........G-5
Wilkie............E-1
Willow Bunch......H-3
Wolseley..........G-4
Wynyard...........E-4
Yellow Grass......G-4
Yorkton...........F-5

MEXICO

Population 67,395,826
(1980 Census)
Land Area: 761,604 Sq. Mi.
Capital: Mexico City

Cities and Towns

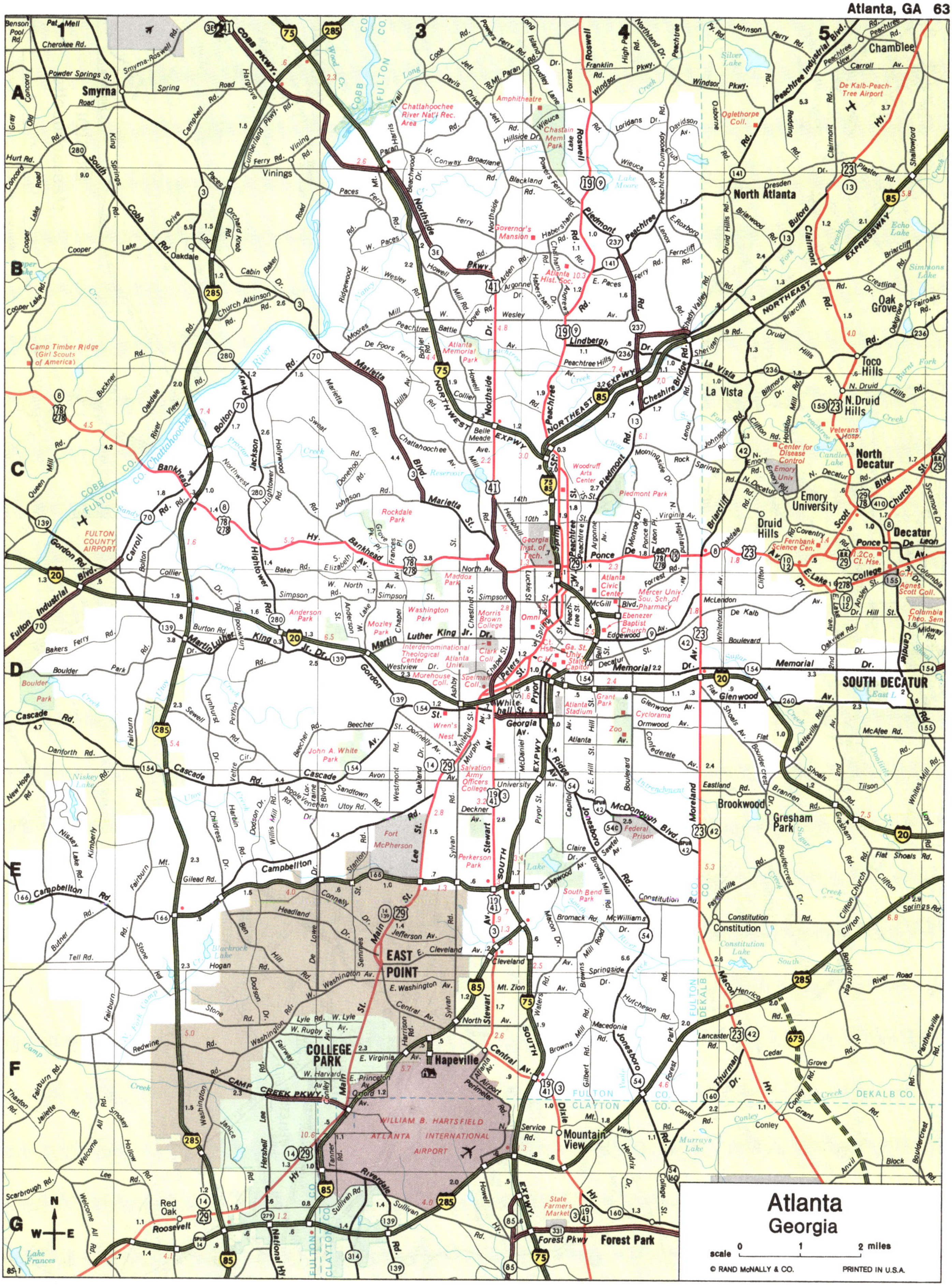
Atlanta
Georgia
scale 0 1 2 miles
© RAND McNALLY & CO.
PRINTED IN U.S.A.
Smyrna
Vinings
Chamblee
North Atlanta
Oak Grove
Toco Hills
N.Druid Hills
La Vista
North Decatur
Emory University
Druid Hills
Decatur
SOUTH DECATUR
Brookwood
Gresham Park
Constitution
EAST POINT
COLLEGE PARK
Hapeville
Mountain View
Forest Park
Red Oak
WILLIAM B. HARTSFIELD ATLANTA INTERNATIONAL AIRPORT
FULTON COUNTY AIRPORT
De Kalb-Peach-Tree Airport
Fort McPherson
Georgia Inst. of Tech.
Atlanta Univ.
Atlanta Stadium
Federal Prison
Camp Timber Ridge (Girl Scouts of America)
Chattahoochee River Nat'l Rec. Area
Governor's Mansion
Center for Disease Control
Agnes Scott Coll.
Columbia Theo. Sem.
Oglethorpe Coll.
State Farmers Market
CAMP CREEK PKWY.
NORTHEAST EXPWY.
NORTHWEST EXPWY.
SOUTH EXPWY.
NORTHEAST EXPRESSWAY
FULTON CO.
DEKALB CO.
CLAYTON CO.
COBB CO.

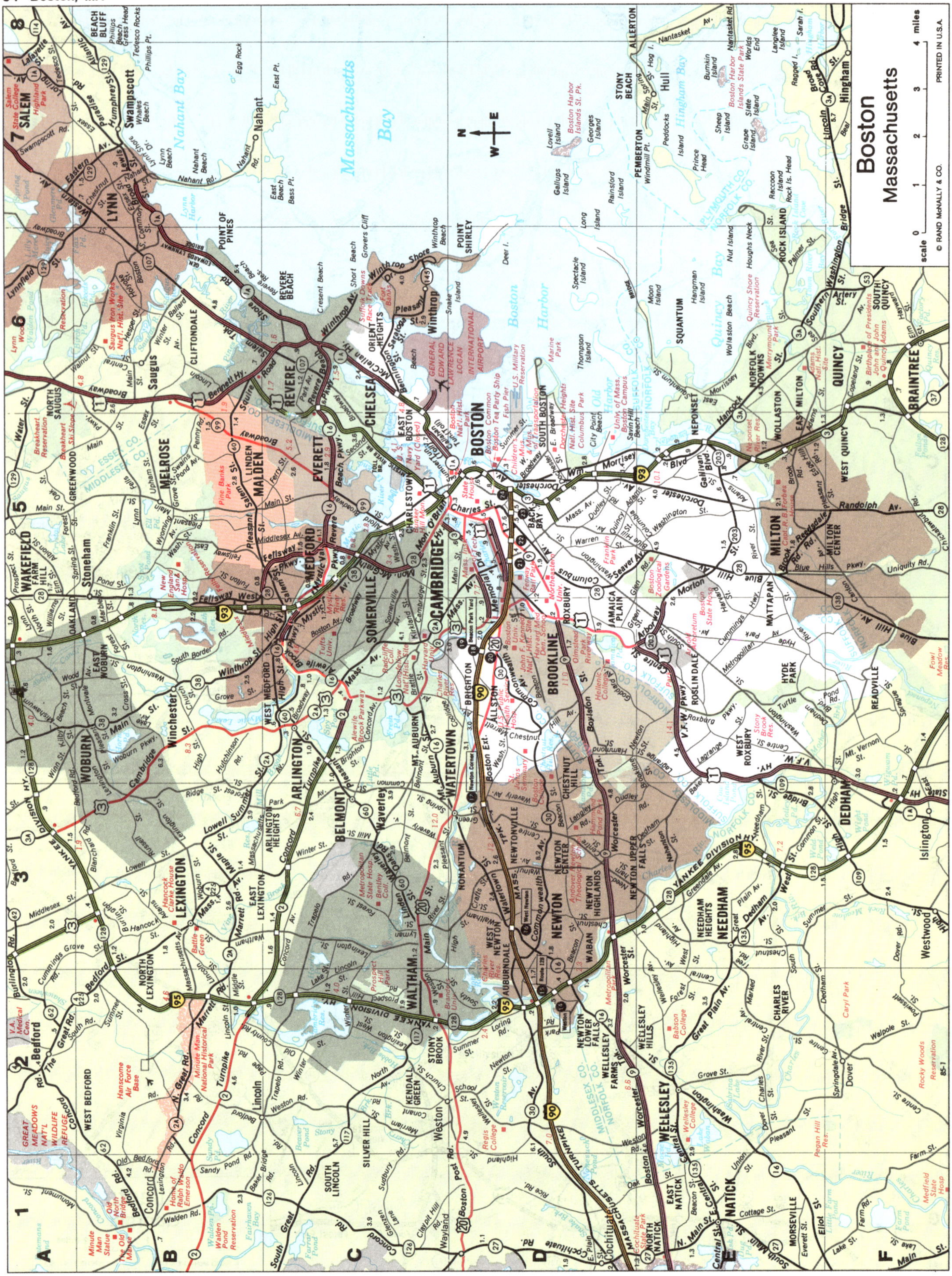
Boston
Massachusetts
scale
miles
© RAND McNALLY & CO.
PRINTED IN U.S.A.
Massachusetts Bay
Boston Harbor
Nahant Bay
BOSTON
CAMBRIDGE
BROOKLINE
NEWTON
WALTHAM
QUINCY
LYNN
SALEM

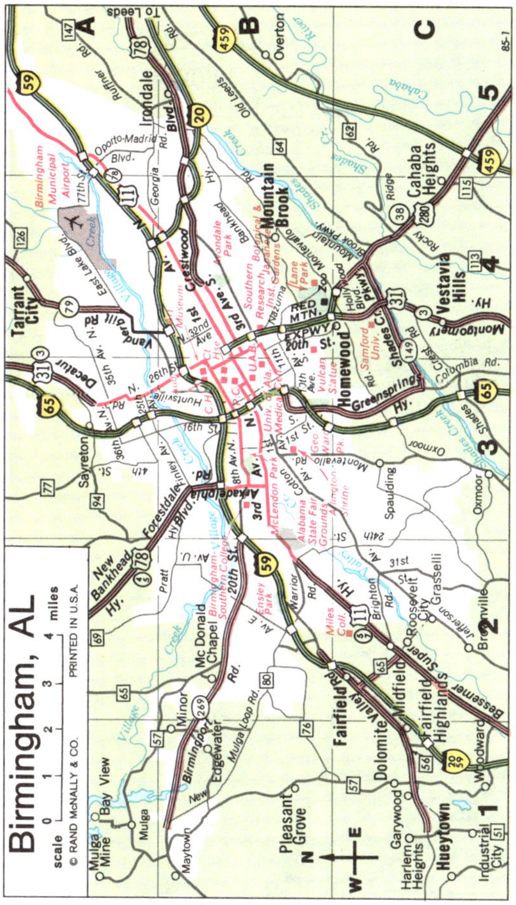
Birmingham, AL
scale 0 1 2 3 4 miles
© RAND McNALLY & CO. PRINTED IN U.S.A.

Buffalo, NY
Niagara Falls
scale 0 1 2 3 4 miles
© RAND McNALLY & CO. PRINTED IN U.S.A.

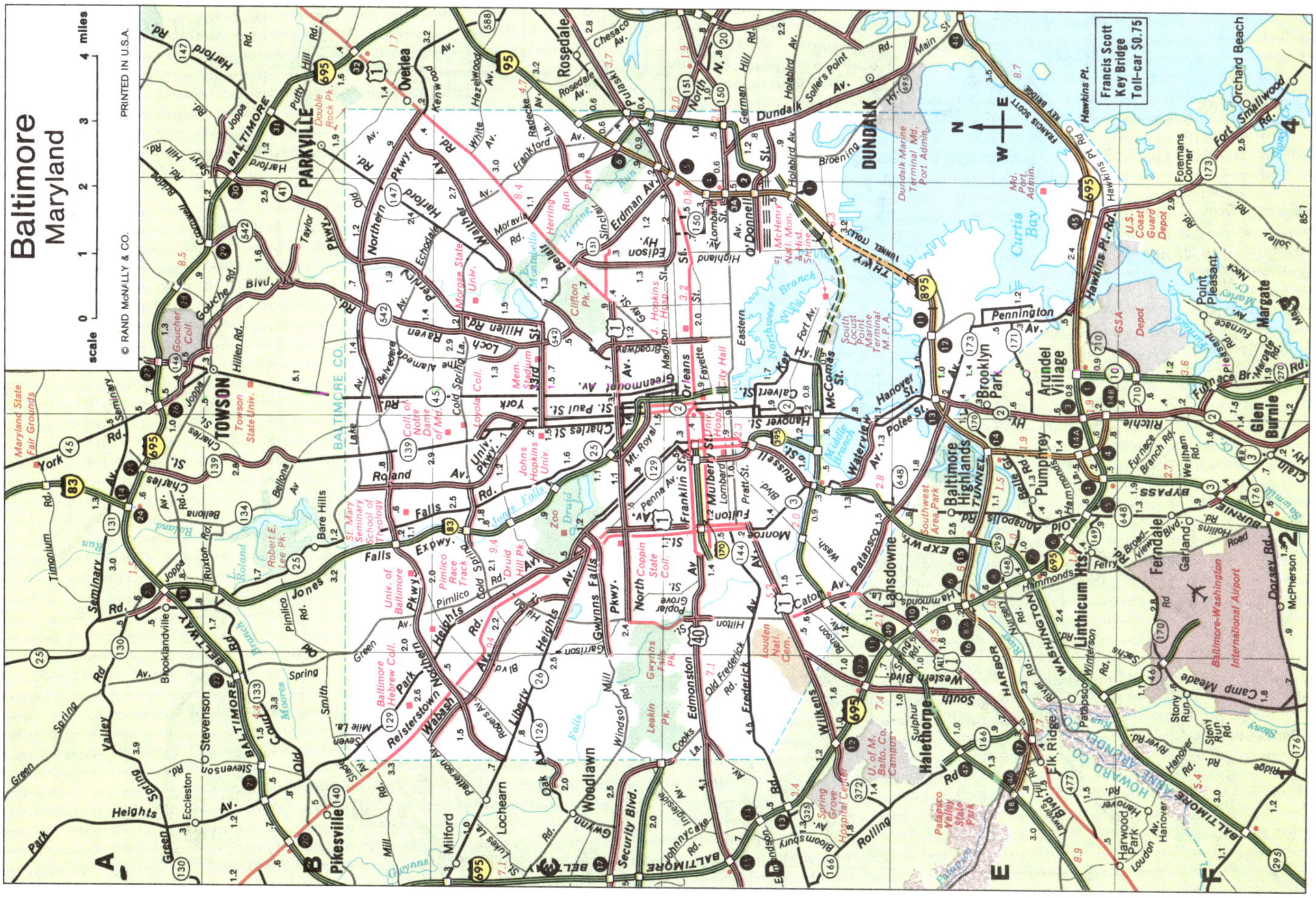
Baltimore
Maryland
scale 0 1 2 3 4 miles
© RAND McNALLY & CO. PRINTED IN U.S.A.
Francis Scott Key Bridge Toll-car $0.75

Chicago
Illinois
scale 0 1 2 3 4 5 miles
© RAND McNALLY & CO.
PRINTED IN U.S.A.
Lake Michigan
CHICAGO
HIGHLAND PARK
Glencoe
Winnetka
Kenilworth
WILMETTE
EVANSTON
SKOKIE
Lincolnwood
MORTON GR.
NILES
GLENVIEW
Northfield
Northbrook
Deerfield
Wheeling
Buffalo Gr
ARLINGTON HTS.
Prospect Hts.
MT. PROSPECT
DES PLAINES
PARK RIDGE
Rosemont
CHICAGO O'HARE INTERNATIONAL AIRPORT
ELK GROVE VIL.
SCHAUMBURG
HOFFMAN ESTATES
Palatine
Rolling Meadows
Roselle
Itasca
Wood Dale
Bensenville
Schiller Park
Franklin Park
Norridge
Harwood Hts.
Elmwood Park
River Gr.
MELROSE PARK
Northlake
Stone Park
OAK PARK
River Forest
MAYWOOD
Bellwood
Berkeley
Hillside
ELMHURST
Villa Park
LOMBARD
Glen Ellyn
WHEATON
Carol Stream
Addison
Bloomingdale
Glendale Hts.
Forest Park
BERWYN
CICERO
Broadview
Westchester
Riverside
N. Riverside
LaGrange Park
LaGrange
Brookfield
Western Sprs.
Hinsdale
Oak Brook
DOWNERS GR.
Lisle
Westmont
Clarendon Hills
Darien
Countryside
Summit
Bedford Park
BURBANK
Justice
Willow Sprs.
Hickory Hills
OAK LAWN
Evergreen Park
Chicago Ridge
Palos Hills
Worth
Alsip
Blue Island
Calumet Park
Riverdale
Dolton
Crestwood
Robbins
Posen
Midlothian
Oak Forest
HARVEY
Phoenix
SOUTH HOLLAND
CALUMET CITY
Burnham
Markham
Orland Park
Palos Hts.
Lemont
BOLINGBROOK
Romeoville
Woodridge
ARGONNE NATIONAL LABORATORY
Hometown
Garden Homes
Merrionette Park
EISENHOWER EXPWY.
STEVENSON EXPWY.
DAN RYAN EXPWY.
KENNEDY EXPWY.
EDENS EXPWY.
CALUMET EXPWY.
SKYWAY
TRI-STATE TOLLWAY
EAST-WEST TOLLWAY
NORTHWEST TOLLWAY
Chicago Midway Airport
GRANT PARK
JACKSON PARK
Museum of Science and Industry
Univ. of Chicago
Loyola University
Northwestern University
Lincoln Park Zoo
Buckingham Fountain
Shedd Aquarium
Adler Planetarium
Field Museum
Merrill C. Meigs Airport
Mc Cormick Place
A B C D E F
1 2 3 4 5

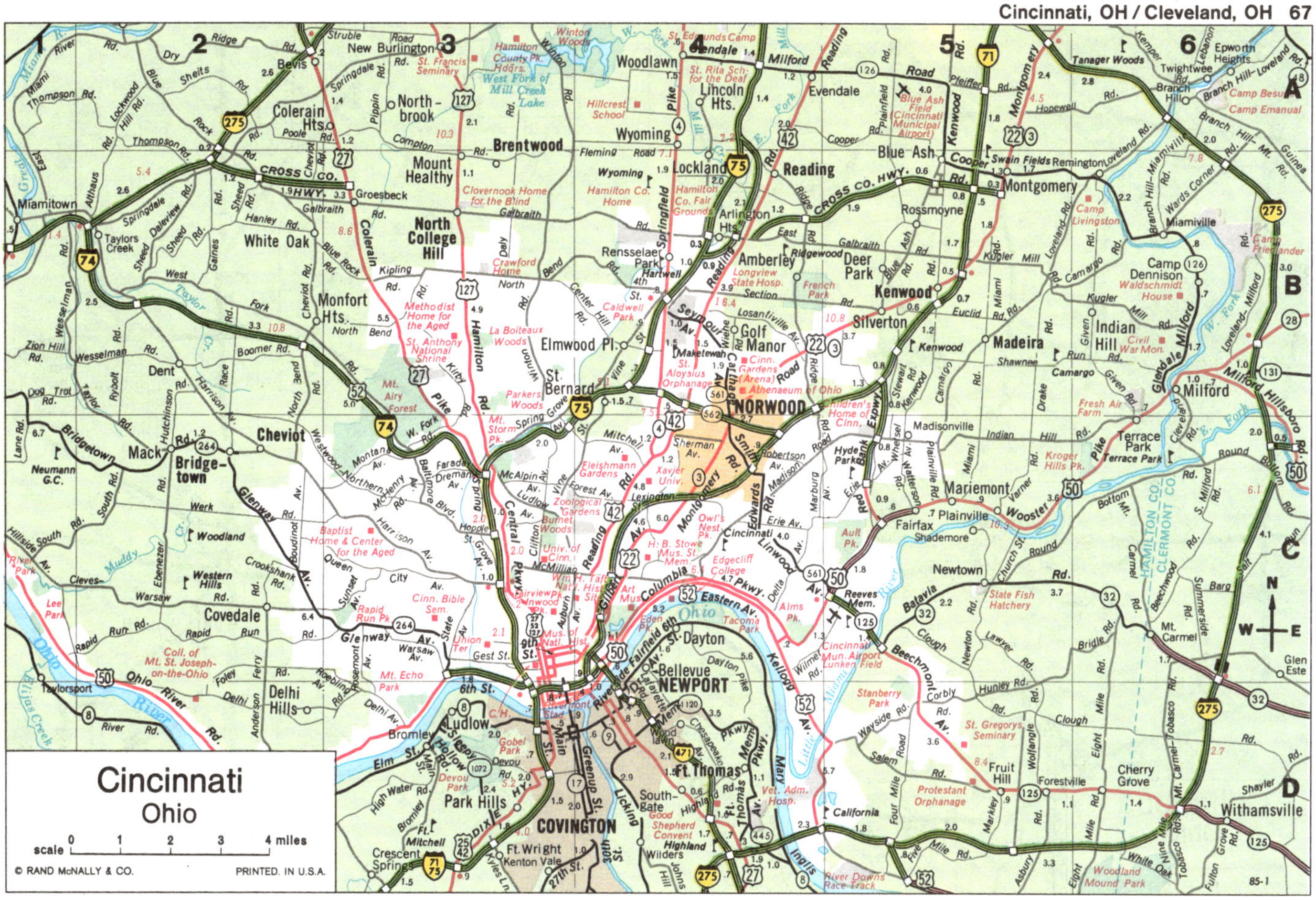
Cincinnati
Ohio
scale 0 1 2 3 4 miles
© RAND McNALLY & CO.
PRINTED. IN U.S.A.
New Burlington
Woodlawn
Glendale
Milford
Evendale
Colerain Hts.
North-brook
Brentwood
Wyoming
Lockland
Reading
Blue Ash
Montgomery
Mount Healthy
Miamitown
Taylors Creek
White Oak
North College Hill
Arlington Hts.
Rossmoyne
Miamiville
Camp Dennison
Monfort Hts.
Elmwood Pl.
Golf Manor
Deer Park
Kenwood
Silverton
Madeira
Indian Hill
Milford
Dent
St. Bernard
NORWOOD
Cheviot
Mack
Bridge-town
Terrace Park
Mariemont
Fairfax
Plainville
Newtown
Covedale
Delhi Hills
Taylorsport
Dayton
Bellevue
NEWPORT
Ludlow
Ft. Thomas
Park Hills
COVINGTON
South-Gate
Fruit Hill
Forestville
Cherry Grove
Withamsville
Mt. Carmel
Crescent Springs
Ft. Wright
Kenton Vale
Wilders
Ohio River
85-1

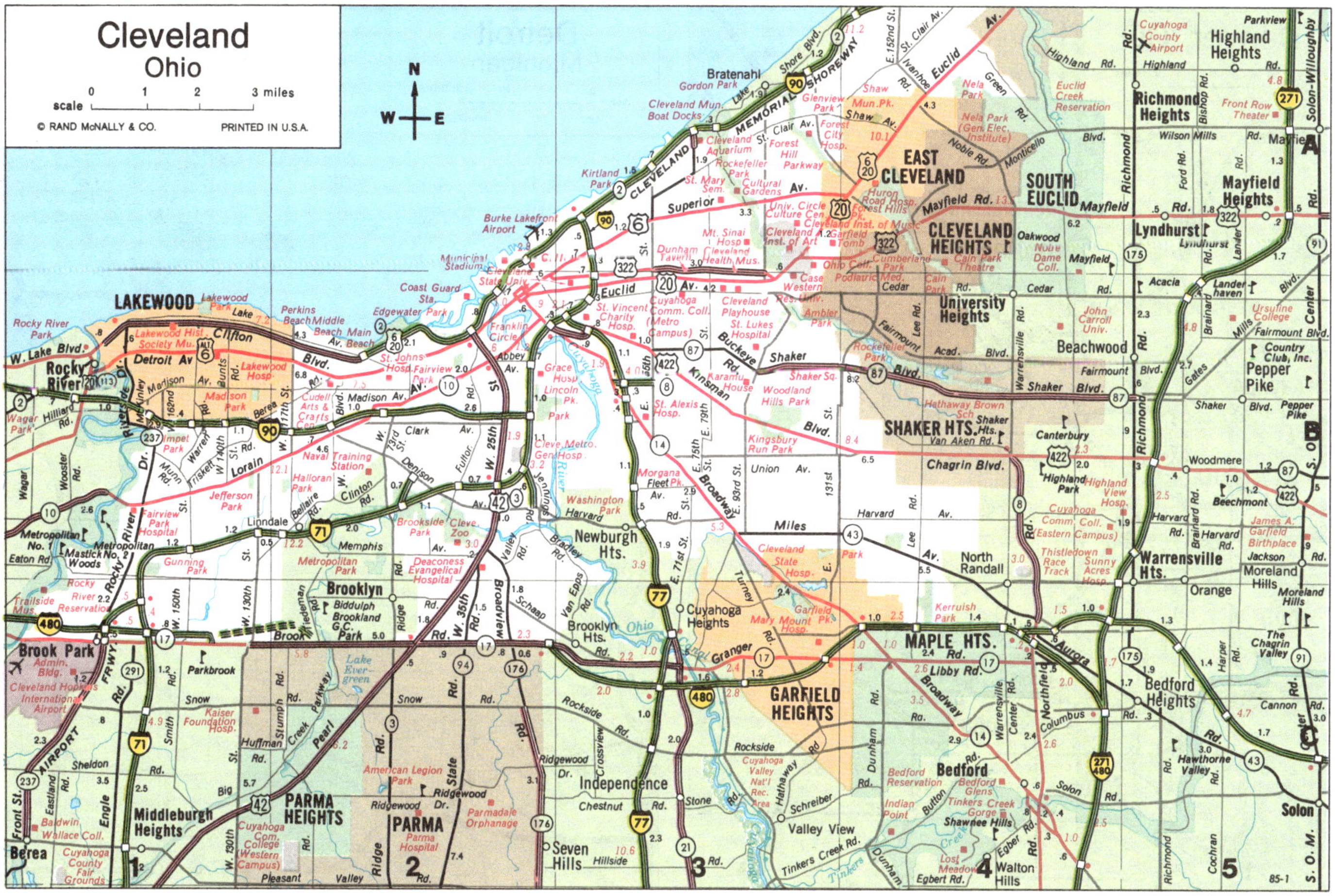
Cleveland
Ohio
scale 0 1 2 3 miles
© RAND McNALLY & CO.
PRINTED IN U.S.A.
Bratenahl
Highland Heights
Richmond Heights
Mayfield
EAST CLEVELAND
SOUTH EUCLID
Mayfield Heights
Lyndhurst
CLEVELAND HEIGHTS
University Heights
Beachwood
Pepper Pike
LAKEWOOD
Rocky River
SHAKER HTS.
Newburgh Hts.
North Randall
Warrensville Hts.
Orange
Moreland Hills
Brooklyn
Cuyahoga Heights
MAPLE HTS.
Bedford Heights
Brook Park
Brooklyn Hts.
GARFIELD HEIGHTS
Bedford
PARMA HEIGHTS
PARMA
Independence
Valley View
Solon
Walton Hills
Seven Hills
Middleburgh Heights
Berea
85-1

Columbus
Ohio
scale 0 1 2 3 miles
© RAND McNALLY & CO. PRINTED IN U.S.A.
85-1

Dallas, TX
Fort Worth
scale 0 1 2 3 miles
© RAND McNALLY & CO. PRINTED IN U.S.A.

Denver, CO
scale 0 2 4 miles
© RAND McNALLY & CO. PRINTED IN U.S.A.
85-1

Detroit
Michigan
scale 0 1 2 3 miles
© RAND McNALLY & CO. PRINTED IN U.S.A.

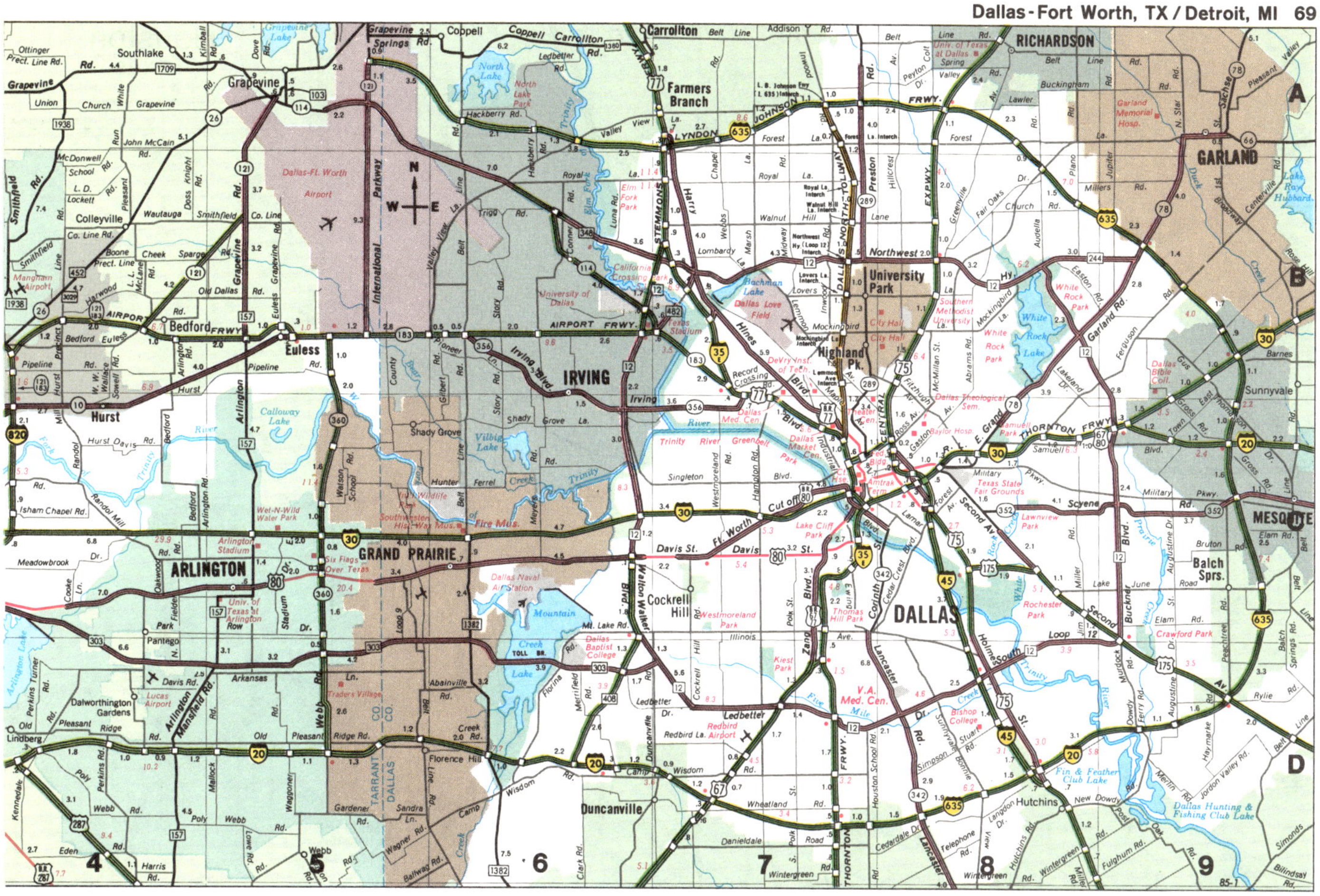
Grapevine
Southlake
Coppell
Carrollton
Farmers Branch
RICHARDSON
GARLAND
Dallas-Ft. Worth Airport
University Park
Highland Pk.
Colleyville
Bedford
Euless
Hurst
IRVING
GRAND PRAIRIE
ARLINGTON
Cockrell Hill
DALLAS
MESQUITE
Balch Sprs.
Duncanville
Hutchins
Sunnyvale
A
B
C
D
4
5
6
7
8
9

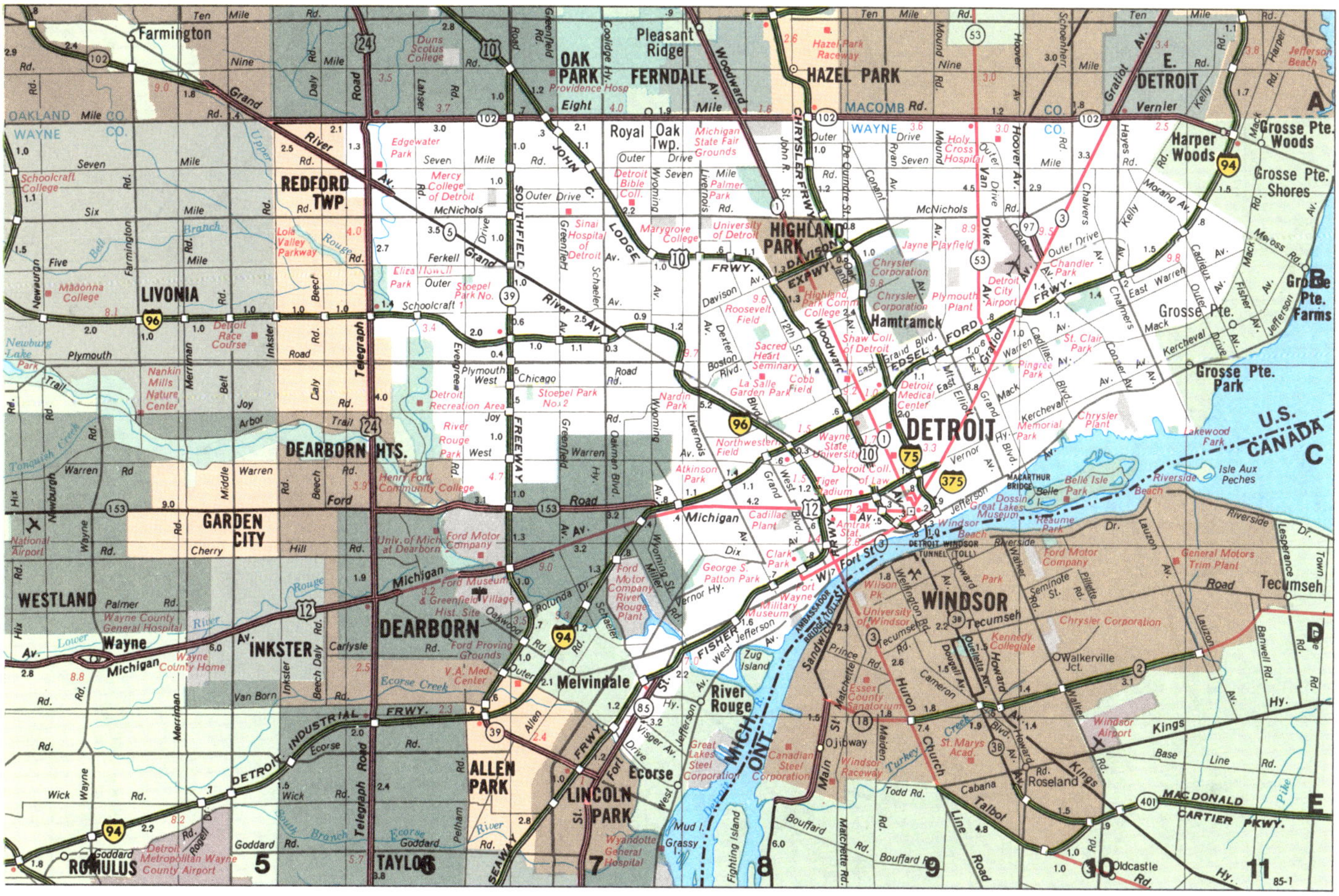
Farmington
OAK PARK
FERNDALE
Pleasant Ridge
HAZEL PARK
E. DETROIT
Harper Woods
Grosse Pte. Woods
Grosse Pte. Shores
Grosse Pte. Farms
Grosse Pte. Park
REDFORD TWP.
LIVONIA
HIGHLAND PARK
Hamtramck
DETROIT
DEARBORN HTS.
GARDEN CITY
WESTLAND
Wayne
INKSTER
DEARBORN
Melvindale
River Rouge
WINDSOR
ALLEN PARK
Ecorse
LINCOLN PARK
ROMULUS
TAYLOR
Tecumseh
U.S.
CANADA
A
B
C
D
E
5
6
7
8
9
10
11

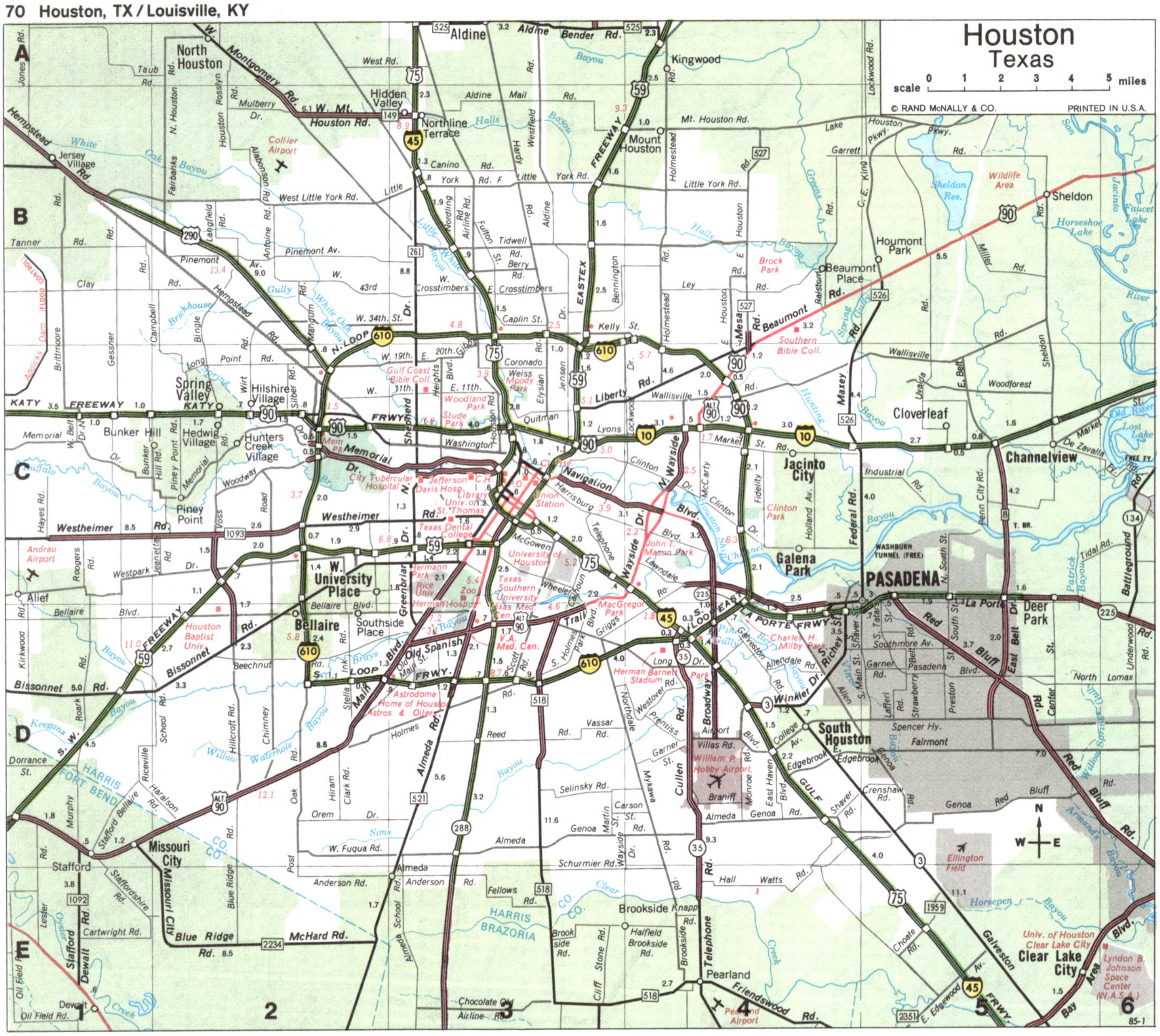
Houston
Texas
scale 0 1 2 3 4 5 miles
© RAND McNALLY & CO.
PRINTED IN U.S.A.
North Houston
Aldine
Kingwood
Mount Houston
Sheldon
Houmont Park
Spring Valley
Hilshire Village
Hedwig Village
Hunters Creek Village
Bunker Hill
Piney Point
W. University Place
Bellaire
Southside Place
Cloverleaf
Channelview
Jacinto City
Galena Park
PASADENA
Deer Park
South Houston
Missouri City
Stafford
Pearland
Clear Lake City
85-1

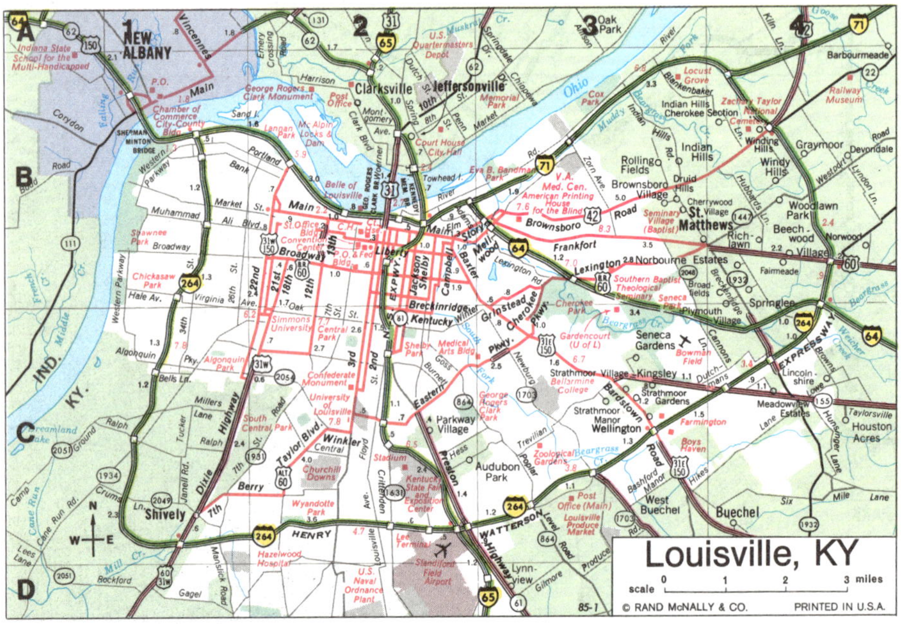
Louisville, KY
scale 0 1 2 3 miles
© RAND McNALLY & CO.
PRINTED IN U.S.A.
NEW ALBANY
Clarksville
Jeffersonville
St. Matthews
Shively
Buechel
85-1

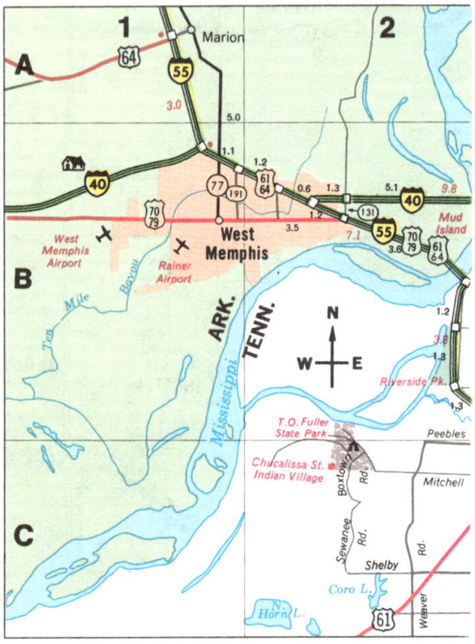
Marion
West Memphis
ARK.
TENN.

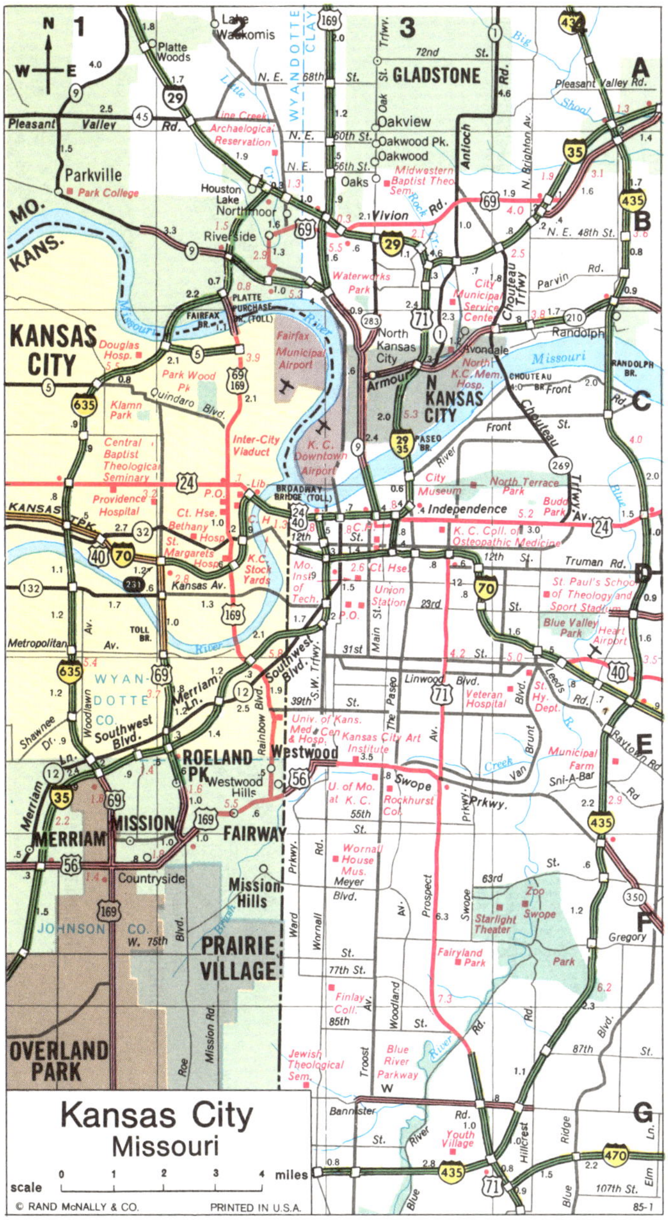
Kansas City
Missouri
scale 0 1 2 3 4 miles
© RAND McNALLY & CO.
PRINTED IN U.S.A.
85-1
GLADSTONE
KANSAS CITY
N KANSAS CITY
North Kansas City
Parkville
Riverside
Northmoor
Houston Lake
Platte Woods
Lake Waukomis
Oakview
Oakwood Pk.
Oakwood
Oaks
Avondale
Randolph
Independence
ROELAND PK.
Westwood
Westwood Hills
MISSION
MERRIAM
FAIRWAY
Mission Hills
PRAIRIE VILLAGE
OVERLAND PARK
Countryside
WYANDOTTE CO.
JOHNSON CO.
MO.
KANS.
Missouri River
K.C. Downtown Airport
Fairfax Municipal Airport

Memphis, TN
scale 0 1 2 3 4 miles
© RAND McNALLY & CO.
PRINTED IN U.S.A.
85-1
Bartlett
Germantown
Cordova
Capleville
Memphis Int'l. Airport
DeWitt Spain Airport
Civic Center
Memphis State Univ.
Rhodes Coll.

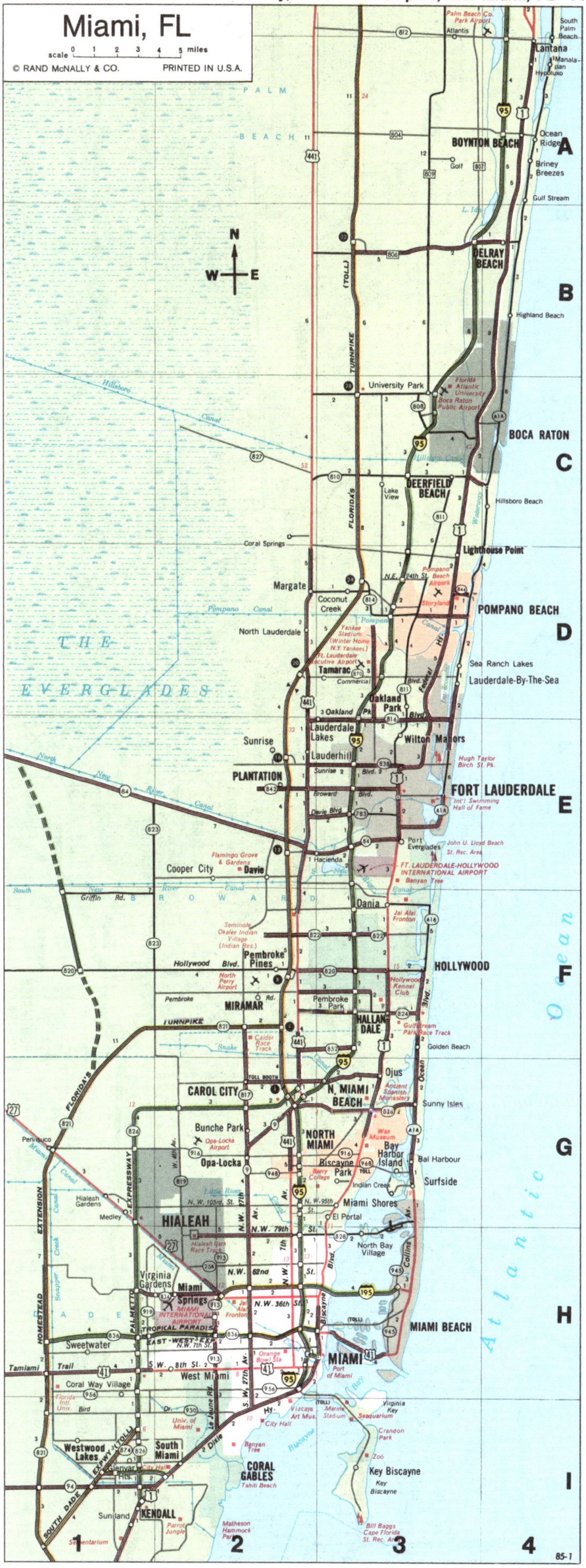
Miami, FL
scale 0 1 2 3 4 5 miles
© RAND McNALLY & CO.
PRINTED IN U.S.A.
85-1
THE EVERGLADES
PALM BEACH
BROWARD
DADE
Atlantic Ocean
Lantana
South Palm Beach
Manalapan
Hypoluxo
BOYNTON BEACH
Ocean Ridge
Briney Breezes
Gulf Stream
DELRAY BEACH
Highland Beach
BOCA RATON
DEERFIELD BEACH
Hillsboro Beach
Lighthouse Point
POMPANO BEACH
Sea Ranch Lakes
Lauderdale-By-The-Sea
Coral Springs
Margate
Coconut Creek
North Lauderdale
Tamarac
Oakland Park
Lauderdale Lakes
Lauderhill
Sunrise
PLANTATION
Wilton Manors
FORT LAUDERDALE
Cooper City
Davie
Dania
HOLLYWOOD
Pembroke Pines
MIRAMAR
Pembroke Park
HALLANDALE
CAROL CITY
N. MIAMI BEACH
NORTH MIAMI
Opa-Locka
HIALEAH
Miami Springs
MIAMI
MIAMI BEACH
Sweetwater
West Miami
CORAL GABLES
South Miami
KENDALL
Key Biscayne

Los Angeles
California
scale
0 1 2 3 4 5 6 7 8 9 10 miles
RAND McNALLY & CO.
PRINTED IN U.S.A.
LOS ANGELES
SANTA MONICA
BEVERLY HILLS
WEST HOLLYWOOD
CULVER CITY
INGLEWOOD
HAWTHORNE
TORRANCE
LONG BEACH
PASADENA
GLENDALE
BURBANK
ANAHEIM
SANTA ANA
HUNTINGTON BEACH
POMONA
ONTARIO
FULLERTON
COMPTON
DOWNEY
WHITTIER

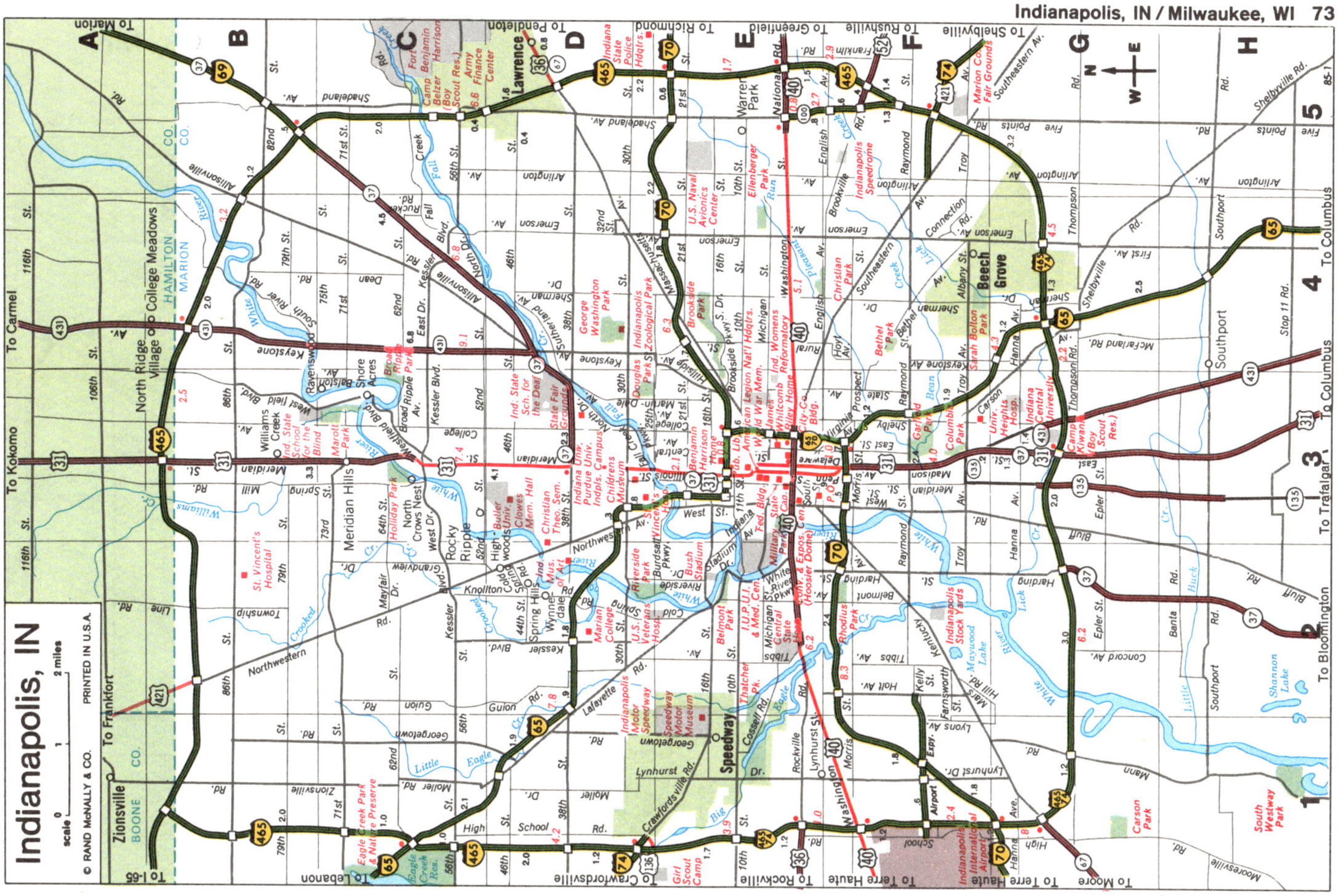
Indianapolis, IN
scale 0 1 2 miles
© RAND McNALLY & CO.
PRINTED IN U.S.A.

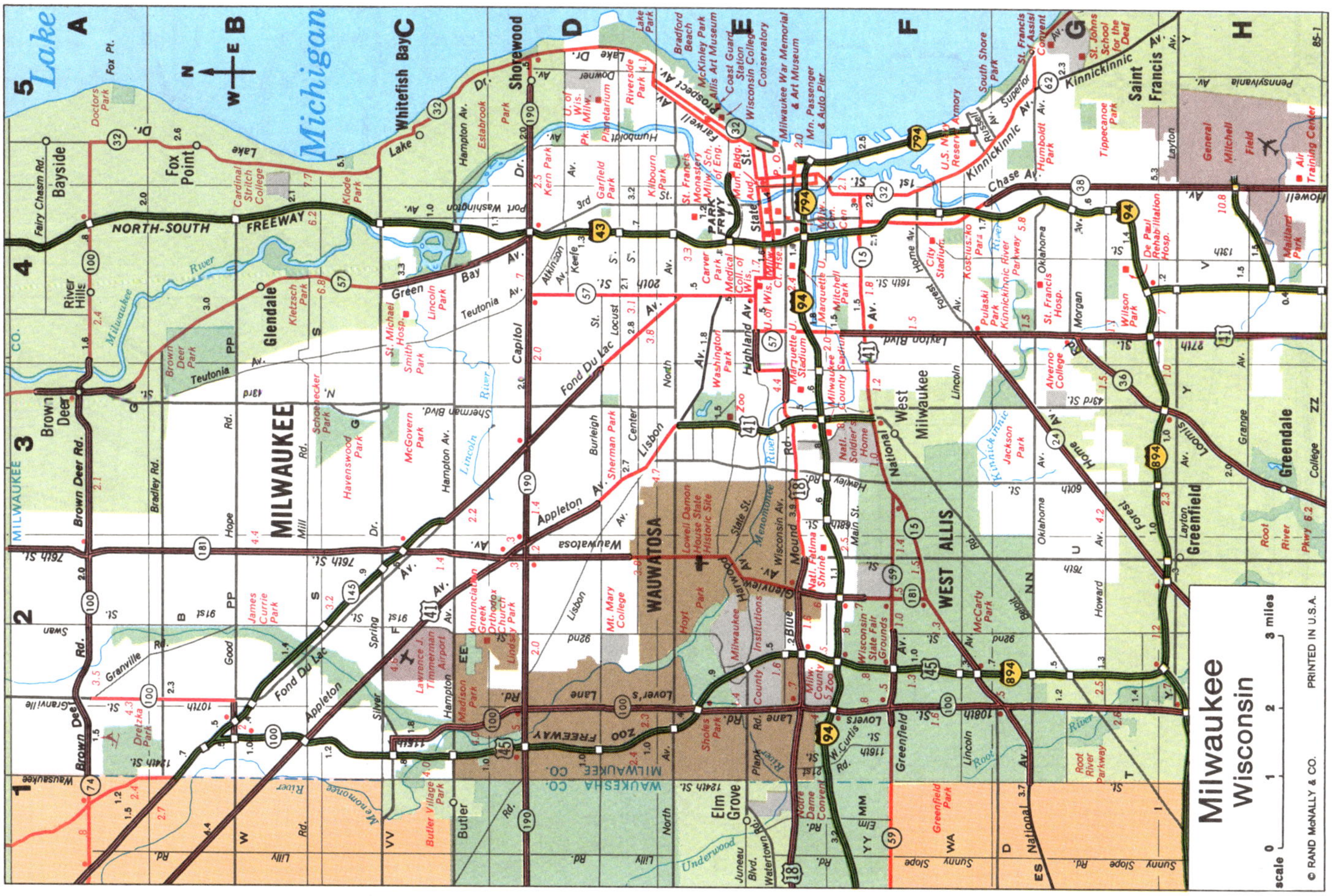
Milwaukee Wisconsin
scale 0 1 2 3 miles
© RAND McNALLY & CO.
PRINTED IN U.S.A.

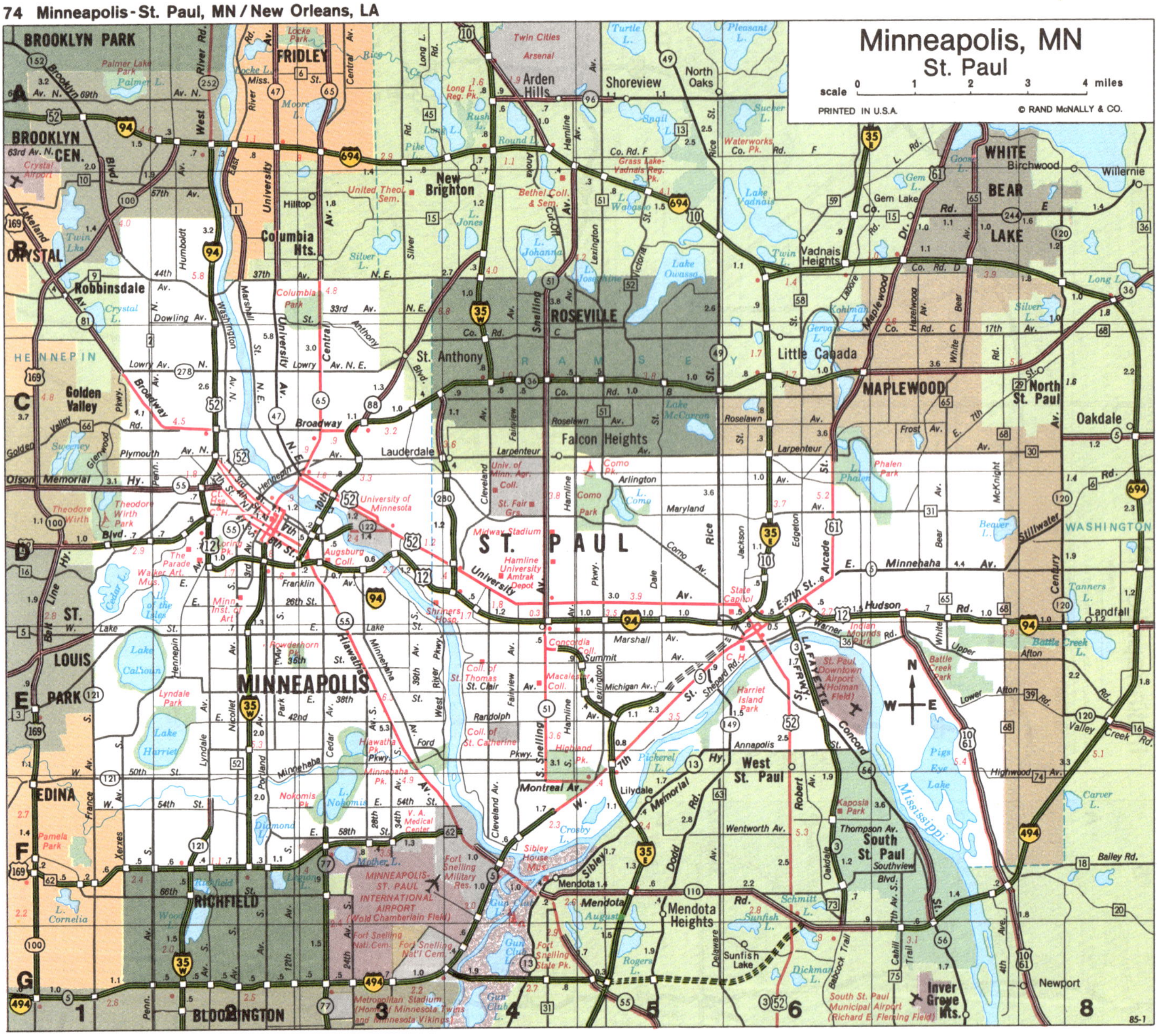
Minneapolis, MN
St. Paul
scale 0 1 2 3 4 miles
PRINTED IN U.S.A.
© RAND McNALLY & CO.
BROOKLYN PARK
FRIDLEY
Arden Hills
Shoreview
North Oaks
BROOKLYN CEN.
New Brighton
WHITE BEAR LAKE
CRYSTAL
Columbia Hts.
Robbinsdale
ROSEVILLE
Vadnais Heights
Little Canada
St. Anthony
MAPLEWOOD
North St. Paul
Golden Valley
Falcon Heights
Oakdale
Lauderdale
ST. PAUL
MINNEAPOLIS
ST. LOUIS PARK
EDINA
West St. Paul
South St. Paul
RICHFIELD
Mendota Heights
BLOOMINGTON
Inver Grove Hts.
Newport
Landfall
HENNEPIN
RAMSEY
WASHINGTON
Mississippi
MINNEAPOLIS-ST. PAUL INTERNATIONAL AIRPORT (Wold Chamberlain Field)
St. Paul Downtown Airport (Holman Field)
South St. Paul Municipal Airport (Richard E. Fleming Field)
Metropolitan Stadium (Home of Minnesota Twins and Minnesota Vikings)
University of Minnesota
Univ. of Minn. Agr. Coll.
State Capitol
85-1

New Orleans, LA
Downtown
scale 0 0.1 0.2 0.3 0.4 0.5 miles
© RAND McNALLY & CO.
PRINTED IN U.S.A.
Tulane Ave.
Canal St.
N. Rampart St.
Elysian Fields
Louis Armstrong Park
Mississippi River
GRETNA
85-1

New Orleans, LA
scale 0 2 4 6 miles
PRINTED IN U.S.A.
© RAND McNALLY & CO.
Lake Pontchartrain
LAKE PONTCHARTRAIN CAUSEWAY (TOLL)
New Orleans Lake Front Airport
Univ. of New Orleans
METAIRIE
ARABI
CHALMETTE
Jefferson
Harahan
Avondale
Waggaman
Westwego
GRETNA
Marrero
Harvey
Timberlane
Meraux
Little Woods
ORLEANS
ST. BERNARD
JEFFERSON
Mississippi River
U.S. Coast Guard Reservation
85-1

New York City
New York
scale
0 1 2 3 4 miles
PRINTED IN U.S.A.
© RAND McNALLY & CO.
YONKERS
MT. VERNON
NEW ROCHELLE
Larchmont
Pelham
Pelham Manor
Haworth
Demarest
Oradell
New Milford
Cresskill
Alpine
River Edge
Dumont
BERGENFIELD
Tenafly
PARAMUS
Maywood
Rochelle Park
HACKENSACK
ENGLEWOOD
Englewood Cliffs
TEANECK
Bogota
LODI
Leonia
Teterboro
Ridgefield Park
Palisades Pk.
Fort Lee
Little Ferry
Hasbrouck Hts.
Wood-Ridge
Moonachie
Ridgefield
Edgewater
Cliffside Park
Secaucus
NORTH BERGEN
Guttenberg
W. NEW YORK
Weehawken
UNION CITY
HOBOKEN
JERSEY CITY
Riverdale
ASTORIA
LONG ISLAND CITY
JACKSON HTS.
COLLEGE POINT
FLUSHING
BAYSIDE
LITTLE NECK
GREENPOINT
MASPETH
FOREST HILLS
WILLIAMSBURG
RICHMOND HILL
JAMAICA
ST. ALBANS
OZONE PARK
SOUTH OZONE PARK
EAST NEW YORK
FLATBUSH
CANARSIE
BAY RIDGE
BENSONHURST
CONEY ISLAND
FAR ROCKAWAY
EDGEMERE
SPRINGFIELD GARDENS
ELMONT
QUEENS VILLAGE
Bellerose
NEW HYDE PARK
VALLEY STREAM
South Valley Stream
Woodmere
Inwood
Cedarhurst
Lawrence
Atlantic Beach
East Atlantic Beach
Great Neck
Great Neck Estates
Kings Point
Saddle Rock
Kensington
Thomaston
Russell Gardens
Lake Success
Manorhaven
Sands Point
Plandome
Baxter Estates
NEW BRIGHTON
ST. GEORGE
TOMPKINSVILLE
STAPLETON
Long Island Sound
Upper Bay
Jamaica Bay
Flushing Bay
Eastchester Bay
Rockaway Inlet
Hudson River
East River
Harlem River
LaGuardia Airport
John F. Kennedy International Airport
Teterboro Airport
Statue of Liberty Natl Mon.
Ellis I.
Governors Island
Rikers Island
City Island
Hart Island
Throggs Neck
Rodman Neck
Hunters Island
Twin I.
Davids I.
Huckleberry I.
Premium Pt.
Long Beach Pt.
Delancey Pt.
Prospect Pt.
Barker Pt.
Plum Pt.
Willets Pt.
Norton Pt.
Breezy Pt.
Gateway National Recreation Area
Floyd Bennett Field
Coast Guard Heliport
Brooklyn Museum & Botanic Gardens
Prospect Park
Central Park
Bronx Zoo
Crotona Park
Van Cortlandt Park
Pelham Bay
Shea Stadium
Yankee Stadium
Jamaica Bay Wildlife Refuge
Aqueduct Race Track
Belmont Park Race Track
Sheepshead Bay
Gravesend Bay
Coney Island
Manhattan Beach
Brighton Beach
Rockaway Beach
Holland Tunnel
Lincoln Tunnel
Queens Midtown Tunnel
George Washington Br. (Toll)
Verrazano Narrows Bridge
Marine Pkwy. Bridge (Toll)
Cross Bay Bridge (Toll)
Triboro Br. (Toll)
Williamsburg Br.
New Jersey Tpk.
Long Island Expwy.
Cross Bronx Expwy.
Belt Pkwy.
Grand Central Pkwy.
Van Wyck Expwy.
Hutchinson River Pkwy.
Bronx River Pkwy.
New England Thruway
Palisades Interstate Pkwy.
Henry Hudson Pkwy.
Major Deegan Expwy.
Bruckner Expwy.
Brooklyn-Queens Expwy.
Gowanus Expwy.
Prospect Expwy.
Interborough Pkwy.
Southern State Pkwy.
Staten Island Expwy.
Shore Pkwy.
Cross Island Pkwy.
Clearview Expwy.
Whitestone Expwy.
Queens Blvd.
Atlantic Av.
Flatbush Av.
Ocean Pkwy.
Eastern Pkwy.
Linden Blvd.
Hillside Av.
Northern Blvd.
Broadway
Grand Concourse
N
W
E
S
A
B
C
D
E
F
G
1
2
3
4
5

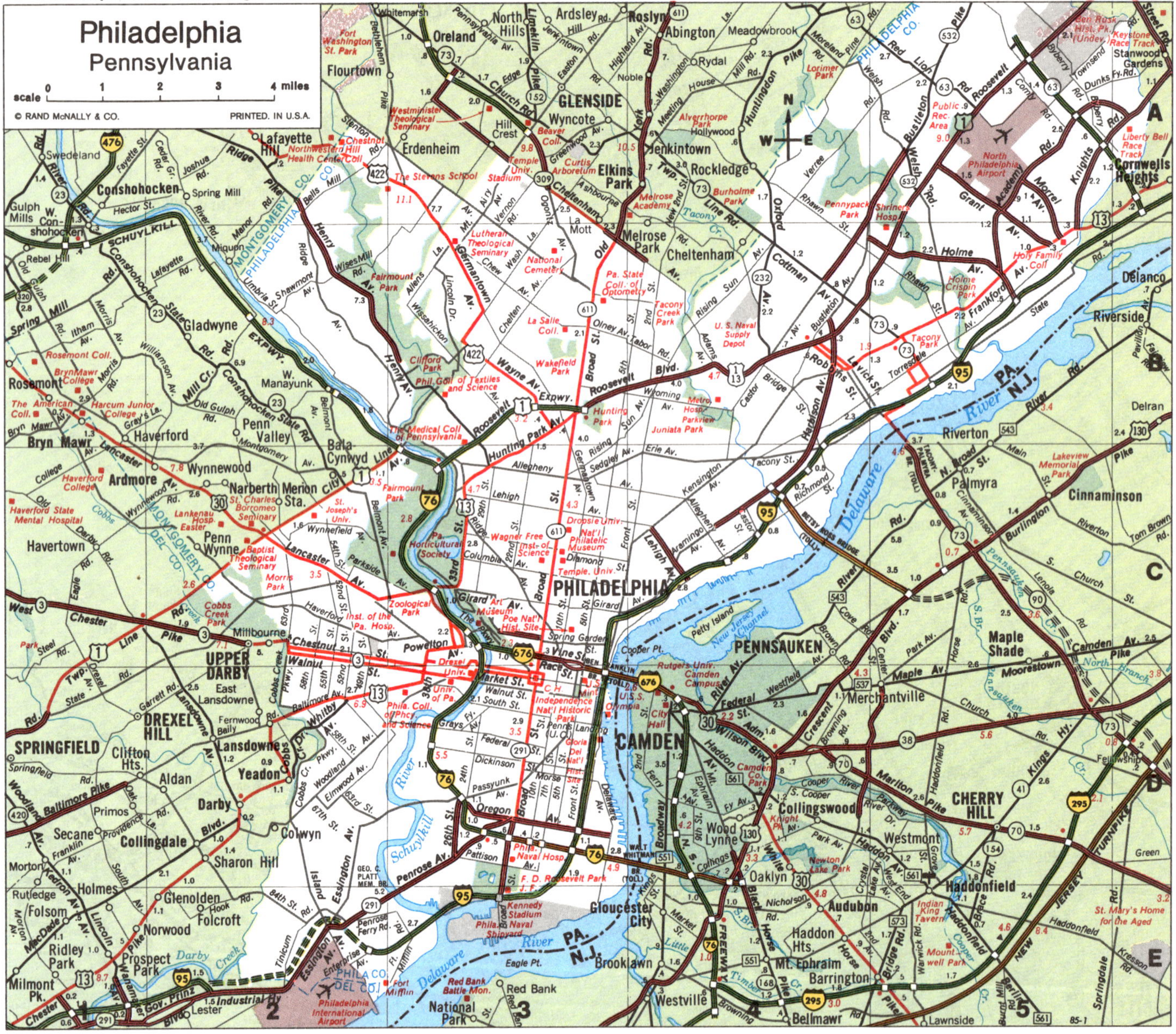
Philadelphia
Pennsylvania
scale 0 1 2 3 4 miles
© RAND McNALLY & CO.
PRINTED. IN U.S.A.
PHILADELPHIA
CAMDEN
PENNSAUKEN
UPPER DARBY
DREXEL HILL
SPRINGFIELD
CHERRY HILL
Delaware River
Schuylkill River
Philadelphia International Airport
North Philadelphia Airport

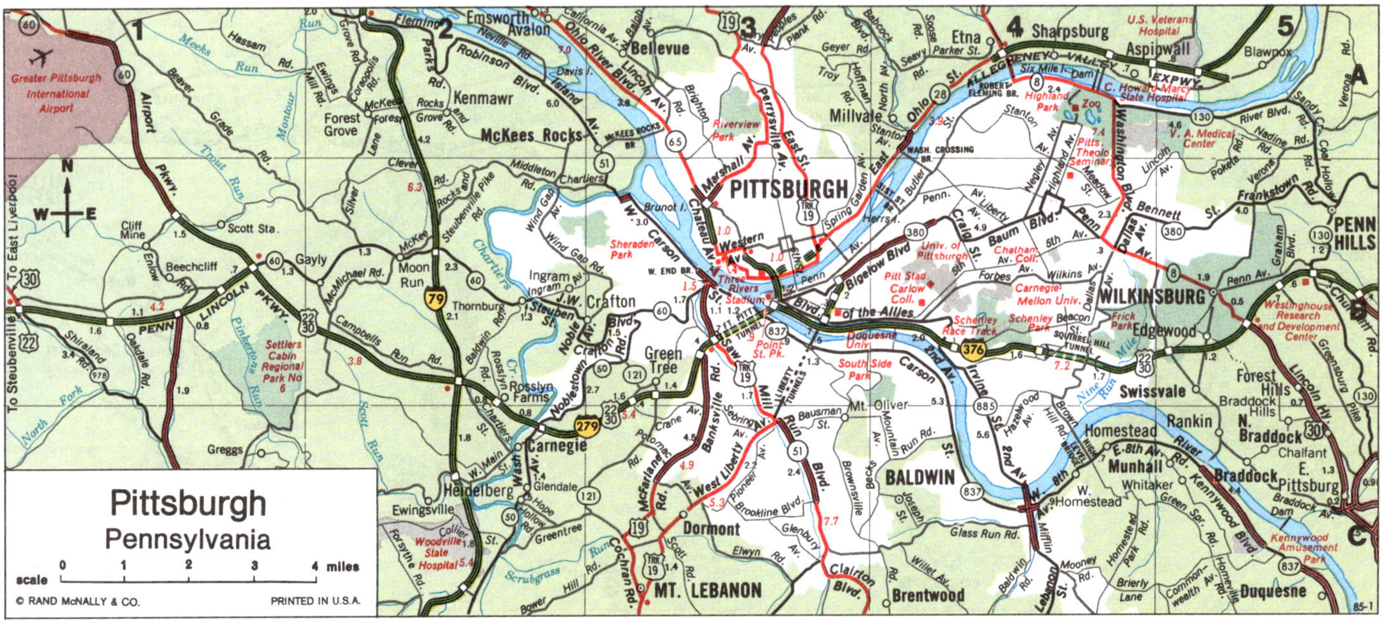
Pittsburgh
Pennsylvania
scale 0 1 2 3 4 miles
© RAND McNALLY & CO.
PRINTED IN U.S.A.
PITTSBURGH
WILKINSBURG
MT. LEBANON
BALDWIN
PENN HILLS
Greater Pittsburgh International Airport

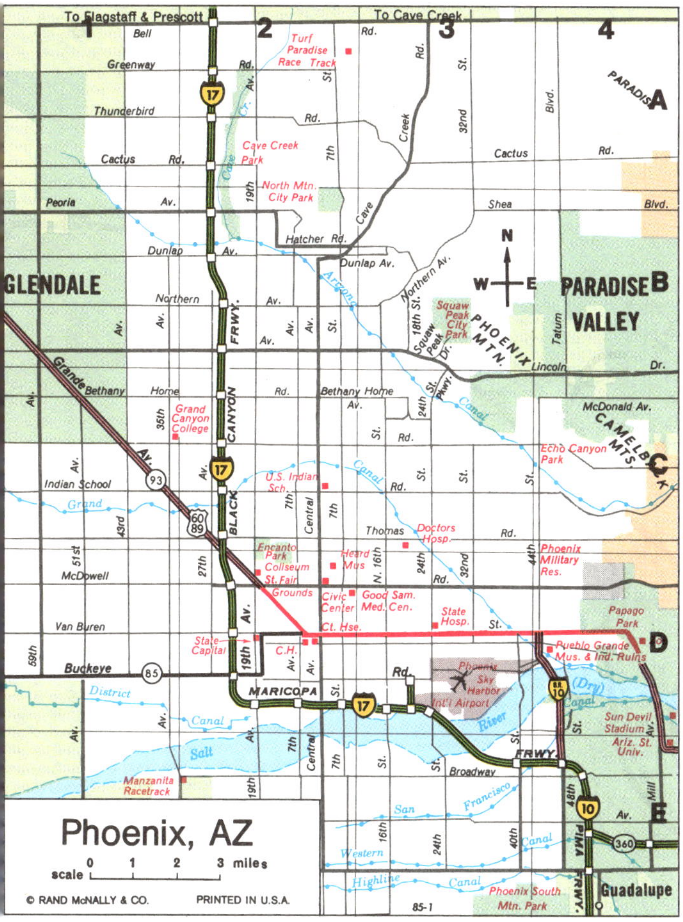
Phoenix, AZ
scale 0 1 2 3 miles
© RAND McNALLY & CO.
PRINTED IN U.S.A.
85-1
To Flagstaff & Prescott
To Cave Creek
GLENDALE
PARADISE VALLEY
PHOENIX MTN.
CAMELBACK MTS.
Turf Paradise Race Track
Cave Creek Park
North Mtn. City Park
Squaw Peak City Park
Grand Canyon College
Echo Canyon Park
Encanto Park
Coliseum
St. Fair Grounds
State Capitol
Civic Center
Good Sam. Med. Cen.
Phoenix Military Res.
Papago Park
Pueblo Grande Mus. & Ind. Ruins
Phoenix Sky Harbor Int'l Airport
Sun Devil Stadium
Ariz. St. Univ.
Manzanita Racetrack
Phoenix South Mtn. Park
Guadalupe
BLACK CANYON FRWY.
MARICOPA FRWY.
PIMA FRWY.
Salt River
Thunderbird
Cactus Rd.
Peoria Av.
Dunlap Av.
Northern Av.
Bethany Home Rd.
Indian School Rd.
Thomas Rd.
McDowell Rd.
Van Buren St.
Buckeye
Broadway
Grand Av.

Portland, OR
scale 0 1 2 3 miles
© RAND McNALLY & CO.
PRINTED IN U.S.A.
85-1
WASH.
OREG.
Columbia River
Ft. Vancouver Natl. Hist. Site
Pearson Airport
Portland International Airport
Portland Air Base
Portland Speedway
Delta Park
West Delta Park
Univ. of Portland
Columbia Pk.
PARK ROSE
Maywood Park
Russellville
PORTLAND
Portland State Univ.
Washington Pk.
Rose Gardens
Portland Zoological Gardens
Oregon Museum
Univ. of Oregon Health Sciences Center
W. SLOPE
RALEIGH HILLS
Garden Home
Metzger
Tigard
LAKE OSWEGO
MILWAUKIE
OAK GROVE
ERROL HEIGHTS
Mt. Tabor Park
Reed College
Multnomah School of the Bible
Warner Pacific College
Columbia Christian Coll.
Willamette Natl. Cem.
Tryon Creek State Park
N. Clackamas Central Park
MULTNOMAH CO.
WASHINGTON CO.

Salt Lake City, UT
scale 0 1 2 3 4 miles
© RAND McNALLY & CO.
PRINTED IN U.S.A.
85-1
BOUNTIFUL
West Bountiful
Woods Cross
VAL VERDA
N. Salt Lake
WASATCH NATIONAL FOREST
FORT DOUGLAS MIL. RES. (Inactive)
Salt Lake City International Airport
State Capitol
Temple Sq.
Univ. of Utah
Westminster College
SALT LAKE
Redwood
Park Terrace
Eastwood Hills
MILLCREEK
Mount Olympus
HOLLADAY
Mt. Olympus El. 9026
Granite Park
HUNTER
WEST VALLEY CITY
TAYLORSVILLE
KEARNS
MURRAY
COTTONWOOD
Cottonwood Hts.
Bennion
WEST JORDAN
MIDVALE
Union
Sherwood Park
Alta Airpark
Peruvian Park
Belmont Heights
Sandy
Granite
White City
Salt Lake Mun. Airport No. 2

San Diego California
scale 0 1 2 3 4 miles
© RAND McNALLY & CO.
PRINTED IN U.S.A.
85-1
To Oceanside
To Escondido
To Ensenada
MIRAMAR NAVAL AIR STATION
SAN DIEGO
La Jolla
Univ. of Calif. San Diego
Torrey Pines St. Beach & Res.
Mission Bay
Sea World Aquatic Museum
Old Town San Diego
Univ. of San Diego
San Diego St. Univ.
Balboa Park
San Diego Int'l Airport-Lindbergh Field
NORTH ISLAND NAVAL AIR STATION
Coronado
Coronado Beach
NATIONAL CITY
San Diego Bay
Pacific Ocean
Point Loma
Cabrillo Nat'l Mon.
La Mesa
Lemon Gr.
Spring Val.
EL CAJON
Santee
Lakeside
La Presa
Bonita
CHULA VISTA
Castle Park
Harbor Side
Imperial Beach
Palm Av.
Otay
Brown Airport
U.S. MEXICO
SAN DIEGO CO.

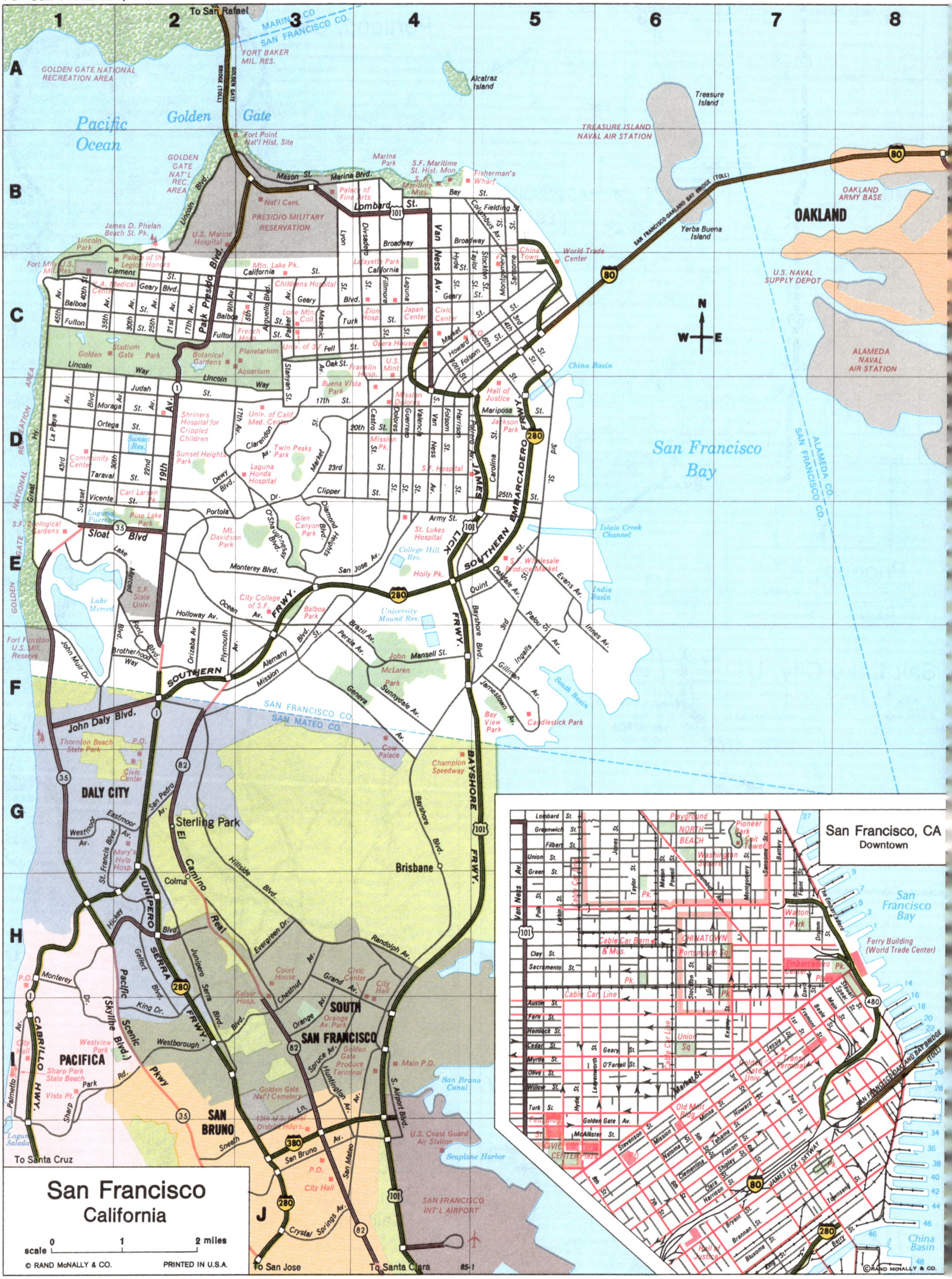

San Francisco
California
scale 0 1 2 miles
© RAND McNALLY & CO.
PRINTED IN U.S.A.
85-1
To San Rafael
MARIN CO.
SAN FRANCISCO CO.
FORT BAKER MIL. RES.
GOLDEN GATE NATIONAL RECREATION AREA
Pacific Ocean
Golden Gate
Alcatraz Island
Treasure Island
TREASURE ISLAND NAVAL AIR STATION
Fort Point Nat'l Hist. Site
GOLDEN GATE NAT'L REC. AREA
Marina Park
S.F. Maritime St. Hist. Mon.
Fisherman's Wharf
Palace of Fine Arts
Nat'l Cem.
PRESIDIO MILITARY RESERVATION
SAN FRANCISCO-OAKLAND BAY BRIDGE (TOLL)
Yerba Buena Island
OAKLAND
OAKLAND ARMY BASE
U.S. NAVAL SUPPLY DEPOT
ALAMEDA NAVAL AIR STATION
World Trade Center
China Town
Lincoln Park
Fort Miley U.S. Mil. Res.
Golden Gate Park
China Basin
Hall of Justice
Jackson Park
San Francisco Bay
ALAMEDA CO.
SAN FRANCISCO CO.
Islais Creek Channel
India Basin
S.F. Wholesale Produce Market
Twin Peaks Park
Laguna Honda Hospital
Sunset Heights Park
S.F. Zoological Gardens
Pine Lake Park
Mt. Davidson Park
Glen Canyon Park
St. Lukes Hospital
College Hill Res.
Holly Pk.
City College of S.F.
Balboa Park
University Mound Res.
John McLaren Park
Lake Merced
S.F. State Univ.
Fort Funston U.S. Mil. Reserve
SOUTHERN FRWY.
SAN FRANCISCO CO.
SAN MATEO CO.
South Basin
Bay View Park
Candlestick Park
Cow Palace
Champion Speedway
Thornton Beach State Park
DALY CITY
Sterling Park
Colma
Brisbane
BAYSHORE FRWY.
JUNIPERO SERRA FRWY.
El Camino Real
SOUTH SAN FRANCISCO
Orange Av. Park
Golden Gate Produce Terminal
Main P.O.
PACIFICA
Sharp Park State Beach
CABRILLO HWY.
Pacific (Skyline Blvd.)
Scenic Pkwy
SAN BRUNO
Golden Gate Nat'l Cemetery
San Bruno Canal
U.S. Coast Guard Air Station
Seaplane Harbor
SAN FRANCISCO INT'L AIRPORT
To Santa Cruz
To San Jose
To Santa Clara
San Francisco, CA
Downtown
NORTH BEACH
Washington Square
Pioneer Park
Coit Tower
CHINATOWN
Portsmouth Sq.
Cable Car Barn & Mus.
Cable Car Line
Walton Park
Ferry Building (World Trade Center)
Embarcadero Center
Union Sq.
Transit Terminal
Golden Gate Univ.
Old Mint Bldg.
JAMES LICK SKYWAY
CIVIC CENTER Plaza
Hall of Justice
China Basin
©RAND McNALLY & CO.

San Antonio, TX
scale 0 1 2 3 4 miles
© RAND McNALLY & CO.
PRINTED IN U.S.A.
Castle Hills
Balcones Heights
Alamo Heights
Terrell Hills
Olmos Park
Leon Valley
Monte Robles Park
Kirby
Windcrest
Kelly A.F.B.
Lackland A.F.B.
Brooks Aero Medical Center
85-1

Seattle, WA
scale 0 1 2 3 4 miles
© RAND McNALLY & CO.
PRINTED IN U.S.A.
EDMONDS
MOUNTLAKE TERRACE
RICHMOND BEACH
RICHMOND HIGHLANDS
KENMORE
BOTHELL
KIRKLAND
SEATTLE
BELLEVUE
MERCER ISLAND
NEWPORT HILLS
REDMOND
RENTON
WHITE CENTER
RIVERTON HTS.
BURIEN
VASHON ISLAND
85-1

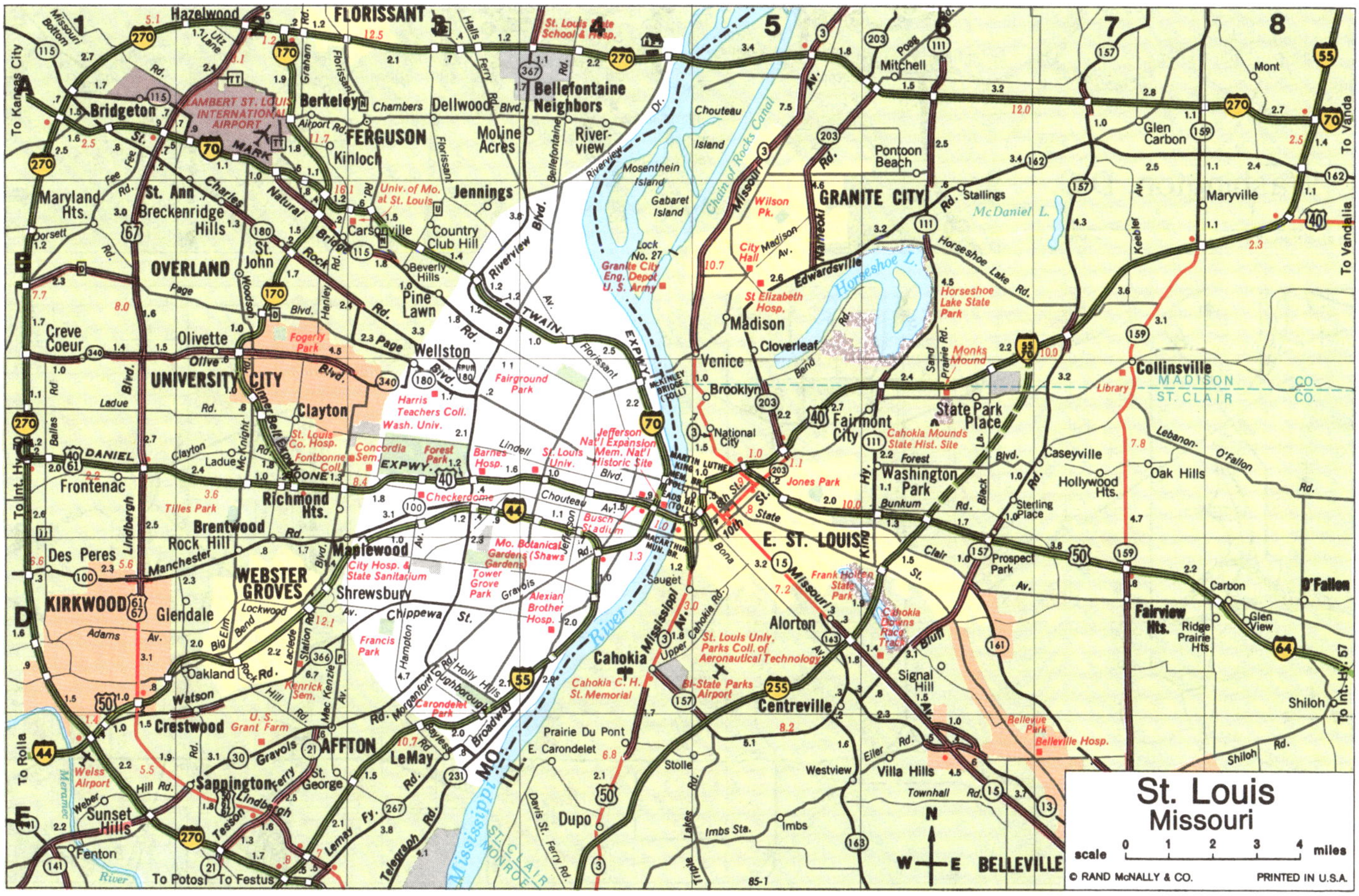
St. Louis
Missouri
scale 0 1 2 3 4 miles
© RAND McNALLY & CO.
PRINTED IN U.S.A.
FLORISSANT
Hazelwood
Bridgeton
Berkeley
FERGUSON
Bellefontaine Neighbors
OVERLAND
UNIVERSITY CITY
Clayton
Richmond Hts.
Brentwood
Maplewood
WEBSTER GROVES
KIRKWOOD
Crestwood
AFFTON
GRANITE CITY
Madison
Venice
Collinsville
E. ST. LOUIS
Cahokia
Centreville
BELLEVILLE
O'Fallon
85-1

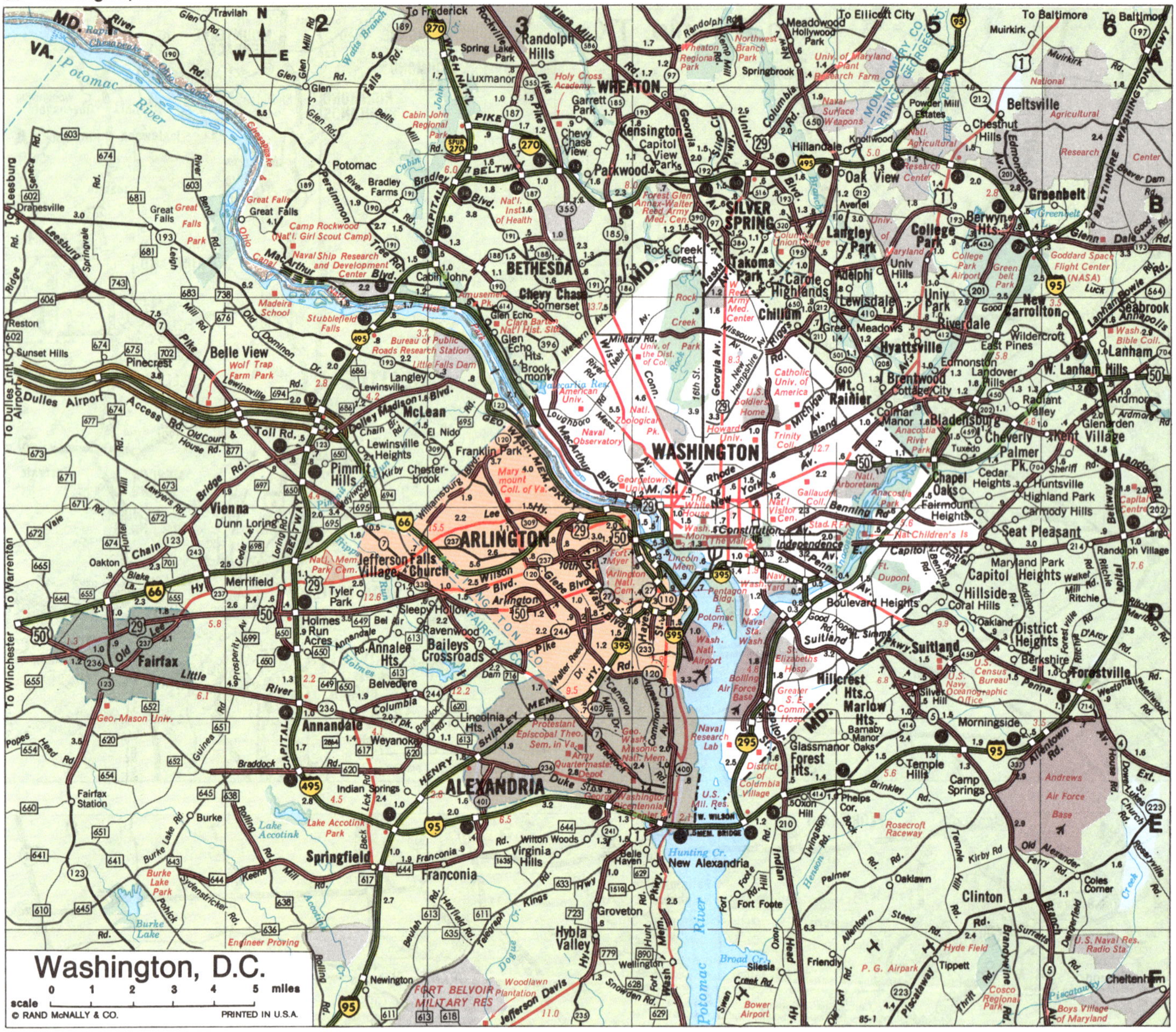
Washington, D.C.
scale 0 1 2 3 4 5 miles
© RAND McNALLY & CO.
PRINTED IN U.S.A.
WASHINGTON
ARLINGTON
ALEXANDRIA
BETHESDA
SILVER SPRING
WHEATON
Fairfax
Springfield
Annandale
Vienna
McLean
Franconia
Greenbelt
College Park
Hyattsville
Takoma Park
Potomac
Chevy Chase
Andrews Air Force Base
To Baltimore
To Frederick
To Ellicott City
To Leesburg
To Winchester
To Warrenton
Dulles Airport Access Rd.
Potomac River
Anacostia River
85-1

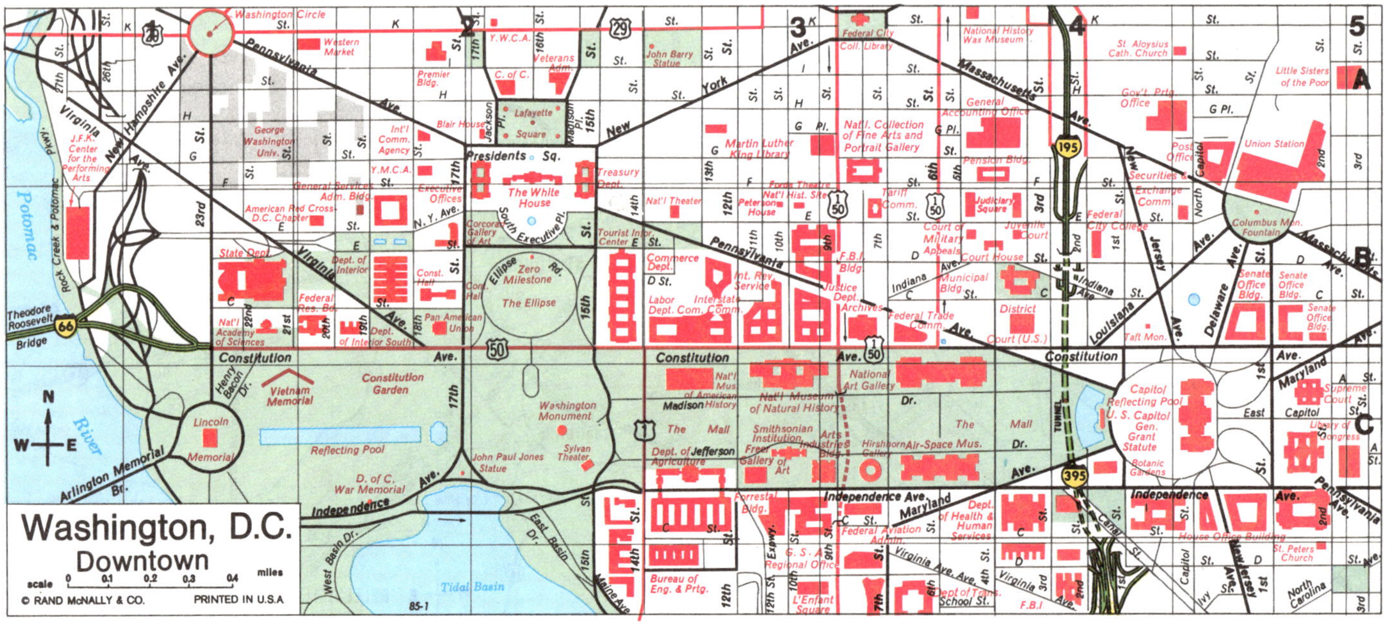
Washington, D.C.
Downtown
scale 0 0.1 0.2 0.3 0.4 miles
© RAND McNALLY & CO.
PRINTED IN U.S.A.
The White House
The Ellipse
Washington Monument
Lincoln Memorial
Reflecting Pool
Constitution Garden
Tidal Basin
Capitol
The Mall
Union Station
Pennsylvania Ave.
Constitution Ave.
Independence Ave.
Potomac River
85-1

Along the Road, *continued*

Memorial, Swope Park and Zoo, Art Institute, and John Wornall House, a restored Greek Revival plantation house of 1858 with period furnishings. Approximately 13 miles northeast of downtown is Worlds of Fun, top theme park. Depicts five "worlds": America, Europe, Africa, Scandinavia, and the Orient.

Lake of the Ozarks State Park, D-4. The state's largest, located near the center of a huge resort-vacation area. Fronting on a portion of giant Lake of the Ozarks (1,375 miles of shoreline), the park offers camping, swimming, fishing. Numerous motels and resorts (rustic to lavish) nearby.

Ste. Genevieve, D-6. Missouri's oldest community and one of the oldest in the Louisiana Purchase. A number of structures are from the late 1700s and are considered among the finest examples of French Colonial architecture in the U.S.

St. Joseph, B-2. The point at which the first Pony Express rider began the first lap of the nearly 2,000-mile run to Sacramento, California, in 1860 is now the Pony Express Museum. The cottage in which Jesse James was fatally shot is now owned by the Patee House (Hotel) Museum.

St. Louis, C-6 (see map p. 79). Outstanding landmark is the 630-foot-tall catenary-curved arch on the riverfront that signifies the Gateway to the West. It is part of the Jefferson National Expansion Memorial, that includes the Museum of Westward Expansion. Adjacent are the Old Courthouse where the Dred Scott decision was made, and the Old Cathedral, both worth visiting. Special almost-vertical trains carry visitors up the arch legs to the top, for a view of Missouri and Illinois, and back down. Everything on wheels is displayed at the National Museum of Transport. Important also are Missouri Botanical Garden and Museum of Science and Natural History and McDonnell Planetarium. Forest Park, with a fine zoo, is one of the nation's great city parks. Tour Anheuser-Busch Brewery, which also operates Grant's Farm, a wild-animal park.

Silver Dollar City, west of Branson, F-3. This theme park is patterned after an old mining village of a century ago.

Six Flags Over Mid-America, C-5. Newest of the Six Flags operations (after Texas and Georgia). Less than an hour's drive west of downtown St. Louis.

Taum Sauk Mountain, D-5. This highest point in the state (1,772 feet) is at the center of a rugged portion of the Ozarks and is adjacent to some of the state's most interesting natural attractions. Nearby, Elephant Rocks State Park, with megaton boulders strewn about; Johnson's Shut-ins State Park, with granite shapes carved by running water; St. Joe State Park, formerly an immense iron mining operation; and some of Missouri's most spectacular caves.

MONTANA / Map page 29

Anaconda, D-2. The Anaconda Copper Company smelter utilizes a smokestack 585 feet tall, said to be made of some 7,000,000 bricks.

Billings, D-5. Visit Yellowstone County Museum, Yellowstone Art Center, Western Heritage Center, and drive Chief Black Otter Trail, a scenic road offering a view of the mountains and city. See Indian pictographs at Pictograph Caves, 5 miles from Billings.

Bozeman, D-4. Montana Agricultural Station, a leading experimental ranch, can be visited, along with the Museum of the Rockies.

Browning, A-3. Largest community on the Blackfoot Indian Reservation, this is an excellent place to purchase genuine Blackfoot handicrafts.

Butte, D-3. View Anaconda Berkeley Pit Mine, one of the world's largest, from a special platform; from another platform at the precipitating plant observe how copper is drawn from mine water.

Custer Battlefield National Monument, D-6. Site of the infamous Battle of the Little Bighorn where Custer and his men came to a crushing defeat.

Gates of the Mountains Wilderness, C-3. On I-15 between Great Falls and Helena, this is a beautiful scenic portion along the headwaters of the Missouri River. Lewis and Clark named it because the mountains seemed to swing open like a giant gate.

Glacier National Park, A-2. Motor along Going-to-the-Sun Highway between St. Mary and West Glacier (good weather only) at nearly 10,000 feet.

Great Falls, B-3. Location of great western artist Charles M. Russell's original cabin and adjacent museum, which contains watercolors, models, illustrated notes, and correspondence of the prolific Russell. Giant Springs, 4 miles northeast, is one of the world's largest; flows 389,000 gallons a day.

Helena, C-3. Originally dubbed "Last Chance Gulch," gold was struck on what is now Main Street. Helena has been the state capital since 1875. Take the tour on the jeep-pulled train "The Last Chancer." Visit the fine Historical Society Museum.

Lewis and Clark Caverns State Park, D-3. Between Three Forks and Whitehall on I-90. Giant cave; one of the largest in the Northwest.

Missoula, C-2. Visitors watch smoke jumpers practice parachuting at the Forest Service Aerial Fire Depot, Missoula County Airport. National Forest Fire Laboratory welcomes visitors. University of Montana here.

National Bison Range, B-2. On U.S. 93 northwest of Missoula. Drive through this national range to view buffalo and other wildlife on designated routes.

Pompey's Pillar, D-5. A short drive northeast of Billings, a huge sandstone formation on which Captain William Clark carved his name in 1806. Hundreds have left their names here since.

Virginia City, west of Ennis, D-3. A Historical Museum, Second Territorial Capitol Restoration, and other buildings from early mining-camp days.

NEBRASKA / Map page 30

Bellevue, south of Omaha, C-8. Located next to Offutt Air Force Base, the Strategic Air Command Museum has a large display of military aircraft and missiles.

Boys Town, C-8. World's most famous community for homeless boys, founded by the late Father Flanagan. The chapel, trade school, field house, and farm buildings can be visited. Open daily.

Bridgeport, C-1. Chimney Rock National Historic Site is centered on a 500-foot-tall tapered rock that was a landmark on the old Oregon Trail. The Mobile Museum features local historical exhibits.

Brownville, D-8. Nebraska's territorial capital city has restored homes, shops, a summer theater, and Missouri River rides on the *Spirit of Brownville.*

Chadron, A-2. Museum of the Fur Trade depicts the lives of American fur traders from colonial times to the present day. Chadron State Park offers camping, picnicking, and recreational facilities. Located nearby.

Fort Robinson State Park, B-1. Visitors can sleep at the fort in the actual homes where army officers were stationed during the Indian wars. The bugle is heard at sunset just as in the old days.

Grand Island, D-6. The Stuhr Museum of the Prairie Pioneer is a tribute to the settlers of the Great Plains; Railroad Town is a turn-of-the century outdoor museum with more than 50 original buildings.

Kearney, D-5. Fort Kearny State Historical Park is a restoration of the fort that guided pioneers along the Oregon Trail; museum, reconstructed buildings, and camping facilities.

Lincoln, D-7. A statue of the sower of grain tops the Capitol. This agricultural state's Capitol is regarded as among the most impressive and unique in the nation. Executive Mansion is on opposite street. Other points of interest are William Jennings Bryan's home "Fairview," a tribute to the "silver-tongued orator of the Platte"; the University of Nebraska, which has the State Museum, Ralph Mueller Planetarium, Sheldon Memorial Art Gallery and Sculpture Garden; Children's Zoo; Antelope Park; and Pioneers Park.

Minden, D-5. Harold Warp Pioneer Village keeps alive the frontier past, with 24 buildings full of collections and craftsmen to show how America grew.

Nebraska City, D-8. Arbor Lodge, in a beautiful arboretum, was the home of Sterling Morton, founder of Arbor Day. Now a state historical park. Wildwood Period House, a reconstructed home, is nearby.

North Platte, C-4. Buffalo Bill Ranch State Historical Park is the setting for the ranch house furnished with mementoes of the famous army scout and showman.

Ogallala, C-3. Front Street has a re-creation of trail-drive days with an old-time saloon show.

Omaha, C-8. Joslyn Art Museum houses a large collection of western, Indian, and modern art. Union Pacific Museum depicts the construction of the railroad across the plains. Other points of interest are Henry Doorly Zoo, Omaha Children's Museum, Mormon Cemetery, and Old Market.

Red Cloud, E-6. The Willa Cather Pioneer Memorial Museum houses the office letters, manuscripts, and other memorabilia of the famous Nebraska writer. Her childhood home also is open.

Scotts Bluff National Monument, C-1. Visitors can walk in the ruts left in solid rock by the wagons on the Oregon Trail. From the summit of the bluff there's a magnificent view of the high plains.

Glacier National Park, Montana

Courtesy Montana Travel Promotion

NEVADA / Map page 31

Austin, C-3. This county seat is a silver boomtown of the 1860s and a contemporary of Virginia City.

Boulder City, G-5. Visitors can view Hoover Dam, one of the highest ever constructed, from parking places on both sides of Black Canyon. Elevators carry passengers down to the power plant. Daily guided tours. An Exhibit Building tells the construction story.

Carson City, D-1. Named after Kit Carson, this is the state's capital city. The original Capitol, still in use, has a silver-like dome.

Ely, D-5. Ghost towns, such as Hamilton, are numerous in the sagebrush valley near Ely. The White Pine Public Museum in town has a collection of historic items and minerals.

Eureka, C-4. Complete and unspoiled, a classic example of an old Nevada mining town.

Lake Tahoe, D-1. Beautiful mountain lake on the Nevada-California border. Ski areas and swinging resort towns line the shores.

Las Vegas, G-5. The town that began as a Mormon settlement has become a world-famous entertainment center and 24-hour-a-day gambling capital. Visitors enjoy lavish hotels, glittering stage shows, and casinos of their choice.

Lehman Caves National Monument, D-5. One of the most handsome cave systems in the country, its caverns are of light gray and white marble.

Reno, C-1. "The biggest little city in the world" is an open town, with 24-hour-a-day stage shows and gambling, great tourist attractions.

Virginia City, D-1. Careful restoration has re-created the 1870s appearance of the West's mining metropolis. Rich Comstock Lode was responsible for the town's early prosperity. The Castle and the Piper's Opera House are open; Virginia and Truckee Railroad operates daily during the summer.

NEW HAMPSHIRE / Map page 32

Colebrook, B-5. The Connecticut (River) Lakes Region stretches to the northeast. A heavily forested wilderness area close to the Canadian border, it is noted for fishing and hunting. Plenty of camping areas, sportsmen's camps, provisions. Guides.

Franconia, C-4. Visitors study the "Great Stone Face"—the natural granite likeness of a man's profile hovering over Profile Lake in Franconia Notch State Park. Nearby is Cannon Mountain aerial tramway, a mile-long funicular rising 4,200 feet to observation points and walking trails. South on U.S. 3 is The Flume, an 800-foot gorge that ends in a scenic waterfall. A boardwalk traverses walls of granite.

Glen, D-5. Story-Land is a theme park built around familiar nursery rhymes and children's stories. Nearby is Heritage, New Hampshire, a three-century journey backward in "living history" to 1634.

Hampton Beach, G-6. One of several locations along the state's 18-mile-long seacoast that affords fine salt-water bathing beaches. There are also a casino, summer-long entertainment programs, small picturesque harbors, and many historic features.

Hanover, E-3. Hopkins Center is a performing arts complex with two theaters, a concert hall, art galleries, sculpture court, recital halls, and studios.

Lake Winnipesaukee, E-5. State's largest lake spreads its 72 square miles along the east-central portion. Popular for salmon fishing; also contains many other species. Bathing, water skiing, boating facilities, and excursions. Nearby Squam and Winnisquam lakes are noted for a variety of water activities.

Pinkham Notch, D-5. Headquarters of the Appalachian Mountain (hiking) Club. Enjoy spectacular views of Mt. Washington (accessible by the Cog Railway and an auto road starting at State 16) and the Presidential Range of the White Mountains, scenic Glen Ellis Falls, and Wildcat Mountain tramway.

Sunapee, F-3. Sunapee State Park, one of the state's most beautiful. Also a ski area.

New York Convention & Visitors Bureau

Brooklyn Bridge, New York

White Mountain National Forest, C-5–D-4. Contains the Appalachian Trail, a large network of other hiking trails, and scenic campgrounds. Kancamagus Highway, one of the East's most scenic, runs 34 miles through the forest from Lincoln to Conway. Spectacular views, numerous camping areas. Beautiful in fall.

NEW JERSEY / Map page 33

Asbury Park, D-5. A large amusement area with white sand public beaches and famed boardwalk.

Atlantic City, G-4. Excellent beach, amusement piers connecting with famous boardwalk. Highly popular casino gambling was begun in 1978.

Batsto, F-3. Restored Batsto Area of Wharton State Forest; part of the more than 99,000 acres of the Old Joseph Wharton Estate. The iron works were of military importance during the American Revolution.

Lakehurst, E-4. Famous Naval Air Station displays blimp hangars, firehouse, and parachute rigging.

Trenton, D-3. State capital. History buffs will enjoy inspecting the barracks where Hessian troops were housed at the time Washington and his men crossed the Delaware River a few miles upstream.

West Orange, B-4. See replicas of Thomas A. Edison's many inventions at his home and laboratory.

NEW MEXICO / Map page 36

Acoma, C-2. The 1,000-year-old Acoma pueblo atop a mesa is the nation's oldest continuously inhabited community. The Indians are master potters.

Albuquerque, C-3. Sandia Peak Tramway runs daily to the top of 10,378-foot-high Sandia Crest. Picturesque Old Town offers everything from strolling singers to Mexican food; shops feature Indian, Mexican, and American jewelry, art and crafts.

Capulin Mountain National Monument, A-5. Drive up a spiral road to the crater rim of the extinct volcano.

Carlsbad, F-5. Living Desert State Park, on the west edge of town, exhibits native wildlife and several thousand varieties of cactus.

Carlsbad Caverns National Park, F-5. Tour the largest underground chambers yet discovered. There's even a lofty dining room 700 feet below ground. Open daily.

Chama, A-3. Ride the Cumbres & Toltec Scenic Railroad between Chama and Antonito, Colorado, through magnificent Toltec Gorge. Round trip includes one way by train, the other by bus; early June–mid-October.

Los Alamos, B-3. The Bradbury Science Museum of the Los Alamos National Laboratory, at Canyon Bridge, has exhibits on thermonuclear bombs, rockets, and peaceful uses of atomic energy.

Santa Fe, B-4. The Palace of the Governors, bordering the central plaza, was erected by the Spanish in 1609; the San Miguel Mission was begun at the same time. There are fine museums; Santa Fe Opera operates July-August.

Taos, B-4. Visit Kit Carson Home, Mission of St. Francis of Assisi, and Taos Pueblo.

White Sands National Monument, F-3. Included in the over 145,000 acres are snow-white dunes of white gypsum sands, some 40 feet high.

Zuni, C-1. A live pueblo, where ceremonial dances may be viewed during the year; famous for its fine inlaid silver jewelry, which is crafted here.

NEW YORK / Map pages 34–35

Albany, E-9. Visit the State Capitol and Empire State Plaza, south of the building. New York State Museum has an outstanding Adirondack Wilderness exhibit.

Ausable Chasm, A-9. This 1½-mile-long gorge can be traveled partly by boat and by a 4,000-foot walkway.

Buffalo, E-2 (see map p. 65). The Albright-Knox Art Gallery and Buffalo Museum of Science are outstanding.

Cooperstown, E-8. Visit James Fenimore Cooper's home, National Baseball Hall of Fame, and Doubleday Field, where the first game of baseball was played.

Corning, F-5. See exhibits covering 3,500 years of glassmaking at the Corning Glass Center and Western American art at Rockwell Museum of the Western Frontier.

Hempstead, (on Long Island, H-2). Of special interest in this Long Island community, settled in 1643, are Hofstra University, Christ's First Presbyterian Church, founded in 1644; St. George's Episcopal Church, chartered in 1730 by George II; and the Black History Museum.

Hyde Park, G-9. The Franklin D. Roosevelt Library and Museum are at the birthplace of the 32nd president. Franklin and Eleanor Roosevelt are buried in the beautiful rose garden, now a national historic site.

Lake Placid, B-9. Visit the Olympic Arena built for the 1932 Winter Games. The same site was used for the Winter Games of 1980. Year-round resort.

Massena, A-7. On Barnhart Island, learn about the St. Lawrence Seaway and Power Project at the Moses-Saunders Visitors Center.

New York, H-1. (see map p. 75). A short list of places to visit should include the American Museum of Natural History, Metropolitan Museum of Art, Museum of Modern Art, Whitney Museum of Art, The Cloisters (medieval art), Guggenheim Museum, Rockefeller Center, the many theatres, restaurants, and shops. Several skyscrapers have observation points from upper floors. Tour the United Nations buildings. Ride the Staten Island Ferry for a view of the city's skyline. Visit Chinatown, Statue of Liberty, New York and American Stock Exchanges, World Trade Center, Lincoln Center, St. Patrick's Cathedral, Cathedral Church of St. John the Divine, Hayden Planetarium, and Riverside Church; famous bridges.

Niagara Falls, D-3 (see map p. 65). Enjoy the view from Prospect Point, then take a *Maid of the Mist* boat from either a Canadian or an American dock through the turbulent waters to the spray at the foot of the falls.

Rochester, D-6. See the International Museum of Photography in the former home of photographic pioneer George Eastman, whose company was chief sponsor of the great Rochester Symphony Orchestra.

Saratoga Springs, D-9. Visit Saratoga Spa State Park, Saratoga Performing Arts Center, Race Track, Harness Track, National Museum of Racing, President Grant Cottage, Casino and Congress Park, Petrified Gardens, and the Saratoga National Historic Park, American Revolution turning-point battle site.

Syracuse, D-6. This city has Syracuse University, Everson Museum of Art, Onondaga Lake Park (with historical exhibits), Daniel Parrish Witter Agricultural Museum, and Canal Museum.

Tarrytown, G-2. Fine old estates, including Washington Irving's Sunnyside and Philipsburg Manor.

Ticonderoga, C-9. A real cannon shoot can be witnessed at the old restored French-built fort.

Watkins Glen, F-5. A fine view of the glen's cascading waterfalls. One of the nation's top auto racing events, the U.S. Grand Prix, held here in October.

West Point, H-9. Watch the cadets' precision marching at parades. Visitor Center at Thayer Gate.

NORTH CAROLINA / Map pages 38–39

Asheville, C-3. Biltmore House and Gardens is the estate of George W. Vanderbilt. Take a self-guided tour of the 250-room mansion, gardens, and dairy barns. Biltmore Homespun Shops has mountain craftsmen.

Banner Elk, southwest of Sugar Grove, B-3. Dorothy and the Wizard are among the characters which come to life at the Land of Oz, Beech Mountain.

Beaufort, D-9. Take a walking tour of this quaint old seacoast town. Hampton Mariners Museum has salt-water aquaria, birds and shells, marine items.

Blowing Rock, B-4. Tweetsie Railroad takes visitors on a scenic ride. There are also a general store, saloon, blacksmith shop, sheriff's office and jail. Throw a piece of paper over Blowing Rock, 2 miles south of town, and an updraft will blow it back.

Blue Ridge Parkway, C-2. Drive this scenic road to magnificent overlooks and Parkway Craft Center, where mountain crafts are demonstrated. Mountain textiles are sold at Brinegar Cabin.

Boone, B-4. Daniel Boone's cabin has been re-created. *Horn of the West* drama performed in summer, late June to late August.

Cape Hatteras National Seashore, C-10. Forty-five miles of unspoiled beaches for exploration. Watch water-fowl from a bird observation platform.

Cashiers, C-2. A toll road leads up Whiteside Mount to a viewpoint atop a precipitous cliff.

Charlotte, C-5. Textile capital. Mint Museum of Art was the Federal Mint from 1837 to 1913, when Charlotte was a gold mining center. Carowinds amusement park is shared by both North and South Carolina.

Cherokee, C-2. The Museum of the Cherokee Indian has unique displays; Oconaluftee Indian Village has colorful Cherokee guides. *Unto These Hills* pageant is presented during the summer months.

Chimney Rock Park, C-3. Take an elevator or hike to the top of a granite monolith, "the chimney."

Durham, A-7. Bennett Place State Historic Site includes the spot where the Civil War ended when General Johnston surrendered to General Sherman. Visitors come to see Duke University, Sarah P. Duke Gardens, and North Carolina Museum of Life and Science. Visitors also come to hear the chant of tobacco auctioneers from September to December.

Flat Rock, C-3. Visit "Connemara," the 240-acre farm where poet Carl Sandburg lived for 22 years.

Fontana Dam, C-1. Ride the incline from the overlook to the powerhouse of the dam. Nearby Fontana Village is a popular year-round resort.

Great Smoky Mountains National Park, C-1. Park roads lead to scenic points in the Smokies (also in Tennessee), east of the Black Hills. Diversified and luxuriant plant life. Take a nature walk and stay for a campfire program in this magnificent wilderness park.

Kitty Hawk, B-10. At Kill Devil Hill, where the Wright brothers made their first flight in 1903, are a memorial and hangar museum. Now a historic landmark.

Linville, B-3. Just a mile from the Blue Ridge Parkway is Grandfather Mountain, with unusual rock formations and a mile-high swinging bridge. Many interesting events here from April to mid-November.

New Bern, C-9. Tyron Palace served as the capitol and residence of the governor of the colony from 1770 until the outbreak of the Revolution. Built by royal governor William Tryon. Now beautifully restored.

Raleigh, B-7. Start at the Capital Area Visitor Center. Both the Museum of History and the Museum of Natural History have outstanding collections.

Wilmington, E-8. The U.S.S. *North Carolina,* mighty battleship of World War II, is docked in Cape Fear River. See *The Immortal Showboat* June-August.

Winston-Salem, B-5. Visit the old Moravian buildings (watch Moravian crafts demonstrated in Single Brothers House) and Reynolda House, Museum of American Art.

NORTH DAKOTA / Map page 37

Bismarck, D-4. Relics of early settlers are at Camp Hancock State Historic Site. Dakota Zoo features domestic and exotic animals. Short distance to the south is Oahe Game Management Area with primitive camping, seasonal hunting, boating, and fishing on 24,000 acres. From the skyscraper State Capitol observation level visitors enjoy a sweeping view of the Great Plains. Indian artifacts and natural science material are displayed at State Historical Museum on the mall. Statue of Sakakawea, interpreter for Lewis and Clark, is on the Capitol grounds. Nearby is historic Mandan.

Dunseith, B-5. International Peace Garden is a 2,300-acre man-made botanical masterpiece nestled in the Turtle Mountains featuring thousands of flowers in the formal garden area, with Peace Chapel and International Music Camp. (1,442 acres in Manitoba.)

Fargo, D-7. Prize-winning new Civic Center and several excellent city parks. North Dakota State University is noted for its experimental farms.

Fort Lincoln State Park, D-4. At the fort, three block-houses have been restored. From here George Armstrong Custer led his men to disaster on the Little Bighorn. Ancient Indian village nearby.

Jamestown, D-6. Frontier Village reconstruction with three-story-high bison statue. Jamestown Dam Recreation Area has water sports facilities.

Lake Metigoshe, A-4. In the Turtle Mountains north of Bottineau. State park along the lake features swimming, canoeing, hiking trails. Cabins available.

Lake Sakakawea, C-3. Over 200 miles, begins at Garrison Dam on the Missouri River. Tours of powerhouse and national fish hatchery. State park, with marina and modern campground, nearby. Three other state parks adjacent to the large lake, with great fishing, water skiing and sailing area, and more.

Medora, D-1. Ruins of the chateau of the Marquis de Mores and packing plant he built open to visitors. Also built in 1883 are Rough Riders Hotel, carefully restored, and a country store patronized by Theodore Roosevelt, whose ranch was nearby.

Theodore Roosevelt National Park, C-1. Includes the Rough Rider president's Elkhorn Ranch in 70,000 acres along the Little Missouri.

West Fargo, D-8. Bonanzaville USA is a pioneer town from Red River Valley communities buildings.

OHIO / Map pages 40–41

Akron, D-7. Visit lovely Stan Hywet Hall and Gardens, former estate of Frank A. Seiberling.

Canal Fulton, D-6. Fulton Heritage Society operates a full-size replica of the original mule-drawn barge on Lock 4 in summer; two-mile trip.

Canton, D-7. Football fans enjoy displays and films at the Pro Football Hall of Fame. Open daily.

Chillicothe, G-4. Adena is the former estate of Thomas Worthington, sixth governor of Ohio. Two miles north is Mound City Group National Monument, a complex of 23 burial mounds. The outdoor drama *Tecumseh!* is performed at Sugarloaf Mountain in summer.

Cincinnati, H-1 (see map p. 67). The "Queen City of the West" has a revitalized downtown, a fine zoo, and several excellent museums, including Taft Museum, Contemporary Arts Center, Cincinnati Museum of Natural History, Cincinnati Art Museum.

Cleveland, C-6 (see map p. 67). Visit the Cleveland Museum of Art, Natural Science Museum, Cleveland Aquarium, Western Reserve Historical Museum, Metroparks Zoological Garden. Within easy driving distance of Akron or Cleveland is Blossom Center, where the Cleveland Symphony Orchestra performs in summer. Twenty miles southeast is Sea World, complete entertainment park; open June through August.

Columbus, F-4 (see map p. 68). State Capitol grounds statuary outstanding. Modernistic Ohio Historical Center and reconstructed Ohio Village, contrasting. Take a walking tour through restored German Village.

Dayton, F-2. Visit Carillon Park and the Air Force Museum, one of the oldest and largest aviation museums, at Wright-Patterson Air Force Base.

King's Island, G-2. Large entertainment center has over 1,600 acres of rides, shows, shops, and resort facilities. North of Cincinnati on I-71.

Mansfield, E-5. Kingwood Center & Gardens are of interest. South is Snow Trails Ski Resort; 12 miles southeast of Lucas is the former home and model farm of noted author Louis Bromfield.

Marietta, G-7. Learn Ohio's history at Campus Martius Museum and Ohio River Museum State Memorial.

Sandusky, C-4. Gateway to the Lake Erie islands. Cedar Point amusement park calls itself the world's ride capital.

Toledo, C-3. Crosby Gardens are beautiful from early spring until late fall. Toledo Museum of Art has a famous glass collection, and the zoo has a large freshwater aquarium, all in a complex.

Wapakoneta, E-2. Armstrong Air & Space Museum commemorates the first walk on the moon by its native son Neil Armstrong. Open daily, March–November.

OKLAHOMA / Map page 42

Anadarko, C-5. In the Federal Building see beautiful murals by Kiowa Indian artists. Home of the American Indian Exposition, mid-August. Indian City, a Plains Indians village, is south of town. Visit Southern Plains

Indians Arts and Crafts Museum and National Hall of Fame for American Indians.

Bartlesville, A-7. The state's first oil town displays Nellie Johnstone No. 1, the first successful oil well drilled in Oklahoma. Visit Woolaroc Ranch and Museum for a look at one of the best collections of western art and artifacts, about 14 miles southwest of town. Exhibit Hall of Phillips Petroleum Co. tells about petroleum technology achievements.

Cache, C-5. Eagle Park Old West Town has 18 historical buildings. Wichita Mountains Wildlife Refuge shelters a large buffalo herd; also longhorn cattle.

Chickasaw National Recreation Area, D-6. The man-made Lake of the Arbuckles provides water recreation; numerous cold mineral- and freshwater springs and bromide waters surface here.

Claremore, B-7. The great Will Rogers Memorial, just west of town, has an outstanding collection of Rogers memorabilia. Home site planned by Rogers.

Dewey, A-7. Tom Mix Museum has items belonging to the late cowboy movie star.

Guthrie, B-6. Territorial Museum depicts the story of life in Oklahoma Territory from 1889 to 1907.

Lawton, C-5. Fort Sill Military Reservation is the army's artillery and missile center. The vast installation is built around the Old Post, where you can see the guardhouse that once imprisoned Geronimo. Artillery pieces from both world wars are on exhibit along Winston Walk. The old corral also of interest.

Muskogee, B-7. The site of the Five Civilized Tribes Museum, with authentic artifacts of the Cherokee, Chickasaw, Choctaw, Creek, and Seminole nations. Visit Honor Heights Park on Agency Hill; tour the submarine U.S.S. *Batfish* in War Memorial Park.

Oklahoma City, B-6. A rare State Capitol without a dome sits astride a sizable oil pool, which has been slant-drilled for access to the "black gold." The National Cowboy Hall of Fame and Western Heritage Center contains extraordinary exhibits concerning the cowboy's way of life then and now. Other attractions are State Museum of Oklahoma, National Softball Hall of Fame, Kirkpatrick Center, Oklahoma Firefighter's Museum, Oklahoma City Zoo, Oklahoma Heritage Center, and Frontier City Amusement Park.

Ponca City, A-6. See the famous Pioneer Woman Statue and Museum and the 30-acre estate of E. W. Marland, former governor and oilman.

Tahlequah, B-8. The capital of the Cherokee Indian Nation has a Capitol, Old Prison, and Supreme Court Building. At nearby Tsa-La-Gi Indian village the Cherokees maintain ancient way of life. The famous drama *Trail of Tears* is presented in summer.

Tulsa, B-7. The "Oil Capital of the World" is also an important art, music, and culture center. Outstanding are Gilcrease Institute of American History and Art, the Philbrook Art Center, and the Rebecca and Gershon Fenster Gallery of Jewish Art.

OREGON / Map page 43

Ashland, F-2. The Oregon Shakespearean Festival's outdoor Elizabethan playhouse in Lithia Park is a replica of London's Old Fortune Theatre. The festival is one of the oldest in America.

Astoria, A-1. Named for John Jacob Astor, whose fur trading enterprises led to the building of Fort Astoria, the first permanent American outpost west of the Mississippi. Climb Astoria Column's 125 feet of steps to an observation deck atop Coxcomb Hill, 700 feet above the Columbia River. Lewis and Clark spent the winter of 1805-6 at Fort Clatsop, now a national memorial.

Bend, C-3. Gateway to winter and summer mountain recreation areas on the east slope of the Cascades. Tumalo, Sawyer, and Pilot Butte state parks in immediate vicinity. Lava Lands south of the city.

Bonneville, B-3. Watch the salmon fighting their way up the torrent during spawning season at vantage points along the fish ladders at Bonneville Dam.

Burns, D-5. Gateway to Malheur National Wildlife Refuge, 30 miles south on State 205.

Bob Frerck/Odyssey

Pacific Coast, Ecola State Park, Oregon

Crater Lake National Park, E-3. From the Rim Drive vantage points, motorists can look down almost 1,000 feet in the bright blue water of the lake.

Florence, C-1. Visitors can take an elevator down to the Sea Lion Caves. Said to be the only mainland sea rockery where you can view the amphibians at home as the tides go in and out.

Gold Beach, E-1. From the mouth of Rogue River, jet boat trips take visitors as far as 52 miles upstream. Charterboat fishing available. See spectacular coastal landscapes here. Diggers seek clams, not gold.

Hood River, A-3. On a clear day enjoy the view of snow-capped Mount Hood from Panorama Point.

Newport, C-1. At south end of the coastal resort area extending from Lincoln City. Visit the wharf and Oregon State University's Marine Science Center.

Oregon City, B-2. Pounding surf has left interesting terraces. The home of Dr. John McLoughlin, "Father of Oregon," is a national historic site.

Pendleton, A-6. The famous woolen mill offers a guided tour. Umatilla Reservation Indians participate in the famous Pendleton Roundup in early September. Just outside the city is Umatilla National Forest.

Portland, B-2 (see map p. 77). Fine museums include the Western Forestry Center, Portland Art Museum, and Oregon Museum of Science and Industry. The International Rose Test Gardens are here. The world-famous Rose Festival is held each June. Roses flourish until fall.

Salem, B-2. Take a tour of the State Capitol, an unusual building with a modernistic fluted tower topped by a golden statue of a pioneer. Magnificent view of snow-capped Cascades from the tower.

PENNSYLVANIA / Map page 43

Allentown, E-11. During the British occupation of Philadelphia, the Liberty Bell was removed to Allentown for safekeeping at the Zion Reformed Church. A replica of the bell is housed in a shrine in the church, along with historic murals and other art. Tour nearby Schaefer Lehigh Valley Brewery, west of town.

Bedford, G-5. First settled in 1751, some of the colonial buildings are still in use. Fort Bedford Museum is a reproduction of one of the fort's blockhouses; one mile north of town is Old Bedford Village, a "live" reproduction of a colonial village.

Conneaut Lake, B-1. Largest natural lake in the state is a popular summer resort and amusement center.

Erie, A-2. Commodore Oliver Hazard Perry's second flagship in the victory over the British on Lake Erie, 1813, is on display at the foot of State St. Five miles north is Presque Isle State Park, with seven miles of white sand beach, many plants and birds.

Gettysburg, G-7. The National Civil War Wax Museum presents the entire story of the Civil War era and the Battle of Gettysburg. Drive the 30 miles of road to see the battlefield's important points, then climb the Gettysburg National Battlefield Tower for a panoramic view.

Harrisburg, F-8. The State Capitol, on the banks of the Susquehanna River, is reminiscent of St. Peter's in Rome. Nearby is the five-story, circular William Penn Memorial Museum; extensive exhibits.

Hershey, F-8. Hershey's Chocolate World tells the complete story of chocolate making. Hersheypark, next door, has over 35 spectacular rides and entertaining stage shows.

Johnstown, F-4. Ten miles north is the Johnstown Flood National Memorial, commemorating the disastrous flood of 1889 when over 2,000 drowned.

Lancaster, F-9. Farmers' markets tempt visitors with Pennsylvania Dutch delicacies. The Pennsylvania Farm Museum of Landis Valley, 3 miles north of town, is a 100-acre area re-creating Pennsylvania rural life back in the last century. The area is in the heart of Amish and Mennonite country.

Longwood Gardens, G-10. Beautiful grounds include fountains, formal gardens, lakes, natural woodlands; summer open-air theatre performances.

Morrisville, F-12. Pennsbury Manor, the 40-acre estate of William Penn, was his country home built in 1683. Reconstructed, the home and outbuildings are open to visitors daily except holidays. Formal gardens.

New Hope, F-12. Mule-drawn barges offer canal boat rides during the summer, and canoe and raft trips on the Delaware River are available from April through October. Bucks County Playhouse has Broadway productions year-round.

Philadelphia, G-11 (see map p. 76). Start at the Visitor Center of Independence National Historical Park, site of Independence Hall (see the desk where the Declaration of Independence was signed), the Liberty Bell, Carpenters' Hall, Congress Hall, First and Second Banks of the United States, and more. Franklin Institute Science Museum and Planetarium contains many do-it-yourself exhibits; the U.S. Mint, Philadelphia Museum of Art, Rodin Museum are outstanding. Fairmount Park has over 8,000 acres of natural beauty along the Schuylkill River; historic mansions.

Pittsburgh, E-2 (see map p. 76). Point State Park, with its interesting Fort Pitt Museum, occupies the site of an area chosen for a fort by George Washington. Today it's called the "Golden Triangle"—where the Monongahela, Allegheny, and Ohio rivers meet. Of interest are the University of Pittsburgh and its cultural complex, Phipps Conservatory, Buhl Science Center, and The Pittsburgh Zoo. Ride the incline to the top of Mount Washington for a breathtaking view.

Scranton, C-10. Nay Aug Park is a favorite spot for residents during summer. Visit the Museum of Natural History, Science and Art and the zoo.

Valley Forge National Historical Park, F-11. The bitter winter of 1777-78 is commemorated at the site where Washington's troops camped. Be sure and include the National Memorial Arch, Washington's Headquarters, and the Washington Memorial Chapel.

Warren, B-4. Stop at the Visitor Center to learn about the Kinzua Dam, which creates a 27-mile-long Allegheny Reservoir on the Allegheny River.

Wellsboro, B-7. Gateway to Pennsylvania's "Country," Canyon, more than 2,857 square miles of ruggedly beautiful country. Rich in history and scenic beauty, also a fisherman's paradise.

West Mifflin, F-2. Kennywood Park is a popular spot, with 34 major rides and attractions.

Williamsport, C-8. Every August the Little World Series is played at Little League headquarters.

RHODE ISLAND / Map pages 10–11

Block Island, G-6. Twelve miles at sea off the southern Rhode Island coast, the island has great scenic beauty and is a popular swimming and fishing spot. Auto ferries depart from Providence, Newport, and Point Judith. Fine beaches; major flyway for birdwatchers.

Bristol, E-7. Hope Street's fine houses are a legacy of the China Trade. The Haffenreffer Museum of Anthropology has splendid Indian, Eskimo, African, and Pacific area collections. Shipbuilding area.

Narragansett, F-6. The fishing village of Galilee is picturesque; many commercial fishing boats.

Newport, F-7. Bellevue Avenue is lined with the mansions of nabobs of the Gilded Age, several open to visitors. Newport is the home of the International Tennis Hall of Fame.

Pawtucket, E-7. America's Industrial Revolution started here. Slater Mill Historic Site has been restored to its early 1800s appearance.

Providence, E-6. See the Gilbert Stuart portrait of George Washington in the State Capitol. Architectural masterpieces on historic streets east of city center include University Hall, Brown University. City has an exceptional number of notable churches: the First Baptist (1775), the First Unitarian (1816), Friends Meeting House (1723), and Greek Revival Beneficent Congregational Church (1810); other Greek revival structures.

Warwick, E-7. Rocky Point Amusement Park has rides and games. Rhode Island shore and clam dinners are popular.

SOUTH CAROLINA / Map pages 38-39

Camden, E-5. At Historic Camden, four restored houses of the Revolutionary War period are filled with museum exhibits. Winding trails, picnic areas.

Charleston, G-5. Charleston's Battery still has blocks of handsome antebellum homes. Boats take tourists from the Municipal Marina to Fort Sumter, where the Civil War broke out. Among the city's gardens are Middleton Gardens, Cypress Gardens, and Magnolia Gardens, with azaleas, cypress groves.

Columbia, E-4. The state capital has outstanding historical museums, antebellum homes, and historic churches. The zoo has a large group of Patagonian sea lions. University of South Carolina here.

Hilton Head Island, H-5. This year-round resort has beautiful beaches, woodlands, and marshes.

Myrtle Beach, F-7. A 55-mile stretch of wide sandy beaches, with Myrtle Beach as its hub, is known as the Grand Strand. Good fishing, camping, fine shops.

Orangeburg, F-5. From spring to frost, flowers bloom in beautiful Edisto Memorial Gardens.

SOUTH DAKOTA / Map page 46

Badlands National Park, D-3. Awesome landscape contains animal fossils of 40 million years ago.

Custer State Park, D-1. There are bison, sheep, and deer in this scenic park of mountains, forests, and lakes. Black Hills Playhouse has summer plays.

Deadwood, C-1. Wild Bill Hickok was shot in the back in No. 10 Saloon; the chair in which he was sitting when shot now hangs over the door. Bill and Calamity Jane are buried in Mt. Moriah Cemetery overlooking the town. Area now has winter sports.

Hot Springs, D-1. Gateway to a large area popular with hunters and fishermen. Evans Plunge is the world's largest indoor swimming pool, spring fed with a natural temperature of 87 degrees Fahrenheit.

Jewel Cave National Monument, D-1. One of the world's largest mapped caves offers matchless beauty.

Keystone, D-1. Visit Big Thunder gold mine and ride the Rushmore Aerial Tramway for a view of Mount Rushmore National Memorial in the Black Hills.

Mitchell, D-7. Every year the town redecorates its famed Corn Palace with new designs, which are created of local seeds and grasses.

Mount Rushmore National Memorial, D-1. Giant-size faces of Presidents Washington, Jefferson, Lincoln, and Theodore Roosevelt were sculptured by Gutzon Borglum on the face of Mount Rushmore.

Pierre, C-5. Tour Oahe Dam, 5 miles north on the Missouri River. Lake Oahe stretches almost to Bismarck, North Dakota, and is great for camping, fishing, and boating. Large rolled earth dam.

Rapid City, C-2. Visit Sioux Indian Museum; the Museum of Geology at the School of Mines; Stavekirke, reproduction of an 800-year-old Norwegian church; Dinosaur Park.

Sioux Falls, D-8. The Great Plains Zoo has an attractive adjoining children's park. EROS Data Center is the national center for processing information on the earth's surface using space age technology.

Spearfish, C-1. In summer the Black Hills Passion Play reenacts the last seven days of Christ's life.

Vermillion, E-8. The W. H. Over Museum at the University of South Dakota has fine exhibits. Shrine to Music Museum has antique musical instruments.

Watertown, B-8. Visit the superbly restored home of Arthur Mellette, South Dakota's last territorial governor and the state's first elected one.

Wind Cave National Park, D-1. You'll see herds of buffalo and other animals grazing in this 28,000-acre park. Strong winds blowing through the chambers of the limestone caverns gave the cave its name.

TENNESSEE / Map pages 20–21

Bristol, E-11. Trails on several levels can be enjoyed at Bristol Caverns, southeast of here; underground river.

Chattanooga, G-7. The Chattanooga Choo-Choo and Terminal Station, downtown on Market Street, commemorates the 1880 rail linkup between the North and South. Take the incline railway to the top of Lookout Mountain, site of a Civil War battle. Ruby Falls in Lookout Mountain Caverns and Rock City Gardens worth visiting.

Columbia, F-5. The ancestral home of James K. Polk, 11th U.S. President, has many of Polk's personal belongings.

Gatlinburg, F-10. Gateway to the Great Smoky Mountains National Park. Resort town with many shops.

Greeneville, E-10. Andrew Johnson, president after Lincoln, is remembered in his hometown at the 17-acre Andrew Johnson National Historic Site. Davy Crockett was born in Greene County.

Jonesboro, E-11. The oldest town in the region west of the Allegheny Mountains, this served as the capital of the State of Franklin in 1784 and as the home of Andrew Jackson during his first law practice.

Knoxville, F-9. Visit the mansion of William Blount, governor of the Territory of the United States South of the Ohio, built in 1792. Also see Confederate Memorial Hall; University of Tennessee; site of the 1982 World's Fair.

Memphis, G-1 (see map p. 71). Take a Mississippi River

Badlands National Park, South Dakota

Courtesy South Dakota Department of Economic and Tourism Development sightseeing cruise on the *Memphis Queen,* from the foot of Monroe St. Beale St., immortal street of the blues, is where the great W. C. Handy composed "Memphis Blues" and wrote the "St. Looie woman with her diamond rings." The city has many historic homes and notable museums. Visit Chucalissa Indian Village and T. O. Fuller State Park southwest of the city.

Nashville, E-6. Visit the State Capitol (Ionic design) and Parthenon (full-size resemblance of Athens building) in Centennial Park. Opryland U.S.A. is a 120-acre entertainment park that is the new home of Grand Ole Opry of radio fame. The Hermitage, northeast of the city, was the home of Andrew Jackson.

Oak Ridge, F-9. American Museum of Science & Energy has largest energy exhibit known.

Shelbyville, G-6. Annual national competition held here in late August by the Tennessee Walking Horse Association. Some horse farms may be toured.

Sweetwater, F-9. A boat ride on the underground "Lost Sea" is a popular feature of cave exploring via glass-bottom boats, about 3 miles east of town.

TEXAS / Map pages 48–49

Abilene, B-6. Three colleges, many parks, and the nearby Dyess Air Force Base add variety to the city.

Amarillo, G-2. Quarries in the Alibates Flint Quarries National Monument have been used for more than 12,000 years. In Amarillo are the Western Stockyard auctions on Mondays and Tuesdays, and the Discovery Center (Harrington Planetarium).

Austin, D-7. The country's largest State Capitol is good for a visit of several hours. Old French Legation is the only building every erected in Texas for a representative of a foreign government. Governor's Mansion is a handsome antebellum home. On the campus of the University of Texas is Lyndon Baines Johnson Presidential Library.

Big Bend National Park, F-3. A magnificent wilderness park with trails for hikers and horseback riders. Mountain scenery contrasts with desert in this great bend of the Rio Grande River. Check in at the Visitor Center; don't wander far from the highways.

Corpus Christi, G-7. Causeways lead to Padre Island National Seashore and to other beach island resorts. Visit Corpus Christi Museum and Art Museum of South Texas.

Dallas, B-8 (see map pp. 68–69). Dallas is an important cultural and entertainment center. In October, visit the Texas State Fair. See Texas Hall of State, Aquarium, Garden Center, Music Hall; museums of natural history, art, and science.

El Paso, C-1. Three Spanish Missions in lower valley area. Ysleta Mission, established 1682, is open daily. Tours. Take the aerial tramway to the top of Ranger Peak for an impressive view of the city.

Fort Davis National Historic Site, D-3. A sound system presents recorded bugle calls, band music, and sounds of horses and troops in a frontier post retreat, hourly during the day at this historic fort.

Fort Worth, B-7 (see map pp. 68–69). Amon Carter Museum of Western Art, Kimbell Art Museum, and the Fort Worth Museum of Science and History are outstanding. Casa Mañana, a unique aluminum-domed theatre-in-the-round, offers popular entertainment.

Galveston, E-9. Enjoy miles of beach. Sea-Arama has a porpoise stadium and oceanarium.

Harlingen, H-7. The Confederate Air Force maintains a vast collection of flyable foreign and U.S. war planes.

Houston, E-9 (see map p. 70). Jesse Jones Hall for the Performing Arts is home to the Houston Symphony Orchestra, opera, and ballet; Alley Theatre and the Museum of Fine Arts are outstanding. Tour Astrodome. Adjacent Astroworld has rides and attractions. A half-hour's drive south of downtown at NASA's LBJ Space Center, see films about the manned space program. Visit nearby San Jacinto Battleground State Historic Park, site where Texas won independence in 1836. Moored nearby is Battleship *Texas,* open daily for tours.

Johnson City, D-7. Ride a mule-drawn wagon tour at the home of President L. B. Johnson, whose birthplace, 14 miles away in Stonewall, is close to the family cemetery where he is buried.

Kingsville, G-7. A loop drive takes motorists on a trip through part of fabulous King Ranch, once the nation's largest, where the Santa Gertrudis Cattle breed was developed. Ranch started in 1853.

Langtry, E-5. Crusty Judge Roy Bean presided at a courtroom that has been kept much as it was when he was known as "Law West of the Pecos."

Houston, Texas

Walter Frerck/Odyssey

Monahan's Sandhills State Park, C-3. Dwarf oak trees with roots sunk 80 feet into the sand, and dunes you can "toboggan" on.

New Braunfels, E-7. German food, bands, and festivals are featured in this town founded 1845 by German settlers led by Prince Carl of Solms-Braunfels.

Odessa, C-4. From June through August see Shakespearean plays at the Globe Theatre.

Padre Island National Seashore, G-8. Wide sand beaches, excellent fishing, marine and bird life.

San Antonio, E-7 (see map p. 79). One of America's most beautiful cities. HemisFair's Tower of the Americas rises over the fairgrounds, with an elevator for viewing. HemisFair Plaza has notable museums. Walk the Paseo del Rio along the concrete and stone banks of the San Antonio River, which winds through the downtown area. Visit La Villita, the town of two centuries ago. Nearby is the Alamo. Four 18th-century missions south of the city.

Six Flags over Texas, B-8 (see map pp. 68–69). At Arlington, halfway between Dallas and Fort Worth, this pioneer theme park has re-created the historic periods of the six flags that have flown over Texas—Spain, France, Mexico, Republic of Texas, the Confederacy, and U.S.

Waco, C-7. Visit the Texas Ranger Hall of Fame, where every kind of pistol and rifle and knife used by the Rangers is on display; ride on the *Brazos Queen,* a steamboat-type craft unique in Texas.

UTAH / Map page 47

Alta, near Park City, C-3. This old silver mining town is now a famous ski resort with year-round facilities.

Arches National Park, E-6. Visitors may drive or hike to see this large assemblage of giant stone arches, windows, pinnacles, and pedestals, which change color constantly as the sun moves overhead.

Bluff, G-6. First permanent town in southeastern Utah, it is dotted with pioneer homes, trading posts, and Anasazi ruins among the canyon walls.

Bryce Canyon National Park, F-3. A series of "breaks" in gigantic amphitheaters 20 miles long and 3,000 feet down through colorful bands of limestone.

Canyonlands National Park, E-5. Utah's largest park has a variety of spectacular geological formations and mesas rising over 7,800 feet. Indian petroglyphs.

Capitol Reef National Park, E-4. Explore canyons filled with colorful goblin formations, vast arches, and stone temples.

Cedar Breaks National Monument, F-2. Huge natural amphitheater eroded into pink cliffs. Nearby Brian Head has alpine skiing and snowmobiling.

Cedar City, F-2. A Shakespeare Festival is staged July–August in an Elizabethan Theatre.

Dinosaur National Monument, C-6 (also in Colorado). Watch scientists at work from the Quarry Visitor Center. Fossilized dinosaur bones on display.

Glen Canyon National Recreation Area, G-4. One hundred-eighty-six-mile-long Lake Powell offers water sports, boating, fishing, marinas, and resorts.

Moab, E-6. Gateway to Canyonlands and Arches national parks. The Moab Museum has interesting Indian, uranium, and geologic displays.

Natural Bridges National Monument, F-5. See the largest display of natural bridges in the world from a paved road along the canyon rim.

Ogden, B-3. Visit Municipal Gardens and historic Union Station. John M. Browning Armory and Firearms Museum has historic and present-day items.

Provo, C-3. Students lead guided tours of Brigham Young University. City edged by majestic mountains.

Rainbow Bridge National Monument, G-4. Three natural bridges, the highest is 220 feet.

Salt Lake City, B-3 (see map p. 77). Mormon Temple, the Tabernacle, and historic shrines of The Church of Jesus Christ of Latter-Day Saints are in Temple Square. Other reminders of the Mormon's historic past are Seagull Monument, a bronze figure of Brigham Young, and Lion and Beehive houses, Young's former homes. Nearby is Great Salt Lake, with water so dense with salt, swimmers can rest on the surface without sinking.

Timpanogos Cave National Monument, C-3. Translucent crystals are beautifully illuminated.

Zion National Park, G-2. One of the oldest national parks, it has a deep, colorful canyon, sheer walls, and impressive formations and landscapes.

VERMONT / Map page 32

Barre, C-3. A world granite center. Watch blasting, drilling, and stonecutting at Rock of Ages quarry; see finishing of the stones from an observation deck.

Bellow Falls, F-3. Adams Grist Mill has early farm and paper manufacturing equipment. An ethnic Heritage Festival is held in late July, with a parade, street dancing, music, exhibits, and dance performances.

Bennington, G-1. Bennington Potters create stoneware and accessories. Bennington Battle Monument commemorates a turning point in the American Revolution. Take an elevator to the top for a fine view.

Burlington, C-1. The University of Vermont's Robert Hull Fleming Museum has Indian relics and pioneer items. Ride the Lake Champlain ferry from Vermont to New York for a memorable experience.

Cabot, southeast of Hardwick, C-3. Watch cheesemaking at Cabot Farmers Cooperative Creamery.

Manchester, F-2. Take the Skyline Drive to the summit of Mount Equinox for a magnificent view; nearby Bromley ski lift and alpine slide operate summers.

Marlboro, G-2. Pianist Rudolf Serkin and Marlboro College sponsor Marlboro Festival in summer.

Middlebury, D-1. This is a busy year-round resort. Vermont State Craft Center is at Frog Hollow.

Montpelier, C-3. Ceres, goddess of agriculture, tops the gilded dome of Vermont's State Capitol. Visit the Historical Society Museum's fine artifacts.

Northfield, D-2. There are covered bridges north of town on State 12. Norwich University also here.

Proctor, E-2. Learn about the history and production of marble from the Marble Exhibit at the Vermont Marble Co. There are bas reliefs of American presidents and demonstrations by a sculptor.

St. Johnsbury, C-4. Stop at Maple Museum and the Maple Grove, Inc. kitchens to see candy and sugar being made. Factory tours weekdays.

Shelburne, C-1. Thirty-five buildings of the Shelburne Museum cover three centuries of Vermont life. See the sidewheeler steamboat *Ticonderoga*, a covered bridge, country store, and more.

Stowe, C-2. Drive the Mount Mansfield Toll Road to the 4,393-foot peak for a view of the surrounding mountains. Trapp Family Lodge, west of town, is the home of the singing family made famous by *The Sound of Music*. The home is now a popular resort hotel.

Woodstock, E-3. On Sabbath days, bells cast by Paul Revere and Sons ring out from four churches across this beautiful Vermont town. There are many old homes in town and exhibits at the Woodstock Historical Society.

VIRGINIA / Map pages 50–51

Abingdon, G-3. Its lovely shops attract buyers of handicrafts, china, and antiques. Famous Barter Theatre stages shows from Shakespeare to Broadway during the summer months.

Alexandria, D-9 (see map p. 80). George Washington lived and worshiped and socialized in this important colonial port. Visit Gadsby's Tavern, the Stabler-Leadbetter Apothecary, Carlyle House, and Lafayette House. Christ Church, where George Washington worshiped, is practically unchanged today.

Arlington, D-9 (see map p. 80). The Tomb of the Unknown Soldier and grave sites of President John F. Kennedy and his brother Senator Robert Kennedy attract millions of visitors every year. The home of Robert E. Lee overlooks the national cemetery. Old Town District has fine restaurants and shops.

Ashland, E-9. Kings Dominion, north on I-95, is the largest theme park in the Middle Atlantic states.

Big Stone Gap, G-2. Visit the Home of John Fox, Jr., whose *Trail of the Lonesome Pine* is presented in musical form June through September.

Charlottesville, E-8. Thomas Jefferson's genius lives on in his home, Monticello, an architectural treasure of original ideas. He also designed Ash Lawn, for President James Monroe, and the University of Virginia.

Fredericksburg and Spotsylvania National Military Park, E-9. Here are portions of four major Civil War battlefields, historic sites, a national military cemetery, and visitors center with a museum relating area's history.

Hampton, G-10. At NASA's Langley Research Center visitors may see a moon rock, the Apollo 12 spacecraft, and the spacesuit worn by Alan Shepard, first U.S. astronaut to venture into space.

Jamestown, F-10. The site of the 1607 settlement has monuments to Capt. John Smith and his beloved Pocahontas; excavations have revealed ruins of some of the original buildings. Jamestown Festival Park has recreations of James Fort, Powhatan's Lodge, a 17th-century pottery, and replicas of the three vessels which brought the settlers to Virginia.

Lexington, E-6. The George C. Marshall Research Library and Museum houses interesting World War II memorabilia; Lee Chapel, on the Washington and Lee University campus, honors the memory of General Lee.

Mount Vernon, D-9. George Washington's estate and final resting place overlook the Potomac River south of Washington, D.C.

Newport News, G-10. The Mariner's Museum has artifacts and displays covering all periods of life on the sea; ship figureheads, model ships.

Norfolk, G-11. Visitors may tour the city by car, following a clearly marked trail. Here are a large naval facility as well as several interesting museums, and Norfolk Gardens-by-the-Sea, beautiful to enjoy from early spring through late summer months.

Portsmouth, G-10. Harbor tours and a Naval History Museum are popular here; to the south is the Dismal Swamp, 600-mile area of Virginia and North Carolina.

Richmond, F-9. The State Capitol planned by Jefferson, the Battle Abbey, Virginia Museum, and the Confederate Museum fascinate visitors. Edgar Allen Poe's house is open to the public; Philip Morris and the American Tobacco Company have weekday tours.

Shenandoah National Park, D-8. Unsurpassed in scenic splendor, the park extends for many miles along the Blue Ridge Mountains crest with vistas of the Shenandoah Valley and the Piedmont.

Virginia Beach, G-11. Miles of boardwalk, fine beaches, and good musical entertainment.

Williamsburg, F-10. Virginia's colonial capital has been handsomely restored, with costumed residents plying their trades as visitors stroll through the town. Among famous restorations are the Governor's Palace, with its formal gardens; the Capitol Building; and Raleigh Tavern. Busch Gardens, with European atmosphere, is a few miles east.

Yorktown, F-10. Visit the battlefield and walk on the ground where the American Revolution came to an end with the surrender of Cornwallis to Washington.

WASHINGTON / Map page 52

Aberdeen-Hoquiam, C-2. Surrounding these twin cities are drives through stately Douglas fir forests.

Bellingham, A-3. Overlooks Puget Sound and the San Juan Islands, and affords a view of the Olympic and the Cascade mountains. Chuckanut Drive, north off I-5, offers breathtaking vistas.

Bremerton, C-3. The Pacific Fleet's Puget Sound naval base includes the naval shipyard. Anchored here is the U.S.S. *Missouri*, on which the Japanese formally surrendered to end World War II in 1945.

Chelan, B-5. A 350-passenger excursion boat makes one round trip daily mid-May to mid-October (periodic in winter) from Chelan to Stehekin and back. All day.

Leith Rohr

Deer in Olympic National Forest, Washington

Coulee Dam National Recreation Area, B-7. Roosevelt Lake was formed by Grand Coulee Dam on the Columbia River.

Mount Rainier National Park, C-4. Greatest single-peak (14,410 ft) glacial system in the U.S. Dense forests and subalpine flowered meadows. Obtain road and weather information before reaching the park.

North Cascades National Park, A-4. This half-million-acre park of high, jagged peaks, glaciers, ice falls, waterfalls, and wild alpine areas is traversed by the North Cascades Highway (State 20).

Olympia, C-2. The impressive State Capitol has guided tours. Visit also the state greenhouse and, in spring, see the Japanese cherry trees and flower gardens blooming on the 35-acre Capitol lawn.

Port Angeles, B-2. Heart-o-Hills Road is a 17-mile-long scenic drive that affords splendid sights from atop Hurricane Ridge. Across the strait is Victoria, B.C.

Puyallup, C-3. This bulb-growing center is a carpet of daffodils from April throughout the summer. Mount Rainier provides a handsome background.

Seattle, B-3 (see map p. 79). From your vantage point on the observation level of the 605-foot-high Space Needle, you can look down on an incomparable panorama of city, Puget Sound, and mountains. Also here at Seattle Center (the old World's Fair Grounds) you can visit the Pacific Science Center, Opera House, Art Pavilion, Food Circus International Fountain, and a 76-acre amusement park. Pioneer Square Historic District has cobblestone streets and outdoor cafes.

Spokane, B-8. Riverfront Park, downtown along the riverfront, is a legacy remaining from Expo '74. Amphitheaters, Opera House, Convention Center, and Japanese Garden are the major features.

Tacoma, C-2. A well-marked city tour takes visitors along the two-hour Kla How Ya Trail (Chinook for "welcome") to 17 points of interest. Point Defiance Park has a replica of an old-time logging camp called Camp Six; also Fort Nisqually, the first regional post of Hudson's Bay Company, includes the state's oldest structure and the Western Washington Forest Industries Museum.

Vancouver, E-2. Fort Vancouver National Historic Site was originally the center of Hudson's Bay Company's widespread fur-trading enterprises (1825-60).

Wenatchee, C-5. This great apple-growing center ships millions of bushels of fruit every year. A famed Apple Blossom Festival is held in April. Ohme Gardens are open April through October; created on a once-arid promontory by an ardent botanist.

Yakima, D-5. Center of Yakima Valley, the "Fruit Bowl of the Nation" ships apples and other fruit throughout U.S. Yakima trolley lines have spring, summer, and fall tours Saturday mornings and Sunday afternoons; costumed conductors and hostesses.

WEST VIRGINIA / Map pages 50–51

Beckley, E-4. Visitors ride a coal car almost 1,000 feet below the surface of New River Park. Scenic Grandview State Park has two summer dramas—*Honey in the Rock* and *Hatfields and McCoys.*

Cass, D-6. Antique logging engines pull train loads of tourists on sight-seeing runs at Bald Knob.

Charleston, D-4. The 300-foot-high dome of the State Capitol rises over the town, famous for its chemical plants. In Museums at Sunrise are an art gallery and a children's museum.

Charles Town, C-8. Thoroughbred racing at Charles Town Turf Club summer and winter. Several historic buildings are in town.

Clarksburg, C-5. Visit Fort New Salem and Salem College, where the arts, crafts, history, music, and folklore of the Mountain State are taught.

Harper's Ferry National Historical Park, C-9. Because of its strategic location at the confluence of the Shenandoah and Potomac rivers, Harpers Ferry changed hands many times during the Civil War. The armory and arsenal and many mills and buildings were completely destroyed; however, the natural beauty of the gorge survived. The park is the site of John Brown's famous raid on the arsenal in 1859. A visit to the area should include the park, Harper's Ferry, and the John Brown Wax Museum.

Huntington, D-3. Heritage Village is a restoration of a 19th-century bank and railroad station. Visit Viking Glass Co. and Pilgrim Glass Corp. Also see Huntington Galleries, a large art complex.

Milton, D-3. Visitors watch highly skilled glassmakers create hand-blown cathedral glass and modern tableware at the Blenko Glass Co.

Morgantown, B-6. Seneca Glass Co., producer of lead-crystal handcrafted glass, offers tours. Area visits include Pricketts Fort State Park at Fairmont, Mother's Day Shrine at Grafton.

Parkersburg, C-4. Places to visit are Blennerhassett Island, Parkersburg Art Center, and the Centennial Cabin Museum in the City Park.

Richwood, E-5. At nearby Cranberry Mountain the U.S. Forest Service operates a Visitor Center. At the Cranberry Glades nature lovers see plants that normally grow in the tundra of the Arctic.

Wheeling, B-5. Olgebay is a public park with museum, zoo, lodging. Visit Wheeling Downs for greyhound racing and Jamboree USA for country western music.

Williamstown, C-4. Fenton Art Glass, which features glass produced early in the century, has factory tours.

WISCONSIN / Map page 53

Apostle Islands National Lakeshore, A-3. Take a ferry trip from Bayfield. La Pointe, on Madeline Island, is one of the state's oldest settlements. Interesting museum, fur company building, and a lighthouse.

Appleton, D-5. Learn the history of papermaking at the Dard Hunter Paper Museum. Open year round.

Baraboo, E-4. Circus World Museum has an extensive collection of memorabilia, music concerts, and performances. Devil's Lake State Park is nearby.

Cassville, F-2. Stonefield includes the homestead of the state's first governor, a museum, and a covered bridge leading to a reconstructed 1890s village.

Cedarburg, north of Mequoin, F-6. Tour the shops and Stone Mill Winery at Cedar Creek Settlement. Nearby is Ozaukee County Pioneer Village.

Eagle, F-5. Old World Wisconsin is a group of pioneer buildings drawn from ethnic group settlers.

Elkhart Lake, E-5. Road America is one of the most challenging raceways for sports-car drivers.

Fish Creek, C-6. During summer Peninsula Players perform in a garden theater; the Peninsula Music Festival brings outstanding musicians to Door County.

Fond du Lac, E-5. Beautifully restored Galloway House and adjacent pioneer village are here.

Green Bay, D-5. Visit the Green Bay Packer Hall of Fame and the National Railroad Museum. The state's oldest city has a wealth of historic attractions: the Roi-Porlier-Tank Cottage (1776), the Cotton House-Baird Law Office (1830-40 vintage), Hazelwood, and Fort Howard buildings.

Hayward, B-2. Interesting demonstrations at Historyland's Indian Village and Logging Camp.

Kenosha, G-6. County Historical Museum and Public Museum are of interest. Harmony Hall is the international headquarters for the Society of the Preservation and Encouragement of Barbershop Quartet Singing in America; library of quartet pieces.

Lake Geneva, G-5. Take a sight-seeing boat to see the beautiful estates, or hike around the lake.

Laona, C-5. Camp Five Farm has a Cracker Barrel Store, blacksmith shop, and logging museum.

Madison, F-4. The State Capitol is open for daily tours. Visit the U.S. Forest Products Laboratory, University of Wisconsin, and Madison Art Center.

Manitowoc, E-6. Climb aboard the submarine U.S.S. *Cobia* and visit the nearby Maritime Museum.

Milwaukee, F-5 (see map p. 73). Outstanding are the War Memorial Center, the Milwaukee Art Museum, Milwaukee Public Museum, Milwaukee County Zoo, Boerner Botanical Garden, and the triple-domed horticultural conservatory. Pabst Brewing Co. offers tours. Summerfest in early July is a good time to visit and enjoy the city.

Mineral Point, F-3. Restored Cornish miners' homes take visitors back to the 1830s lead mining days.

New Glarus, F-4. The center of Swiss culture in the state, famous for its Wilhelm Tell Drama, Heidi Festival, and Volksfest. Visit the Chalet of the Golden Fleece and the Swiss Historical Village.

Rhinelander, B-4. One of the most complete displays of old-time lumbering in the Midwest, includes a working narrow-gauge railroad locomotive.

Shullsburg, east of Gratiot, G-3. Tourists go underground to Badger Mine, a pioneer lead producer. There's also a mining museum with early artifacts.

Spring Green, F-3. Frank Lloyd Wright's Taliesin architectural workshop has a few summer tours.

Sturgeon Bay, D-6. Boat tours from the municipal dock give a great view of the large shipbuilding yards. See the Door County Historical Museum.

Superior, A-1. Drive across the high bridge for views of the busy harbor. One of the nation's last whaleback freighters, *The Meteor,* is now a museum.

Wisconsin Dells, E-5. The Stand Rock Indian Ceremonials, boat trips on the scenic river, a pioneer fort, and many types of recreation and entertainment.

WYOMING / Map page 54

Bighorn Canyon National Recreation Area, A-3. Yellowtail Dam impounds a vast lake for all types of recreation. Pryor Mountain Wild Horse Range adjoins the area. (Also in Montana.) On the Bighorn River.

Buffalo, B-5. The famous old Occidental Hotel still operates; Jim Gatchell Memorial Museum is interesting, and the Chamber of Commerce can arrange for a tour of a working ranch in the area.

Casper, D-5. Old Fort Caspar, named for Lieutenant Caspar (*ar* correct for the fort, *er* for the town) Collins, is a replica of the original. Nearby Independence Rock bears the names of many early pioneers.

Cheyenne, F-6. During Frontier Days in July the town remembers its uproarious past. See the State Museum in the State Capitol complex and new Frontier Days and Old West Museum in Frontier Park.

Cody, B-3. Buffalo Bill Historical Center has the scout's memorabilia; also here the Whitney Gallery of Western Art, the Plains Indian Museum, and the complete Winchester Museum. Old Irma Hotel is unchanged. Local cowboys stage exciting rodeos.

Devils Tower National Monument, B-6. View the great 865-foot-rock and enjoy the prairie dogs' antics near the monument entrance. A trail leads around the base of the tower. First national monument.

Bob Frerck/Odyssey

Picking Pumpkins in Wisconsin

Flaming Gorge National Recreation Area, F-2. Comprises some 201,000 acres of scenic land surrounding Flaming Gorge Reservoir. This colorful desert/lake is known for fine fishing and boating.

Fort Laramie National Historic Site, E-7. See more than 10 of the original structures of this important western frontier fort built by Jim Bridger and his men.

Fossil Butte National Monument, E-1. Just west of Kemmerer, this area's unusual concentration of fossilized aquatic vertebrate remains shows the evolution of freshwater fish, some 40-65 million years old.

Grand Teton National Park, B-1. Jagged peaks make a visit to Grand Teton unforgettable. See the Museum of Fur Trade at Moose and Indian Museum at Colter Bay. Moose can be seen along the shores of Jackson Lake. Take a guided rubber raft trip on the Snake River for an exciting one- or five-day outing.

Jackson, C-1. On summer nights the Cache Creek Posse chases bearded "badmen" through downtown streets; several theaters feature "Old West" melodramas. Teton Village is a famous winter resort; winter visitors help feed elk at National Elk Refuge.

Laramie, F-6. Ten miles southeast of town is a bronze bust of Lincoln, symbolic of the highest elevation on the old Lincoln Highway, now Interstate 80.

Sheridan, B-5. Southwest of town is Bradford Brinton Memorial Ranch, containing an impressive collection of Indian arts, crafts, and works of Western artists.

Yellowstone National Park, B-1. Oldest and largest of our national parks, Yellowstone is a wonderland of geysers, falls, and canyons. Old Faithful is the most spectacular of the some 10,000 geysers. Among the park's other wonders are Mammoth Hot Springs, with its unusual thermal activity; magnificent Grand Canyon of the Yellowstone; and a waterfall twice the height of Niagara Falls. Serene Yellowstone Lake and the bubbling pots are contrasting sights. (Park also extends into Montana and Idaho.)